# Preface

I would like to give thanks and praise to God the Father, God the Son, and the Holy Spirit for creating the universe. God inspired the scripture quoted in **Jesus is Our Friend** and to Him we give glory. I want to thank William Tyndale for translating the Holy Bible into the English language, so common people could read the Holy Bible. Much of William Tyndale's work was used to create the King James Bible. William Tyndale was burned at the stake for his efforts in giving the Holy Bible to the common man to read.[1] Although the subtitle of this book is **A Common Man's Search for Jesus Christ**, I am very humbled by William Tyndale's valiant effort for the common man. Sincere appreciation is also extended to the numerous transcribers of the New Revised Standard Version of the Bible, the New International Version of the Bible, the New American Standard Bible, and the King James Bible.

Appreciation is expressed to the staff and volunteers of the Living Word Outdoor Drama in Cambridge, Ohio. I attended the Living Word Drama several years prior to starting to write this book. Listening and watching the Gospels presented as a live drama gave me a better understanding of Jesus' message. Gaining a better understanding of Jesus' message helped me to locate amazing scripture verses. The Living Word Drama web site is www.livingworddrama.org.

The scripture selections and the interpretation of the Lord's teaching presented in **Jesus is Our Friend** truly exceed my intelligence, training and spiritual worthiness. The poem Persistence by Calvin Coolidge may partially explain how this book was written.

> Nothing in the world can take the place of persistence.
> Talent will not; nothing is more common than unsuccessful men with
>     talent.
> Genius will not; unrewarded genius is almost a proverb.
> Education will not; the world is full of educated derelicts.
> Persistence and determination are omnipotent.[2]

I was not born talented in understanding the Holy Bible. I was not born talented in music either, but I am still learning to play the piano. God gave me skills in deductive logic, systems engineering, engineering design, problem solving, and mentoring others. *Jesus is Our Friend* is a collection of carefully selected Bible verses that are applicable to our daily lives. This book describes my spiritual journey, and discloses many experiences that impacted my life. I am definitely not a genius and do not have a divinity degree.

God created the heavens and the earth; He created us.

As a deer longs for flowing streams, so my soul longs for you, O God. Psalm 42.1

By God's design, like a deer searches for water, our souls search for God. God's gentle Holy Spirit guided me to have questions about God, righteousness, life on earth, the purpose of life, and eternity.

My wife is much appreciated for her suggestions while I wrote this book and for proofreading the book. I also thank her for believing that God called me to write this book. I spent many hundreds of hours writing the book on weekends, after work, and on vacations. My wife mentioned that God seems to enjoy selecting people to do His work that would not be picked by those in the world. Perhaps God picks unqualified people, so they grow in faith and wisdom while doing His work. I know God has a sense of humor because He commanded me to write *Jesus is Our Friend*. I humbly declare myself unworthy and unqualified to write a scholarly book on Jesus Christ. However, God prompted me to write this book from the perspective of a common man. Since I am a common man, I am comfortable in writing a book on Jesus from a common person's perspective. No theological words, created by man, are used in *Jesus is Our Friend*. This book was written to share Jesus' teachings in a clear and concise manner. Jesus spoke with supernatural clarity and used words the common person could understand. With God's constant guidance, persistence, and determination, this book on Jesus, from the common man's perspective, was written.

When I was writing a chapter, I would read the scripture relating to a chapter and pray about God's message in His living Word. Rather than sit at my computer for hours and ponder topics for each chapter, I would live my day filled with the Holy Spirit and God would disclose what I needed to know when I was praying, taking a shower, listening to the Bible on tape, driving my car, drifting off to sleep, waking up in the morning, talking with people, or listening to a sermon. Often, God provided an event in my life to explain a chapter or sent my friends to share a Bible based message to include in this book. I thank my wife, Connie; Mark Johnson; John Dauphin; Jonathan; and Dan Campbell for their inspirational conversations on numerous complex topics regarding God. I also thank my wife, Connie; my son, Carl Butcher II, M.D.; Mark Johnson; and John Blair for proofreading my manuscript. God parted the Red Sea when the people escaping Egypt reached the beach, not beforehand (see Exodus 14.9-16). I walked by faith and patiently let God guide me in writing this book. Rather than being proud of this book, I am humbled that God asked a common man like me to write this book and sent me people to help me succeed in declaring the gospel.

The subtitle of this book is **A Common Man's Search for Jesus Christ**; this refers to me being the common man. However, this book is equally written for women. I am fully aware my wife has greater faith than me and she is a better Christian than me. This book is written to share the good news with everyone.

# Table of Contents

# CHAPTER 1

# A Pearl Necklace to Share with You

*Jesus is Our Friend* is written to be enjoyable, full of good news, and a useful guide to gain insight about Jesus and His teachings. This book is for those starting their Christian journey and for those who study the Holy Bible. My wife and I hosted a high school exchange student from Japan a few years ago. Nana explained that she had not worshipped God, did not attend any church, and religion was not part of her life. My wife and I took Nana to a Christian church with us for the nine months we were her host family. We explained Jesus Christ was the Son of God, was God, and He died so that all who believe in Him will have eternal life. Nana taught me that she and many others truly know nothing about Jesus. She became a member of our family and we remain in contact and visit. Nana grew up and became a physician. Nana told us that the complexity of the human body confirms there is a master designer named God. The blessing to explain the Gospel to someone who knew nothing about God provided me with a unique perspective in how to share the good news of God's love. As an engineering manager, I understand personnel must be trained in both the basic and complex aspects of the job to succeed. To share God's message with clarity, it is best to lovingly explain the basic and the complex aspects of Christianity. *Jesus is Our Friend* quotes Old and New Testament Bible verses that document the foundation for numerous beliefs regarding Jesus Christ. I will present Nana with a copy of this book to further explain that Jesus is indeed our Friend.

A psychology teacher of mine, in 1974, declared learning and knowledge require the acquisition, retention, and retrieval of information. This acquisition-retention-retrieval principle impressed me as a college student and I still embrace the principle many years later. After attending church for several years, and listening to sermons and Bible readings, I wanted to study about Jesus and the Bible myself. I tried to read parts of the Holy Bible myself. I felt totally lost and inadequate reading the Bible without guidance. I joined a study group at church and with the help of the study group, read the entire Holy Bible in one year. To continue to learn the Bible, I listened to many sermons on the radio. I also listened to audio recordings of the Holy Bible while commuting to and from work.

While reading and listening to the Holy Bible, specific profound passages amazed me and I wrote them down for future retrieval. Also, I searched for passages to answer questions pending in my heart and I wrote these passages down. I accumulated more and more inspiring Bible verses. Being an Industrial Engineer and an acquisition-retention-retrieval enthusiast, I began typing the selected Bible verses in my computer. I openly disclose I am unable to recall, word for word, many of the Bible verses listed in this book. As an engineering manager, my expertise is not in retrieving information directly from my mind, but knowing where to find detailed information regarding various subjects. *Jesus is Our Friend* began as a collection of Bible verses that I may not be able to fully remember, but are important to retrieve when necessary. As many Bible verses were accumulated, I began sorting them by topic. I focused on learning the directives from God documented in the Bible rather than following traditions of man. Jesus asked:

"Why do you break the commandment of God for the sake of your tradition?" Matthew 15.3b.

My personal quest for knowledge, faith, and wisdom included finding what God has declared and differentiating this from the traditions of man. Traditions are not necessarily bad to follow, but it is best to know what God directed and what traditions man is propagating.

Since Jesus came to earth and lived amongst us humans 2,000 years ago, and his teachings are recorded in the Bible, it makes sense to read and know the Bible. The Holy Bible is the only way to know what Jesus did and said. *Jesus is Our Friend* contains numerous quotes of Jesus Christ, the most intelligent, wise, and kindest human being who ever lived. Jesus was a co-designer and co-creator of the universe.

As I was completing my third decade of researching and documenting various topics addressed in the Bible, I perceived a directive from God to share His Words that I gathered. I am merely a humble servant who found these pearls of wisdom and truth, and tied them together with string into a pearl necklace. The beauty of God's Word is the pearls; my research is just the piece of string that enables the reader to easily retrieve the many pearls efficiently. Perhaps I can be compared to a pearl diver who searched for thirty years and found many pearls of God's wisdom and truth in the huge ocean of God's Word, the Holy Bible. The string of the pearl necklace is the sequence that God's word is presented. My comments serve as the clasp of the necklace. The clasp keeps the selected pearls of God's Word together for easy use and presentation; the beauty remains in the pearls.

There are many other pearls of wisdom and truth in the Holy Bible not mentioned here; this is just the pearl necklace I humbly share with you. May God be with you as you read portions of His Holy Word. I am honored and humbled to be a servant of God in sharing portions of His good news. Amen.

*Jesus is Our Friend* is structured such that selections from God's Word in the Bible are presented at the beginning of each chapter. God's Word is presented first because He is the Holy One and my ramblings are relatively insignificant. The Holy Spirit speaks through God's living Word, the Bible, and I do not want to interrupt the Holy Spirit while He is speaking with you. Reading God's Holy Word will likely provoke an intellectual, spiritual, and emotional response. I recommend you pause and perhaps re-read the scripture at the beginning of each chapter to be filled with the Holy Spirit. When you are ready to proceed, my commentary and application of God's word will follow.

The living Word of God speaks to us individually. Scripture, messages from God the Father, God the Son, and God the Holy Spirit, has the miraculous ability to communicate different messages when read by different people or even the same person at different eras of his or her life. The Holy Spirit may give you unique insights and lessons when you read the Bible verses that are different than my commentary; that will be excellent. I will rejoice that the Holy Spirit opened your mind to understand the scriptures.

Let us pray. Dear God, please fill the person reading *Jesus is Our Friend* with your Holy Spirit. May the Word of God bring peace that transcends all understanding, discernment between good and evil, and acceptance of God's salvation through faith. Amen.

# CHAPTER 2

# Scripture is the Inspired Word of God

All Scripture is God-breathed and is useful for teaching, rebuking, correcting and training in righteousness, so that the man of God may be thoroughly equipped for every good work. 2 Timothy 3.16, 17 NIV

"Do not think that I have come to abolish the Law or the Prophets; I have not come to abolish them but to fulfill them." Matthew 5.17 NIV

You search the scriptures, because you think that in them you have eternal life; and it is they that testify on my behalf. John 5.39

Then he said to them, "These are my words that I spoke to you while I was still with you-that everything written about me in the Law of Moses, the prophets, and the psalms must be fulfilled." Then he opened their minds to understand the scriptures, and he said to them, "Thus it is written, that the Messiah is to suffer and to rise from the dead on the third day." Luke 24. 44-46

Jesus answered him, "I have spoken openly to the world; I always taught in synagogues and in the temple, where all the Jews come together; and I spoke nothing in secret. John 18.20 NASB

The grass withers, the flower fades; but the word of our God will stand forever. Isaiah 40.8

Indeed, the word of God is living and active, sharper than any two-edged sword, piercing until it divides soul from spirit, joints from marrow, it is able to judge the thoughts and intentions of the heart. Hebrews 4.12

You have been born anew, not of perishable but of imperishable seed, through the living and enduring word of God. I Peter 1.23

Humans seem to be designed with a questioning mind and a longing for God. My questions regarding God and life included the following:

- Why do we exist?
- What is the purpose to life?
- Is the God of the Old and New Testaments the same?
- Does being filled with the Holy Spirit as a human on earth provide earthly rewards?
- What did Jesus teach?
- Why do sickness, death, and bad things occur in life?
- Why do some humans seem to gravitate toward hurting others, not love?
- Is God in control of heaven and earth?
- Is there a spiritual aspect to life on earth in addition to what we physically see?
- Do people have eternal souls?
- If we each have a soul, how is our final destination determined?

Throughout my life, I have enjoyed talking with people about God, creation, life, choices, and relationships. When I talk to people in an open discussion regarding life and existence itself, it appears many people have questions similar to the ones listed above.

Few of the questions that filled my mind throughout much of my life seemed to be answered by the one or two Bible verses read weekly in church or by the sermons. With limited knowledge of the Holy Bible, I did not know how to investigate my questions regarding life and God. However, engineering school taught me how to think differently. Engineers focus on "root cause analysis," that is, review the available data to deduce the root cause or primary causative factor. However, my engineering training did not address my questions regarding this life, God, and eternity. I utilized my engineering training in research to compile data contained in the Holy Bible. My soul longed for God's answers to my questions regarding the purpose of life, love, and eternity. I prayed to God for wisdom. God's answer to my prayer to find his truth was, as usual, brief and clear: If you want to know more about God, **search**.

Searching for knowledge and data, then determining a conclusion is what I do best. God directed me to use my engineering brain and root cause analysis to research God's textbook, the Holy Bible. If I attended a class where an engineering professor or an English professor would read a few sentences from a textbook and lecture once a week, and I did no homework on my own, I would know very little about engineering or writing.

Reading through the Bible in one year is similar to reading through a very complicated textbook once. Reading through the Bible in a year involves a very fast pace and I openly confess I did not retain much detail of the Bible. Jesus indicated in Matthew 28.20 that people are to learn all that Jesus commanded! For a common person like me to learn the Holy Bible, I listened to thirty years of sermons, both in church and daily radio programs, carefully re-read many books of the Holy Bible multiple times, read numerous books explaining the Holy Bible, attended men's retreats on the Bible, attended Bible study classes, and prayed to the Holy Spirit of God Himself to teach me. I researched the teaching of God in a manner similar to the way I learned engineering: logically, thoroughly, and repeatedly.

I initially did not know exactly what God wanted me to teach in *Jesus is Our Friend: A Common Man's Search for Jesus Christ.* I wrote this book in the same manner I function as an engineering manager: I do extensive research and gather all the facts available, document and organize all the data into a logical format and determine the root cause or conclusion. My assigned task from God is to attempt to teach what Jesus taught in a condensed and easy to read format for the common man and woman.

I openly declare I am not able to convey all of Jesus' teachings in one book. My mission in writing this book is to share the good news of Jesus with the common person. With God's guidance, I humbly submit many of the teachings of Jesus in a concise book. Religious scholars may criticize me for writing this book. However, this is nothing new; the Pharisees attacked Jesus Himself when He taught the good news. Teddy Roosevelt must have been a courageous person and took risks. Teddy Roosevelt's speech inspires me:

> It is not the critic who counts; not the man who points out how the strong man stumbles, or where the doer of deeds could have done them better. The credit belongs to the man who is actually in the arena, whose face is marred by dust and sweat and blood; who strives valiantly; who errs, who comes short again and again, because there is no effort without error and shortcoming; but who does actually strive

to do the deeds; who knows great enthusiasms, the great devotions; who spends himself in a worthy cause; who at the best knows in the end the triumph of high achievement, and who at the worst, if he fails, at least fails while daring greatly, so that his place shall never be with those cold and timid souls who neither know victory nor defeat.

President Theodore Roosevelt
Sorbonne, Paris, April 23, 1910[3]

The Holy Bible is a special interactive book. The Word of God is living; the Bible is called the living Word. The Word of God provides a different insight to the reader, contingent upon our situation in life occurring at that time. The Bible provides a personalized living letter from God. A particular verse of scripture can provide an answer to a question at a point in one's life; the same scripture verse can provide additional insight if reread when a different question or different situation arises. As mentioned in Luke 24.46, God must open your mind to understand the Bible. Reading and rereading a portion of the Bible permits us to gain a different and deeper understanding of God and His words. This book, *Jesus is Our Friend*, has many interrelated topics and the same scripture passage is occasionally used in two chapters for different topics.

As we try and live closer to the way Jesus specified, life becomes more joyful and purposeful. The Bible is what the creator of the universe wrote for us to fill us with joy and peace.

I read the Holy Bible and listen to a Bible-based sermon on the radio most days. A miracle in itself, I gain insight on God and how to approach life every time I read or hear the Bible. Reading and understanding God's plan fills me with love, joy and peace. People at work have asked me why I am happy, smile, and have peace. I reply "Jesus."

Although the birth, death, and resurrection of Jesus took place approximately 2,000 years ago, the Holy Bible records the events for mankind to read and understand. It is truly amazing and awe-inspiring that Jesus was walking around with our ancestors two thousand years ago! The Bible provides clear directions to deal with life and people. The Holy Spirit of God will teach us what Jesus told us.

"I have said these things to you while I am still with you. But the Advocate, the Holy Spirit, whom the Father will send in my name, will teach you everything, and remind you of all that I have said to you." John 14.25-26

By reading the words of Jesus, we can learn His teachings and the Holy Spirit can enhance our understanding.

The human soul has an inborn emptiness for God and understanding of life. I personally had many questions about how to live life and be filled with Joy. God, through the Bible, has answered my questions. I started reading the Bible for answers to my own life experience. My spiritual questions were very deep for a twenty-three-year-old man. When I was a carefree eleven-year-old grade school boy, I thought my life was fine. I went to school. I played on a softball team. I took vacations. I had a new bicycle. I attended church. I thought Jesus was my friend. In my mind as an eleven year old, I thought I understood life and it was good. I woke up one morning to my mother's hysterical weeping and was told my father killed himself; I thought I was in the wrong body, the wrong house, and the wrong reality. Unfortunately, I was truly in my body and my father did truly kill himself and left me on planet earth with no father. I was angry with my father. I was disappointed and angry with God for many years for allowing my childhood to spiral into chaos. I had sufficient faith to understand that God is almighty and He could have prevented the destruction of my childhood; He chose not to intervene. I prayed to God for the wisdom to understand why the only life I had was transformed from pleasant to chaos. God evidently was not in a hurry to speak to me directly and I did not understand how life works for several decades. The answers to my deep spiritual questions were available all along in the Holy Bible, but I had to read and study God's Word. God's answers to my question regarding pain in life and other questions are listed in **Jesus is Our Friend**. I can truly and personally declare that the Holy Bible is the inspired Word of God.

As you read the Bible selections in this book, may the Holy Spirit through God's Word answer your questions. May the Holy Spirit ask you questions and may you research more topics for your continued spiritual growth.

Let us pray. Thank you Lord Jesus for coming to earth and teaching us the ways of God. The Gospels of Matthew, Mark, Luke, and John record the words of Jesus spoken as a human. Jesus, the apostle John refers to You as the Word because you came and delivered God's message. Reading your Word in the Gospels clarifies that You are the Son of the Living God because the message delivered is supernatural; no human being could possess that much wisdom. The wisdom you shared is supernatural in that it is applicable throughout time. The Words you spoke are as clear and profound today as when you said them over 2,000 years ago.

# CHAPTER 3

# The Beginning

In the beginning God created the heavens and the earth. Genesis 1.1a.

Then God said, "Let us make humankind in our image, according to our likeness; and let them have dominion over the fish of the sea, and over the birds of the air, and over the cattle, and over all the wild animals of the earth, and over every creeping thing that creeps upon the earth." So God created humankind in his image, in the image of God he created them; male and female he created them. Genesis 1.26, 27

In the beginning was the Word, and the Word was with God, and the Word was God. He was in the beginning with God. All things came into being through him, and without him not one thing came into being. John 1.1-3

Isaac Newton's first law, the law of inertia indicates, "Every object persists in its state of rest or uniform motion in a straight line unless it is compelled to change that state by forces impressed on it."[4] Isaac Newton also said, "Gravity explains the motions of the planets, but it cannot explain who set the planets in motion. God governs all things and knows all that is or can be done."[5] My humble compliments to Isaac Newton; he was a brilliant man. Isaac Newton's writings take me directly to intelligent design. God must have designed the planets and put them in orbit.

The world is a beautiful place. God is truly a great designer. My wife, son, daughter, and I enjoy traveling to places where God's creation is extraordinarily beautiful. The Valley of Fire State Park in Nevada has rocks bigger than houses that sparkle red in the sunlight. Monument Valley in Utah has even bigger mesas that protrude from the earth with a majesty that is amazing. A mesa is a lava flow that solidified with straight walls in dirt, then the dirt eroded away over time. Mesas are so big, I clearly understood that I am a very small creature that is alive for only a brief moment in time.

The mesas in Monument Valley were there many years before me and will be standing for thousands of years after I am dead and my spirit is in heaven with God. When standing in Monument Valley, I felt God whisper to me, "Be still and know I am God." God told a Psalmist the same statement; it is recorded in Psalm 46.10. I was very comforted and enlightened that God is in charge and I am just passing through. I felt relieved that I can do my best here on earth, but the creator of the universe has more power than I can even conceive.

As a designer myself, I find the creation of heaven, the earth, and all creatures, including us, by God to make perfect sense. The earth is at a precise distance from the sun so the earth is not too hot or too cold. The tilt of the earth causes the four seasons and the changing of the length of days. The rotation of the earth causes night and day every twenty-four hours. God is truly amazing to have created all of these complex systems. God made water to drink, gravity to keep us from floating away, food, dogs, cats, birds, and all the thousands of species of plants and animals to keep us entertained for a lifetime. The complexity of our human body amazes me. I'm happy my body works as well as it does; I could have never designed a robot as good as me that has auto-focus eyes, moving fingers and a creative brain! Our bodies even repair itself when cut or broken. I have never seen a car get a dent, then repair itself good as new.

Genesis records God made man in "our" image. The "our" is an interesting word, especially since humans were not created yet. Perhaps the "our" is God the Father, the Holy Spirit, and Jesus or God and angels. Either way, the Gospel of John 1.1-3 clearly states Jesus, the Word, was with God and was God in the beginning and all things came into being through him.

As a musician enjoys the craftsmanship of a fine piano or a driver appreciates the quality and performance of a particular model motor vehicle, the consumer comprehends that a designer and manufacturer of the product is responsible. Likewise, when we humans see a loved one's attractive smile, a singing bird, or a beautiful flower, we must comprehend there is a designer and creator. The existence of food to eat, water to drink, and sunlight to keep us warm indicates we are a part of a system working in concert. Regardless of when or how God chose to shape the first man and woman, bird, fish, and grain of wheat, He did it. The amount of scientific knowledge God possesses to design and create life from nothing is beyond the scope of His created creatures: us.

I have seen bumper stickers on a few automobiles over the years that indicate the driver believes in evolution and does not believe in God. As a design engineer, I totally disagree with the notion that evolution somehow proves there is no God. The hypothesis that evolution disproves the existence of God is flawed with the **Fallacy of Irrelevant Conclusion.**[6] The fallacy of irrelevant conclusion is a term in the study of deductive logic. Two examples of statements with the fallacy of irrelevant conclusion follow:

1. Adaptation or evolution of species to the environment proves there is no creator.
2. Adaptation of equipment to the environment proves there is no design engineer.

Let me spend a few moments explaining my opinion of adaptation and evolution. Creatures adapt to their environment to survive. I live in a deep suburban area populated with many deer. Thirty years ago and prior, the deer would often walk in front of a speeding automobile on a road and collide with an automobile. My wife hit a deer many years ago with our family car. In the past decade, I observed that many deer in my area approach the side of the road, stop, and look both ways. If a car is approaching, the deer will wait until the car passes, then it will quickly cross the road. Deer that do not look both ways before crossing a street will likely get killed by a car and subsequently not have offspring. Over many generations of deer living in the deep suburbs, deer that look both ways before crossing the street will live longer and reproduce. Deer living in areas that have automobiles, but are unable to adapt to living with automobiles, will likely be struck and killed. In God's animal kingdom, the most resilient members of a species survive. Climatic changes and other extreme changes may cause extreme adaptations in creatures over time.

I have designed modern heating and air conditioning systems that automatically adapt to the environment. If the weather is cold, the thermostat will cause a gas furnace to cycle and produce heat. During the summer season, the thermostat starts the air conditioner when the internal temperature is too warm. The adaptation of a heating and air conditioning system to the environment provides evidence of an intelligent designer. In my particular case, I was the intelligent design engineer.

Living creatures adapting to the environment provides evidence of a very superior intelligent designer, God. God is so brilliant, He even created people capable of thinking abstract thought and inventing things to make life easier and more productive. Adaptation proves God exists.

Cross species evolution is a more extreme case of adaptation. To the best of my research, there are no fossils found of a bear with bird feathers or a lion with alligator legs. There is little proof that the species on earth evolved from one source. I have personally witnessed a caterpillar, with many little legs, go into a cocoon, and emerge a butterfly with wings. Perhaps the metamorphous of a caterpillar to a butterfly is somewhat similar to a repetitive cross species evolution. If cross species evolution did exist, that is, one species adapting into another species, it would give glory to God, the master designer, and creator of all.

There seems to be an attitude in current media and society that it is politically correct to unconditionally accept the theory of evolution and reject the existence of God. When a society seeks to coerce all to accept the unproven theory of cross species evolution and deny the existence of God, the **fallacy of appeal to authority**[6] is evident. We are each human beings with the God given right to think. I clearly state here that I know an intelligent designer created we humans and all that is seen and unseen. I reject the fallacy that our human life form, and the form of all living creatures came from chaos. As a designer myself, I declare that all functional systems are produced by design and that chaos never produces functionality.

While the arguments regarding the existence of God seem to be focused on the evolution of species on earth, the more important question is who made the earth, the sun, and the universe? Newton's first law of motion prompts the question who started the motion of creation itself and the planets? We humans live only because we have a planet with suitable atmosphere, temperature range, water, and food. The universe declares the glory of God.

Why are so many in our society endorsing evolution and trying to deny God? Some people seek to be their own god and reject accountability to anyone. Belief in God acknowledges an all-powerful being exists. Understanding an all-powerful God exists validates the sense of right and wrong that is placed in our soul. Understanding we have a soul acknowledges we are accountable for our actions. Understanding we have a soul and are accountable for our actions acknowledges judgment by God. Understanding judgment by God acknowledges a reward or punishment for our deeds in the body. Those who disregard right and wrong do not want to receive judgment for their deeds. Those who do wrong and want to avoid judgment may deny the existence of God.

Let us pray. God you are eternal and almighty. Although You are self-sufficient, You chose to create the physical universe and create man in Your image. We stand humbly before You as created beings. Thank You for creating the beautiful world around us. Thank you for creating human beings with an observant and creative brain. Thank You for creating love.

# CHAPTER 4

# Scripture Selections Regarding The Life of Jesus

Kindly note that chapters four and five are different from the other chapters in *Jesus Is Our Friend*; these chapters are more historical and informative. Chapters four and five explain the life of Jesus and why He lived as a human being. These two chapters are important for those unfamiliar with Jesus and will serve as a review for more knowledgeable Christians. It is necessary to know who Jesus is and why He came to earth to understand His message of love and salvation. The remaining chapters of this book disclose personal tragedies, mistakes, and triumphs to explain how the Holy Bible is applicable to the lives of the common man and woman.

Chapter four records important aspects of the life of Jesus through numerous Bible verses. This chapter has the most quotes from scripture. This chapter on the life of Jesus is structured as I previously described; the selected Bible verses are presented first, followed by my commentary. It is important that the Holy Spirit of God speak to you while you read the Gospel of Jesus. God's Word is holy and eternal; my commentary is a humble attempt by a common man to apply the Bible to our daily lives. Let us begin our journey through Jesus' life as recorded in scripture.

Now the birth of Jesus the Messiah took place in this way. When his mother Mary had been engaged to Joseph, but before they lived together, she was found to be with child from the Holy Spirit. Her husband Joseph, being a righteous man and unwilling to expose her to public disgrace, planned to dismiss her quietly. But just when he had resolved to do this, an angel of the Lord appeared to him in a dream and said, "Joseph, son of David, do not be afraid to take Mary as your wife, for the child conceived in her is from the Holy Spirit. She will bear a son, and you are to name him Jesus, for he will save his people from their sins." All this took place to fulfill what had been spoken by the Lord through the prophet: "Look, the virgin shall conceive and bear a son, and they shall name him Emmanuel," which means, "God is with us." When Joseph awoke from sleep, he did as the angel of the Lord commanded him; he took her as his wife, but had no marital relations with her until she had borne a son; and he named him Jesus. Matthew 1.18-25

And the Word was made flesh, and dwelt among us, (and we beheld his glory, the glory as of the only begotten of the Father,) full of grace and truth. John 1.14 KJV

In Him was life, and that life was the light of all people. The light shines in the darkness, and the darkness did not overcome it. John 1.4-5

Behold, an angel of the Lord appeared to Joseph in a dream and said, "Get up! Take the Child and His mother and flee to Egypt, and remain there until I tell you; for Herod is going to search for the Child to destroy Him." So Joseph got up and took the Child and His mother while it was still night, and left for Egypt. He remained there until the death of Herod. This was to fulfill what had been spoken by the Lord through the prophet: "OUT OF EGYPT I CALLED MY SON." Matthew 2.13b-15 NASB

And Jesus, when he was baptized, went up straightway out of the water: and, lo, the heavens were opened unto him, and he saw the Spirit of God descending like a dove, and lighting upon him: And lo a voice from heaven, saying, This is my beloved Son, in whom I am well pleased. Matthew 3.16-17 KJV

These are the names of the twelve apostles: first, Simon (who is called Peter) and his brother Andrew; James son of Zebedee, and his brother John; Philip and Bartholomew; Thomas and Matthew the tax collector; James son of Alphaeus, and Thaddaeus; Simon the Zealot and Judas Iscariot, who betrayed him. Matthew 10.2-4 NIV

And when they wanted wine, the mother of Jesus saith unto him, They have no wine. Jesus saith unto her, Woman, what have I to do with thee? mine hour is not yet come. His mother saith unto the servants, Whatsoever he saith unto you, do it. And there were set there six water pots of stone, after the manner of the purifying of the Jews, containing two or three firkins apiece. Jesus saith unto them, Fill the water pots with water. And they filled them up to the brim. And he saith unto them, Draw out now, and bear unto the governor of the feast. And they bare it. When the ruler of the feast had tasted the water that was made wine, and knew not whence it was: (but the servants which drew the water knew;) the governor of the feast called the bridegroom, And saith unto him, Every man at the beginning doth set forth good wine; and when men have well drunk, then that which is worse: but thou hast kept the good wine until now. This beginning of miracles did Jesus in Cana of Galilee, and manifested forth his glory; and his disciples believed on him. John 2.3-11 KJV

They came to Jericho. As he and his disciples and a large crowd were leaving Jericho, Bartimaeus son of Timaeus, a blind beggar, was sitting by the roadside. When he heard that it was Jesus of Nazareth, he began to shout out and say, "Jesus, Son of David, have mercy on me!" Many sternly ordered him to be quiet, but he cried out even more loudly, "Son of David, have mercy on me!" Jesus stood still and said, "Call him here." And they called the blind man, saying to him, "Take heart; get up, he is calling you." So throwing off his cloak, he sprang up and came to Jesus. Then Jesus said to him, "What do you want me to do for you?" The blind man said to him, "My teacher, let me see again." Jesus said to him, "Go; your faith has made you well." Immediately he regained his sight and followed him on the way. Mark 10.46-52

"For no one does anything in secret when he himself seeks to be known publicly. If You do these things, show Yourself to the world." For not even His brothers were believing in Him. So Jesus said to them, "My time is not yet here, but your time is always opportune." John 7.4-6 NASB

Coming to his hometown, he began teaching the people in their synagogue, and they were amazed. "Where did this man get this wisdom and these miraculous powers?" they asked. "Isn't this the carpenter's son? Isn't his mother's name Mary, and aren't his brothers James, Joseph, Simon and Judas? Aren't all his sisters with us? Where then did this man get all these things?" And they took offense at him. But Jesus said to them, "Only in his hometown and in his own house is a prophet without honor." Matthew 13.54-57 NIV

Then said Jesus unto him, Except ye see signs and wonders, ye will not believe. John 4.48 KJV

And when Jesus entered Capernaum, a centurion came to Him, imploring Him, and saying, "Lord, my servant is lying paralyzed at home, fearfully tormented." Jesus said to him, "I will come and heal him." But the centurion said, "Lord, I am not worthy for You to come under my roof, but just say the word, and my servant will be healed. "For I also am a man under authority, with soldiers under me; and I say to this one, 'Go!' and he goes, and to another, 'Come!' and he comes, and to my slave, 'Do this!' and he does it." Now when Jesus heard this, He marveled and said to those who were following, "Truly I say to you, I have not found such great faith with anyone in Israel. I say to you that many will come from east and west, and recline at the table with Abraham, Isaac and Jacob in the kingdom of heaven; but the sons of the kingdom will be cast out into the outer darkness; in that place there will be weeping and gnashing of teeth." And Jesus said to the centurion, "Go; it shall be done for you as you have believed." And the servant was healed that very moment. Matthew 8.5-13 NASB

Soon afterward, Jesus went to a town called Nain, and his disciples and a large crowd went along with him. As he approached the town gate, a dead person was being carried out - the only son of his mother, and she was a widow. And a large crowd from the town was with her. When the Lord saw her, his heart went out to her and he said, "Don't cry." Then he went up and touched the coffin, and those carrying it stood still. He said, "Young man, I say to you, get up!" The dead man sat up and began to talk, and Jesus gave him back to his mother. They were all filled with awe and praised God. "A great prophet has appeared among us," they said. "God has come to help his people." Luke 7.11-16 NIV

"The Father and I are one." John 10.30 KJV

Jesus said to him, "I am the way, and the truth, and the life. No one comes to the Father except through me." John 14.6.

After six days Jesus took with him Peter, James and John the brother of James, and led them up a high mountain by themselves. There he was transfigured before them. His face shone like the sun, and his clothes became as white as the light. Just then there appeared before them Moses and Elijah, talking with Jesus. Peter said to Jesus, "Lord, it is good for us to be here. If you wish, I will put up three shelters—one for you, one for Moses and one for

Elijah." While he was still speaking, a bright cloud enveloped them, and a voice from the cloud said, "This is my Son, whom I love; with him I am well pleased. Listen to him!" When the disciples heard this, they fell facedown to the ground, terrified. But Jesus came and touched them. "Get up," he said. "Don't be afraid." When they looked up, they saw no one except Jesus. As they were coming down the mountain, Jesus instructed them, "Don't tell anyone what you have seen, until the Son of Man has been raised from the dead. Matthew 17.1-9 NIV

Jesus said to them, "Truly, truly, I say to you, before Abraham was born, I am." John 8.58 NASB

Jesus did many other miraculous signs in the presence of his disciples, which are not recorded in this book. John 20.30 NIV

For God so loved the world, that He gave His only begotten Son, that whoever believes in Him shall not perish, but have eternal life. John 3.16 NASB

Then he began to teach them that the Son of Man must undergo great suffering, and be rejected by the elders, the chief priests, and the scribes, and be killed, and after three days rise again. Mark 8.31

Then the chief priests and the Pharisees called a meeting of the Sanhedrin. "What are we accomplishing?" they asked. "Here is this man performing many miraculous signs. If we let him go on like this, everyone will believe in him, and then the Romans will come and take away both our place and our nation." Then one of them, named Caiaphas, who was high priest that year, spoke up, "You know nothing at all! You do not realize that it is better for you that one man die for the people than that the whole nation perish." John 11. 47-50 NIV

And when He had taken some bread and given thanks, He broke it and gave it to them, saying, "This is My body which is given for you; do this in remembrance of Me." Luke 22.19 NASB

Then he took a cup, and after giving thanks He gave it to them, saying, "Drink from it, all of you; for this is My blood of the covenant, which is poured out for many for forgiveness of sins." Matthew 26.27-28

Pilate said to them, 'Whom do you want me to release for you, Jesus Barabbas or Jesus who is called the Messiah?' For he realized that it was out of jealousy that they had handed him over. While he was sitting on the judgement seat, his wife sent word to him, 'Have nothing to do with that innocent man, for today I have suffered a great deal because of a dream about him.' Now the chief priests and the elders persuaded the crowds to ask for Barabbas and to have Jesus killed. The governor again said to them, 'Which of the two do you want me to release for you?' And they said, "Barabbas." Pilate said to them, "Then what should I do with Jesus who is called the Messiah?" All of them said, "Let him be crucified!" Then he asked, "Why, what evil has he done?" But they shouted all the more, "Let him be crucified!" So when Pilate saw that he could do nothing, but rather that a riot was beginning, he took some water and washed his hands before the crowd, saying, "I am innocent of this man's blood; see to it yourselves." Then the people as a whole answered, 'His blood be on us and on our children!' Matthew 27. 17b-25

Then delivered he him therefore unto them to be crucified. And they took Jesus, and led him away. And he bearing his cross went forth into a place called the place of a skull, which is called in the Hebrew Golgotha: Where they crucified him, and two other with him, on either side one, and Jesus in the midst. And Pilate wrote a title, and put it on the cross. And the writing was JESUS OF NAZARETH THE KING OF THE JEWS. John 19.16- 19 KJV

Later, Joseph of Arimathea asked Pilate for the body of Jesus. Now Joseph was a disciple of Jesus, but secretly because he feared the Jews. With Pilate's permission, he came and took the body away. He was accompanied by Nicodemus, the man who earlier had visited Jesus at night. Nicodemus brought a mixture of myrrh and aloes, about seventy-five pounds. Taking Jesus' body, the two of them wrapped it, with the spices, in strips of linen. This was in accordance with Jewish burial customs. At the place where Jesus was crucified, there was a garden, and in the garden a new tomb, in which no one had ever been laid. Because it was the Jewish day of Preparation and since the tomb was nearby, they laid Jesus there. John19.38-42 NIV

And Joseph took the body and wrapped it in a clean linen cloth, and laid it in his own new tomb, which he had hewn out in the rock; and he rolled a large stone against the entrance of the tomb and went away. Matthew 27.59, 60 NASB

Pilate said to them, "You have a guard of soldiers; go, make it as secure as you can." So they went with the guard and made the tomb secure by sealing the stone. Matthew 27.65, 66

After the Sabbath, as the first day of the week was dawning, Mary Magdalene and the other Mary went to see the tomb. And suddenly there was a great earthquake; for an angel of the Lord, descending from heaven, came and rolled back the stone and sat on it. His appearance was like lightning, and his clothing white as snow. For fear of him the guards shook and became like dead men. But the angel said to the women, "Do not be afraid; I know that you are looking for Jesus who was crucified. He is not here; for he has been raised, as he said. Come, see the place where he lay. Then go quickly and tell his disciples, "He has been raised from the dead, and indeed he is going ahead of you to Galilee; there you will see him." This is my message for you." So they left the tomb quickly with fear and great joy, and ran to tell his disciples. Suddenly Jesus met them and said, 'Greetings!' And they came to him, took hold of his feet, and worshipped him. Then Jesus said to them, 'Do not be afraid; go and tell my brothers to go to Galilee; there they will see me.' Matthew 28.1-10

"Look at my hands and my feet; see that it is I myself. Touch me and see; for a ghost does not have flesh and bones as you see that I have." Luke 24.39

After he said this, he showed them his hands and his side. Then the disciples rejoiced when they saw the Lord. Jesus said to them again, 'Peace be with you. As the Father has sent me, so I send you.' When he had said this, he breathed on them and said to them, 'Receive the Holy Spirit.' John 20. 20-22

After the Lord Jesus had spoken to them, he was taken up into heaven and he sat at the right hand of God. Mark 16.19 NIV

Jesus, the Son of God, left his throne in heaven and lived as a human being on earth. Jesus was conceived by the Holy Spirit and born to a virgin named Mary. The virgin birth of Jesus was prophesized in Isaiah 7.14. Jesus is very different than other prophets, such as Moses, Abraham, or Noah. Moses, Abraham, and Noah were mortal men who lived and died. Jesus was with God in the beginning, and is one with God. All things came into being through Jesus. Jesus was born in the flesh, however, Jesus also remained in the Spirit.

Jesus was fully human and fully God. Jesus was not born into the family of an earthly king. God selected Mary to be Jesus' mother and He selected Joseph, Mary's husband, to care for His Son. Jesus was born to working parents from Nazareth. Joseph worked as a carpenter. Luke 2 records that Jesus was born in a manger for cattle because there was no room in the inn. Jesus was not born as an earthly aristocrat; Jesus Himself lived as a common man. An angel told Joseph to take Mary and Jesus to Egypt because King Herod was in the process of murdering all boys born in Bethlehem who were under the age of two.

As a child, Jesus referred to the temple as His Father's house. Jesus grew and worked as a carpenter (Mark 6.3) until he was about thirty years old (Luke 3.23).

Jesus met His cousin John the Baptist by the Jordan River. Jesus asked John to baptize Him. When John baptized Jesus, God spoke from heaven and indicated He was pleased with His beloved Son. Baptism is an outward expression of one's repentance for sin and commitment to righteousness. Jesus was without sin.

Humans differ from Jesus in that we are born of the flesh and every inclination of our heart gravitates toward carnal instincts. We humans must be born again of the Spirit to be transformed from our inclination to sin and become children of the light. Jesus calls us to repent in acknowledgement of our sins. The carnal nature of man focuses on the wants and needs of the self and disregards one's neighbor.

Jesus chose twelve men to be His apostles. Jesus did not choose His apostles from the educated religious elite. Jesus had common men for apostles. Simon Peter and his brother Andrew were fisherman. James and his brother John were fishermen. Matthew was a tax collector. Jesus also chose women to share His gospel message, such as the woman at the well. Jesus was a Friend to the common human being. As I read and reread the gospels, I perceived a bond to Jesus that He was a common man. Jesus worked as a carpenter and spent much time with common people. Jesus is not only the God of wealthy people in worship in ornate cathedrals; Jesus is the God for all people, rich or poor. We can worship Jesus anywhere.

Jesus' first miracle was turning water into wine at a wedding feast in Cana of Galilee. Mary, Jesus, and His apostles attended a wedding feast and all the wine was drank before the feast was completed. Mary, Jesus' mother, asked Jesus to make more wine. Jesus honored His mother and had the servants fill six large water pots with water; Jesus then changed the water into wine and made his first miracle. The wine Jesus made was better than the wine the host served initially.

The details of Jesus restoring sight to Bartimaeus explain two complex subjects. Bartimaeus, a blind beggar, shouted, "Jesus, Son of David, have mercy on me!" when Jesus passed by. The crowd following Jesus ordered the blind man to be quiet. The crowd selfishly wanted to hoard Jesus to themselves. Bartimaeus continued to cry out for mercy from Jesus. Jesus asked the blind man what he wanted. Bartimaeus asked Jesus to restore his sight. Jesus restored the man's sight and indicated his faith healed him. Although Jesus knows what we want before we ask Him, Jesus wants us to pray and ask for specific needs. A specific request to Jesus indicates we have faith that He can help us. Also, if we are with the crowd following Jesus, believing in Jesus and perhaps attending church, we do not own Jesus. As followers of Jesus, we are not to hoard Jesus to ourselves, but share Jesus with all who need Him.

Jesus had four earthly half brothers, James, Joseph, Simon, and Judas. Jesus also had half sisters, but they are not named in the Holy Bible. Scripture reveals that Jesus' earthly half brothers initially did not comprehend, nor believe, He was the Son of the Living God. After Jesus' miracles and teachings became well known, Jesus' brother James believed and then likely wrote the book of James.

After Jesus cured a person with leprosy, a centurion asked Jesus to heal his paralyzed servant. Jesus kindly offered to travel to the centurion's house. The centurion demonstrated extraordinary faith and humility in the presence of Jesus. The centurion told Jesus he was unworthy to request the Son of God to enter his home. Although Jesus previously healed the sick in His presence, the centurion understood that Jesus had the authority and power to heal his servant from afar. Jesus was pleased with the faith of the centurion. The centurion was not a Jew. Jesus taught in this healing that being a child of God is not based on one's race, but faith in God.

When Jesus went to a town called Nain, He saw a widow's dead son being carried out to be buried. Jesus took pity on the widow and told the woman not to cry. Jesus restored the life into her son and the dead man sat up and talked.

Per Matthew 8.14, Jesus healed Peter's mother-in-law.

Jesus plainly declared that He and God the Father are one. Jesus' declaration that He and the Father are one explained that Jesus is not a human prophet, but the Son of the living God.

Jesus stated that He is the Way, the Truth, and the Life.

Jesus came to earth to show us the way. Jesus is the Way to heaven. We will all each sit before the judgment seat of Jesus Christ. Jesus lived without sin and was perfect. As a human, we cannot be perfect, and we cannot be sinless. Jesus is our example to emulate. Jesus loved God and loved his neighbor. Jesus experienced the joy and pain of being fully human and fully God. It is comforting to me to know that Jesus understands any pain that I experience in my life because He was human. We are forgiven of our sins by Jesus' atoning sacrifice on the cross and by grace through faith in Jesus. God gives us the gift of eternal life when we live and believe in Jesus.

Jesus is the Truth. Jesus taught the commandments and summarized them as loving God and loving your neighbor. Jesus told many parables and made many profound declarations to illustrate applications of the commandments in daily life.

Jesus is the Life. Jesus offers us eternal life in paradise. Jesus died as a perfect sacrifice for all mankind; all who live and believe in Jesus are forgiven of their sins and have eternal life. Jesus also offers us life on earth filled with supernatural contentment and understanding. We are blessed that Jesus came to be the Way, the Truth, and the Life for us, his friends.

Jesus took Peter, James, and John to a mountain. Jesus transfigured Himself such that He displayed His glory. Jesus' face shined like the sun and His clothes were white as light. Moses and Elijah, Old Testament prophets appeared with Jesus. God spoke from heaven and indicated Jesus is His Son and with Him He is well pleased. God also told the apostles to listen to Jesus.

When Jesus visited the workers at the temple, He said before Abraham I AM. In this clear and concise statement, Jesus told the Jew working that He existed before Abraham and He was the great I AM, that is God. God referred to Himself as I AM when he spoke to Moses at the burning bush before the exodus from captivity in Egypt. At that juncture, the Jewish workers picked up stones to throw at Jesus.

More of Jesus' miracles are listed in subsequent chapters of **Jesus is Our Friend**. Jesus performed many miracles that are not recorded in the Holy Bible.

And as Moses lifted up the serpent in the wilderness, even so must the Son of man be lifted up: That whosoever believeth in him should not perish, but have eternal life. John 3.14-15 KJV

Jesus openly taught that He would suffer greatly and be lifted up. Jesus compared His being lifted up to the bronze serpent that Moses held up in Numbers 21.9.

The Lord instructed Moses to make a serpent. Moses made a bronze serpent and lifted it up with a pole. When a deadly snake bit an Israelite, he would look at the bronze serpent and God would allow him to live.

Jesus was lifted up on the cross during His death as the perfect sacrifice for the forgiveness of sin for all who live and believe in Him. Like the bronze serpent that Moses lifted up, Jesus provides eternal life for those who look to Him for salvation.

Jesus fulfilled many roles, and had many names, including:

Christ, Matthew 1.16: Christ translates to the word "annointed."[7]   Jesus Christ is the holy one and loved by God.

Friend, John 15.15: Jesus calls us to a personal relationship as His Friend. Jesus has communicated with us in detail what God the Father has made known.

I AM, John 8.58: Jesus declared before Abraham was born "I AM". "I AM" is what God the Father referred to Himself as when He spoke to Moses at the burning bush in Exodus 3.14. Jesus was with God in the beginning and Jesus is God.

Immanuel, Isaiah 7.14 & Matthew 1.23: The Holy Bible teaches that Immanuel translates to "God with us." Jesus was conceived by the Holy Spirit. Jesus lived with humans on earth.

Jesus, Matthew, 1.21: The angel instructed Joseph to name God's Son Jesus, for He will save the world from their sin. Scripture implies Jesus means Savior.

King of Kings, Lord of Lords, 1 Timothy 6.15: Jesus is more powerful than any king or any Lord.

Light of the World, John 8.12: Jesus brought the light of truth into the world. The light shines in the darkness.

Nazarene, Mark 16.6, Jesus' hometown was Nazareth. Jesus was called the Nazarene. Acts 24.5 documents that the followers of Jesus were referred to as the Nazarene sect.

Prince of Peace, Isaiah 9.6: Jesus brings peace to people of good will, not as the word gives, but peace in their soul. Peace in the soul is based on building one's faith on the rock of Jesus, not in the world.

Savior, John 4.42: Jesus came to save the world from their sins by His atoning sacrifice.

Son of the Living God, Matthew 16.16: Peter was inspired by God to call Jesus the Son of the Living God.

Teacher, Mark 4.1: Jesus taught many truths. We are blessed that God instructed Matthew, Mark, Luke, and John to record Jesus' teaching for us to read. Jesus often taught in figurative language and called them parables.

Word, John 1.14: The apostle John called Jesus the Word. Jesus taught the truth by His Word and example. Jesus loved God and Loved His neighbor as Himself.

As Jesus had known, when the news of Jesus' miracles became widespread, the Pharisees became aware of Jesus' popularity. The Pharisees were concerned that everyone would believe in Jesus. Caiaphas, the high priest that year, spoke up and indicated that Jesus should be murdered, rather than allow the glory of Jesus be known by all. The Pharisees knew Jesus was holy and performed miracles. Caiaphas wanted Jesus murdered because he knew Jesus was truly sent by God and all would believe in Jesus. Caiaphas and the Pharisees envied Jesus and wanted to retain their earthly power.

Jesus and His twelve apostles met for their last supper. Jesus knew He would be murdered the following day. Jesus took bread, gave thanks, and broke it; Jesus indicated the bread represents His body given for us and we are to do that in memory of Him. Jesus then took the cup and indicated we are to drink it. The wine represents Jesus' blood of the new covenant poured out for many for the forgiveness of sin. God Himself created the last supper, commonly renamed communion in contemporary society. Communion is an outward and visible sign of our commitment to Jesus; communion acknowledges that Jesus died, once and for all, for the forgiveness of sins.

During the last supper, one of the twelve apostles left and arranged for guards to seize Jesus. Judas identified Jesus with a kiss of betrayal.

Caiaphas asked Jesus if He was the Christ, the Son of God. Mark 14.61-62 records that Jesus indicated He was Christ, the Son of God. Caiaphas and his fellow Pharisees falsely accused Jesus of blasphemy and declared Jesus was worthy of death. Caiaphas and the Pharisees brought Jesus before Pilate. Pilate knew Jesus was not guilty of any crime, and did not deserve death and did not deserve to be crucified. Pilate tried to avoid making any decision regarding Jesus and offered the people gathered to free a prisoner named Barabbas or Jesus. The chief priest and the elders persuaded those gathered to asked that Barabbas be freed and crucify Jesus. When Pilate asked the crowd for their decision on whom to free, the crowd shouted Barabbas. When Pilate asked the crowd what to do with Jesus, the people demanded

He be crucified. Pilate washed his hands and said he was innocent of Jesus' blood. However, Pilate was the governor and responsible to carry out the law. Caiaphas was the chief priest and facilitated the murder of Jesus Christ. The Pharisees and the crowd answered Pilate when the governor declared he was innocent of Jesus' death:

Then the people as a whole answered, "His blood be on us and on our children!" Matthew 27.25

Jesus was then crucified and died a painful death by torture.

Joseph of Arimathea and Nicodemus took Jesus' dead body and wrapped it with spices and linen. They placed Jesus' body in a new tomb and rolled a great stone to enclose the tomb of Jesus.

Mark 8.31 records that Jesus prophesized that He would be rejected by the elders and the chief priests, would suffer and be killed, then in three days rise again. The chief priests and elders, who arranged Jesus' murder, asked Pilot to place guards at the tomb of Jesus to prevent His followers from moving Jesus' body and claim He rose from the dead. The body of Jesus, the savior of the world, laid dead in the tomb; guards stood outside the tomb.

On the third day, Sunday, Mary Magdalene and the other Mary went to the tomb of Jesus. An earthquake and an angel from God rolled back the great stone of the tomb. The angel sat on the great stone. The guards of the tomb were terrified and appeared to be dead. The angel told the two women named Mary not to be afraid. The angel told the women Jesus has been raised from the dead. As the women left the tomb, Jesus met them and they fell at His feet and worshipped Him. Jesus told the women to tell the others to meet Him in Galilee. Jesus returned to life in His human body; Jesus triumphed over death and sin.

Let us pray. Thank you Jesus for coming to earth and living with us. You chose to live amongst the common people and lived as a common man yourself. Jesus, you are familiar with the joy and disappointments of everyday life. You were betrayed by one of your apostles, Judas. We are able to pray to you and know you understand our struggles and our emotions. All who are weary and heavy laden may come to you and You will give us rest. With Your great love, You taught us how to live. With Your great love, You gave us hope. With Your great love, You gave up your life for us. With Your great love, You offer us the forgiveness of sin and eternal life. Thank You for loving us first. Amen.

# CHAPTER 5

# The New Covenant of Jesus Christ

But the serpent said to the woman, "You will not die; for God knows that when you eat of it your eyes will be opened, and you will be like God, knowing good and evil." So when the woman saw that the tree was good for food, and that it was a delight to the eyes, and that the tree was to be desired to make one wise, she took of its fruit and ate; and she also gave some to her husband, and he ate. And to the man he said, "Because you have listened to the voice of your wife, and have eaten of the tree about which I commanded you, `You shall not eat of it,' cursed is the ground because of you; in toil you shall eat of it all the days of your life; thorns and thistles it shall bring forth to you; and you shall eat the plants of the field. By the sweat of your face you shall eat bread till you return to the ground, for out of it you were taken; you are dust, and to dust you shall return." Genesis 3.4-6, 17-19

And the LORD God said unto the serpent, Because thou hast done this, thou art cursed above all cattle, and above every beast of the field; upon thy belly shalt thou go, and dust shalt thou eat all the days of thy life: And I will put enmity between thee and the woman, and between thy seed and her seed; it shall bruise thy head, and thou shalt bruise his heel. Genesis 3.14-15 KJV

He shall slaughter the goat of the sin offering that is for the people and bring its blood inside the curtain, and do with its blood as he did with the blood of the bull, sprinkling it upon the mercy seat and before the mercy seat. Thus he shall make atonement for the sanctuary, because of the uncleannesses of the people of Israel, and because of their transgressions, all their sins; and so he shall do for the tent of meeting, which remains with them in the midst of their uncleanness. Leviticus 16.15, 16

And according to the Law, one may almost say, all things are cleansed with blood, and without shedding of blood there is no forgiveness. Hebrews 9.22 NASB

And every priest stands day after day at his service, offering again and again the same sacrifices that can never take away sins. But when Christ had offered for all time a single sacrifice for sins, "he sat down at the right hand of God," and since then has been waiting "until his enemies would be made a footstool for his feet." For by a single offering he has perfected for all time those who are sanctified. Hebrews 10.11-14

"I am the good shepherd. The good shepherd lays down his life for the sheep. The hired hand, who is not the shepherd and does not own the sheep, sees the wolf coming and leaves the sheep and runs away - and the wolf snatches them and scatters them. The hired hand runs away because a hired hand does not care for the sheep. I am the good shepherd. I know my own and my own know me, just as the Father knows me and I know the Father. And I lay down my life for the sheep. I have other sheep that do not belong to this fold. I must bring them also, and they will listen to my voice. So there will be one flock, one shepherd. For this reason the Father loves me, because I lay down my life in order to take it up again. No one takes it from me, but I lay it down of my own accord. I have power to lay it down, and I have power to take it up again. I have received this command from my Father." John 10. 11-18

Jesus said to them, "I am the bread of life. Whoever comes to me will never be hungry, and whoever believes in me will never be thirsty. But I said to you that you have seen me and yet do not believe. Everything that the Father gives me will come to me, and anyone who comes to me I will never drive away; for I have come down from heaven, not to do my own will, but the will of him who sent me. And this is the will of him who sent me, that I should lose nothing of all that he has given me, but raise it up on the last day. This is indeed the will of my Father, that all who see the Son and believe in him may have eternal life; and I will raise them up on the last day." John 6.35-40

When many of his disciples heard it, they said, 'This teaching is difficult; who can accept it?' John 6.60

From this time many of his disciples turned back and no longer followed him. "You do not want to leave too, do you?" Jesus asked the Twelve. Simon

Peter answered him, "Lord, to whom shall we go? You have the words of eternal life. We believe and know that you are the Holy One of God." John 6.66-68 NIV

But now, irrespective of law, the righteousness of God has been disclosed, and is attested by the law and the prophets, the righteousness of God through faith in Jesus Christ for all who believe. For there is no distinction, since all have sinned and fall short of the glory of God; they are now justified by his grace as a gift, through the redemption that is in Christ Jesus, whom God put forward as a sacrifice of atonement by his blood, effective through faith. He did this to show his righteousness, because in his divine forbearance he had passed over the sins previously committed; it was to prove at the present time that he himself is righteous and that he justifies the one who has faith in Jesus. Romans 3. 21-26

For by grace you have been saved through faith, and this is not your own doing; it is the gift of God--not the result of works, so that no one may boast. For we are what he has made us, created in Christ Jesus for good works, which God prepared beforehand to be our way of life. Ephesians 2. 8-10

When Jesus came to earth and lived amongst our ancestors, He performed many miracles, including changing water into wine, healing the sick, feeding five thousand people, and walking on water. Unconditional gifts are typically easy to accept. The gifts and healing that Jesus provided were seen and experienced by people in the flesh. Many people followed Jesus for earthly rewards. Jesus then advanced His teachings to a spiritual level and said:

"Do not work for the food that perishes, but for the food that endures for eternal life, which the Son of Man will give you. For it is on him that God the Father has set his seal." John 6.27

Jesus taught that He was the bread of life. Jesus explained that He came from Heaven, He was the Son of God, and we must believe in Him to have eternal life in Heaven after death. Many of Jesus' followers thought Jesus' teaching was hard to accept and then rejected Jesus. The teaching that many of Jesus' initial followers rejected is called "The New Covenant." Jesus Himself named His gift of eternal life to human beings the new covenant:

And when He had taken some bread and given thanks, He broke it and gave it to them, saying, "This is My body which is given for you; do this in remembrance of Me." And in the same way He took the cup after they had eaten, saying, "This cup which is poured out for you is the new covenant in My blood." Luke 22.19, 20 NASB

To understand the holiness and majesty of the new covenant of Jesus Christ, it is critical to understand why we need a covenant with God. It is beneficial to understand the initial covenant between God and man and what is God's new covenant.

Let us first investigate why we humans need a covenant with God. In the beginning, God made man and woman in His image, blessed them, and placed them in the Garden of Eden. God's creation was good. Adam and Eve were initially created to be immortal. However, Adam and Eve questioned God's authority and commands; Adam and Eve ate of the forbidden knowledge of good and evil. Mankind's choice to reject God and embrace evil resulted in God's punishment. God cursed the earth, created thorns and thistles, made hard labor a necessity to survive, and made mankind mortal creatures. The descendents of man grew wicked. God then destroyed all of mankind, except the family of Noah, by causing a great flood. God made a covenant with Noah after the flood subsided.

"Never again will I curse the ground because of man, even though every inclination of his heart is evil from childhood. And never again will I destroy all living creatures, as I have done." "I establish my covenant with you: Never again will all life be cut off by the waters of a flood; never again will there be a flood to destroy the earth." Genesis 8.21b and 9.11 NIV

The great flood purged the earth of numerous wicked people, but did not eradicate mankind's inclination to sin. The descendants of Noah's family were unable to walk in perfect righteousness. Although we humans try to follow God's commandments we stumble into sin.

God made a covenant with Moses to restore his followers and forgive them of their sins. God's forgiveness was attained through the blood of the covenant. God instructed Moses that his brother Aaron and Aaron's sons would serve as priests. The priests would act as a mediator between the people and God. The priest would make atonement for the sins of the people by sprinkling the blood of a goat and a bull in the Holy of Holies area located behind the curtain in the temple. The offerings by the priest must be done again and again to attain atonement for the sins.

The burnt offerings became a revenue generator for the religious authorities. The authorities would sell the animals to be offered and would make additional profit in exchanging the various currencies. When Jesus came to live with us on earth, He drove out the animals in the Temple and overturned the tables of the moneychangers. Jesus objected to the religious authorities using the temple as a marketplace for their greed and self-indulgence.

Jesus, the Son of the Living God, declared the end of the blood of the covenant with the following statement:

I desire mercy, and not sacrifice. Matthew 12.7b

He said to them, "'You shall love the Lord your God with all your heart, and with all your soul, and with all your mind.' This is the greatest and first commandment. And a second is like it: 'You shall love your neighbor as yourself.' On these two commandments hang all the law and the prophets." Matthew 22.37b-40

Prior to Jesus being born as a human and living amongst us, there was a human mediator between God and humans. God called Moses to go to Mount Sinai and receive His commandments. Moses then shared God's message with the people. During the time of Moses, common people were not permitted to enter the Holy of Holies. A mediator would make the sacrifice to God on behalf of the people.

The relationship between God and humans became much more personal when God's only Son was born in Bethlehem. When Jesus walked the earth, people had direct access to the Son of God. Jesus devoted several years preaching the good news. The good news included eternal life through living and believing in Jesus. Jesus knew that after He completed his teaching ministry, He would be insulted and killed. Jesus' death on the cross would be the perfect atoning sacrifice to forgive the sins of mankind, once and for all. Jesus' gift of forgiveness by his perfect blood sacrifice negated the need for any further sacrifices for our sins. When Jesus died on the cross, He gave another gift to mankind:

Then Jesus gave a loud cry and breathed his last. And the curtain of the temple was torn in two, from top to bottom. Now when the centurion, who stood facing him, saw that in this way he breathed his last, he said, "Truly this man was God's Son!" Mark 15. 37-39

Jesus tore the curtain of the temple from top to bottom to make a visible and outward sign that He granted mankind direct access to God Himself! From the death of Jesus and beyond, humans could approach God directly through the forgiveness of Jesus Christ. Jesus, the Son of God, offered Himself to be the mediator between God and mankind:

For there is one God; there is also one mediator between God and humankind, Christ Jesus, himself human, who gave himself a ransom for all - this was attested at the right time. I Timothy 2.5

I am saddened that Jesus loves us so much, and is our greatest friend, that he willingly died to save us from eternal death. My sadness moves to gratitude and comfort at communion when I realize that Jesus is Our Friend. Jesus is such a brave and courageous Friend; He died to defend the people He loves. We are to graciously accept His gift and be filled with joy that we can have eternal life in paradise with God by living and believing in Him.

The crucifixion of Jesus was a difficult concept for me to understand and accept. Like the people who wanted Jesus to be an earthly king on Palm Sunday, I did not understand Jesus' death to save our souls. Jesus died to offer us eternal life in Heaven because eternity is much more important that our brief life here on earth in the flesh.

Jesus answered, "My kingdom is not from this world. If my kingdom were from this world, my followers would be fighting to keep me from being handed over to the Jews. But as it is, my kingdom is not from here." John 18.36

Jesus had the authority to stop His pending death at any time:
Do you think that I cannot appeal to my Father, and he will at once send me more than twelve legions of angels? Matthew 26.53

For Christ also died for sins once for all, the just for the unjust, so that He might bring us to God, having been put to death in the flesh, but made alive in the spirit. I Peter 3.18 NASB

We partake of the bread and cup in remembrance of Jesus. Jesus' love was poured out for us for the forgiveness of sin. Jesus Himself tells us to partake of the bread and the cup in remembrance of Him.

Adam and Eve partaking of the knowledge of good and evil signified their disobedience of God and their rejection of God's authority. In partaking of the bread and the cup, we signify our obedience to God and acknowledge God's power and forgiveness.

Jesus rose from the dead on the third day. Jesus' death was not permanent; Jesus rose from the dead! The happy ending of our forgiveness is that Jesus became the sacrifice and then triumphed over death and rose from the dead. Jesus' resurrection from the dead and triumph over evil fulfilled the promise God made in Genesis 3.14-15. When the devil lured Eve and then Adam into disobeying God and eating of the tree of the knowledge of good and evil, the devil prompted the fall of man. God cursed the devil. God told the devil that He would put an adversary between the devil and an offspring of the woman. The adversary of the devil is Jesus Christ, the Son of the living God! Jesus is the enemy of Satan sent to save mankind from our sins. Jesus crushed Satan's head by Jesus' life, death, resurrection, and triumph over evil. The devil did bruise Christ's heel by Jesus' crucifixion by the children of the devil. The war between good and evil is won; Jesus won the war. God will throw the devil into hell for eternal torment when Jesus returns a second time.

Perhaps the tearing of the curtain in the temple also signified that God would no longer be separated from His people:

"I will not leave you orphaned; I am coming to you. In a little while the world will no longer see me, but you will see me; because I live, you also will live. On that day you will know that I am in my Father, and you in me, and I in you. They who have my commandments and keep them are those who love me; and those who love me will be loved by my Father, and I will love them and reveal myself to them." John 14. 18-21

We are privileged to be living in the time of the New Covenant. Jesus lives in those who love Him and we live in Jesus. God's presence is not confined to the temple. We are the temple of God's Holy Spirit. We are filled with the grace of Jesus Christ, the Son of the Living God!

Luke 24.13-35 explains that Simon Peter did not have the ability to recognize the risen Jesus on the road to Emmaus until he ate bread with Jesus. We do not worship a fallen Friend named Jesus; Jesus is alive and is with us. Communion helps me to remember that Jesus layed down His life to save His friends, but Jesus is alive and with us to eternity. I find peace in communion remembering that Jesus loves me as His friend.

Jesus said to her, "I am the resurrection and the life. He who believes in me will live, even though he dies; and whoever lives and believes in me will never die." John 11.25-26a NIV

Let us pray. Thank You for offering your life to provide eternal life for those who live and believe in you. Thank you for tearing the curtain in the temple in two, from top to bottom. Although we humans are unworthy creatures of instinct, You gave us the gift of direct access to You LORD. You God are holy; we are unworthy to be in Your presence. We humans can never be perfect, and never be without sin. We are cleansed of our sin only through You Jesus. We may come before your throne and ask for Your blessing only because you invite us. We are humbled to be in the presence of the Living God. Thank You for teaching us the Truth and providing a Way to eternal life in Heaven. All You ask from us is that we live and believe in You. Thank You Most High God. Amen.

# CHAPTER 6

# God Controls All

For it was you who formed my inward parts;
You knit me together in my mother's womb.
I praise you, for I am fearfully and wonderfully made.
Wonderful are your works. Psalm 139.13-14a

Just as you do not know how the breath comes to the bones in the mother's womb, so you do not know the work of God, who makes everything. Ecclesiastes 11.5

Ask the animals, and they will teach you;
the birds of the air, and they will tell you;
ask the plants of the earth, and they will teach you;
and the fish of the sea will declare to you.
Who among all these does not know that the hand of the LORD has done this?
In his hand is the life of every living thing and the breath of every human being. Job 12.7b-10

"Is it by your wisdom that the hawk soars, and spreads its wings toward the south? Is it at your command that the eagle mounts up and makes its nest on high? It lives on the rock and makes its home in the fastness of the rocky crag. From there it spies the prey; its eyes see it from far away." Job 39.26-29

Where can I go from your Spirit?
Where can I flee from your presence?
If I go up to the heavens, you are there;
if I make my bed in the depths, you are there.

If I rise on the wings of the dawn,
if I settle on the far side of the sea,
even there your hand will guide me,
your right hand will hold me fast.
If I say, "Surely the darkness will hide me
and the light become night around me,"
even the darkness will not be dark to you;
the night will shine like the day,
for darkness is as light to you. Psalm 139.7-12 NIV

Who will separate us from the love of Christ? Will hardship, or distress, or persecution, or famine, or nakedness, or peril, or sword? No, in all these things we are more than conquerors through him who loved us. For I am convinced that neither death, nor life, nor angels, nor rulers, nor things present, nor things to come, nor powers, nor height, nor depth, nor anything else in all creation, will be able to separate us from the love of God in Christ Jesus our Lord. Romans 8. 35, 38, 39

We know that all things work together for good for those who love God, who are called according to his purpose. Romans 8.28

Can anyone hide in secret places so that I cannot see him?" declares the LORD. "Do not I fill heaven and earth?" declares the LORD. Jeremiah 23.24 NIV

"Every one then who hears these words of mine and acts on them will be like a wise man who built his house on rock. The rain fell, the floods came, and the winds blew and beat upon that house, but it did not fall, because it had been founded on rock. And everyone who hears these words of mine and does not act on them will be like a foolish man who built his house on sand; and the rain fell. The rain fell, and the floods came, and the winds blew and beat against that house, and it fell and great was its fall." Matthew 7.24-27

The LORD said to Satan, "Very well, he is in your power; only spare his life." So Satan went out from the presence of the LORD, and inflicted loathsome sores on Job from the sole of his foot to the crown of his head. Job 2.6, 7

On the day when the LORD gave the Amorites over to the Israelites, Joshua spoke to the LORD; and he said in the sight of Israel, "Sun, stand still at Gibeon, and Moon, in the valley of Aijalon." And the sun stood still, and the moon stopped, until the nation took vengeance on their enemies. The sun stopped in mid-heaven, and did not hurry to set for about a whole day. There has been no day like it before or since, when the LORD heeded a human voice; for the LORD fought for Israel. Joshua 10.12, 13a, c 14

As he walked along, he saw a man blind from birth. His disciples asked him, "Rabbi, who sinned, this man or his parents, that he was born blind?" Jesus answered, "Neither this man nor his parents sinned; he was born blind so that God's works might be revealed in him." John 9.1-3

"I will be gracious to whom I will be gracious and will show mercy on whom I will show mercy." Exodus 33.19b

I will punish the world for its evil, and the wicked for their iniquity; I will put an end to the pride of the arrogant, and lay low the insolence of tyrants. Isaiah 13.11

Life in the flesh, as human beings, involves tensions between God's choices and man's choices; life is balanced between choices. How God controls all is a mystery.

They were amazed, saying, "What sort of man is this, that even winds and sea obey him?" Matthew 8.27

The scriptures declare that God is in control and the wind, waves, and even the rotation of the earth for sunlight (as recorded in Joshua 10.12-14) obey God. However, God's ways are not our ways. The first time I heard that God controls all was at a Christian Businessmen's meeting. The speaker said that either God is the sovereign controller of all or He is not in control. I understood from that day onward that God does control all.

God controlling ALL is often questioned, and is not easily understood at various points in one's life. I have caused more stress to myself by faithless reactions to interim events in life, or worrying about possible events, rather than the consequences of the actual events that occur. Looking back at my life as a fifty-something year old, the worst things that could have happened to me did not happen to me. When an unpleasant event happened, the talents God gave me were sufficient to enable me to successfully resolve the situation or take a suitable alternate path in life.

I started researching if God controls all when I was eleven years old. I was not extraordinarily brilliant to start researching such complex subjects at a young age. My father killed himself when I was eleven years old. My father's suicide caused me to initially have a sense of dazed trauma. As weeks became years, my reactions to my father's suicide became a sense of abandonment, frustration toward my father, and unanswered questions to God. I was a happy child with a father, mother, and two brothers. My dad and I attended a movie together every Wednesday, our special weekly outing. We took a father and son weekend vacation every year to explore caves or go boating. My dad was my best friend on planet earth. My dad was a brave soldier in World War II. He was awarded many medals, including the Purple Heart after being wounded by a mortar in battle. Suddenly he was dead.

Although God controls all, He grants us free will to choose good or bad business decisions and good or bad life choices. God gave us the ability to think and work. To the best of my knowledge, I do not recall God overtly giving me direct guidance to accept or reject a new job offer or select what home to purchase. God expects us to use the talents He gave us to provide a living and take care of our family.

God clearly states we are not in the Garden of Eden, we need to work or we will not have bread. We can choose to work and eat or we can choose to be lazy.

People make choices. The level of brokenness we each have clouds our decisions. My father served in fierce combat in World War II. During a battle, a mortar shell fell from the sky and contacted with my father's back before hitting the ground. The mortar did not explode on impact, otherwise my father would have been killed instantly. The mortar severely damaged my father's back, similar to being grazed by a three-inch diameter bullet. After surgeries and a long recovery, my father returned from the war and returned to his job as a machinist. Most likely my father experienced sufficient change and pain in life and simply wanted to work and live peacefully. Years after the war, the company that employed him encountered financial trouble. The company that employed my father manufactured equipment that was utilized by defense contractors. Ironically, peace caused many of the manufacturing jobs in the United States to be eliminated. Perhaps my father had post-traumatic stress from World War II and more change in life caused a panic attack and depression. In the nineteen-sixties, depression was not a well-known illness and treatment for depression was limited. My father did seek medical treatment, but ultimately chose to kill himself to stop his pain. God chose to not take supernatural actions to prevent my father's death.

Perhaps it is better if we acknowledge what God does control on a daily basis. God keeps the earth rotating at a rate of twenty-four hours per day. God sends the rain and the sun. God grants every breath we take. Every day we are alive is a gift from God. Creation declares God's handiwork. Let us rejoice and be glad in this day.

Let us pray. Thank you God for creating the world and the air that we breathe. We humans truly have no power or right to exist outside of you oh LORD. Our heat and light come from the sun that you hung in the sky. The soil beneath our feet and seeds we sow for food are gifts from you. The hearts that beat in our chests follow your command. The hug from a loved one and the ability to see a sunset are gifts from You. We humans should not complain about what we do not have, but rather praise you for all that you gave us. Amen.

# CHAPTER 7

# Rain Will Fall on the Righteous and on the Unrighteous

"Have you not put a hedge around him and his household and everything he has? You have blessed the work of his hands, so that his flocks and herds are spread throughout the land. Job 1.10 NIV

So Satan went out from the presence of the LORD and afflicted Job with painful sores from the soles of his feet to the top of his head. Then Job took a piece of broken pottery and scraped himself with it as he sat among the ashes. His wife said to him, "Are you still holding on to your integrity? Curse God and die!" He replied, "You are talking like a foolish woman. Shall we accept good from God, and not trouble?" In all this, Job did not sin in what he said. Job 2.7-10 NIV

Job asked God:

"Why did I not perish at birth, and die as I came from the womb?" Job 3.11 NIV

He makes his sun rise on the evil and on the good, and sends rain on the righteous and on the unrighteous. Matthew 5.45b

As you do not know the path of the wind, or how the body is formed in a mother's womb, so you cannot understand the work of God, the Maker of all things. Ecclesiastes 11:5 NIV

"Arise, go to Nineveh the great city and cry against it, for their wickedness has come up before Me." But Jonah rose up to flee to Tarshish from the presence of the LORD So he went down to Joppa, found a ship which was going to Tarshish, paid the fare and went down into it to go with them to Tarshish from the presence of the LORD. The LORD hurled a great wind on the sea and there was a great storm on the sea so that the ship was about to break up. Jonah 1.2-4 NASB

"For my thoughts are not your thoughts, neither are your ways my ways," declares the LORD. "As the heavens are higher than the earth, so are my ways higher than your ways and my thoughts than your thoughts." Isaiah 55.8, 9 NIV

Who does great things beyond understanding, and marvelous things without number? Job 9.10

Though he slay me, yet will I hope in him. Job 13.15a NIV

"If the world hates you, be aware that it hated me before it hated you. If you belonged to the world, the world would love you as its own. Because you do not belong to the world, but I have chosen you out of the world-- therefore the world hates you. Remember the word that I said to you, 'Servants are not greater than their master.' If they persecuted me, they will persecute you; if they kept my word, they will keep yours also. John 15.18-20

God left him to himself, in order to try him and to know all that was in his heart. 2 Chronicles 32.31. Referring to Hezekiah

"You shall remember all the way which the LORD your God has led you in the wilderness these forty years, that He might humble you, testing you, to know what was in your heart, whether you would keep His commandments or not." Deuteronomy 8.2 NASB

Why, O LORD, do you stand far off? Why do you hide yourself in times of trouble? Psalm 10.1b

Therefore, to keep me from being too elated, a thorn was given me in the flesh, a messenger of Satan to torment me, to keep me from being too elated. Three times I appealed to the Lord about this, that it would leave me, but he said to me, "My grace is sufficient for you, for power is made perfect in weakness." So, I will boast all the more gladly of my weaknesses, so that the power of Christ may dwell in me. Therefore I am content with weaknesses, insults, hardships, persecutions, and calamities for the sake of Christ; for whenever I am weak, then I am strong.  2 Corinthians 12.7b-10

Where were you when I laid the foundation of the earth? Tell me, if you have understanding. Job 38.4

"Come to me, all you that are weary and are carrying heavy burdens, and I will give you rest. Take my yoke upon you, and learn from me; for I am gentle and humble in heart, and you will find rest for your souls.  For my yoke is easy, and my burden is light."  Matthew 11. 28-30

Since therefore Christ suffered in the flesh, arm yourselves also with the same intention because (for whoever has suffered in the flesh has finished with sin), so as to live for the rest of your earthly life no longer by human desires, but by the will of God. 1 Peter 4.1, 2

I researched and wrote this chapter to determine what the Bible documents regarding God's involvement in our daily lives.  I searched the Bible for twenty-five years and did not find the exact quote I was intuitively looking for.  While watching the motion picture, "The Gospel of John," adapted to film by John Goldsmith, I heard a scripture verse that explained a man was born blind, but his blindness had no correlation to any sinful behavior.[8]

Jesus answered "Neither this man nor his parents sinned. He was born blind so that God's works might be revealed in him." John 9.3

I feel obligated to interject an aside.  I find it frequently amusing, that God guided me to write this book and share Bible answers to my questions with others.  It is hilarious to me that it took me over twenty-five years to find a particular Bible passage to address a question on one topic: tests. I can personally declare that God has a great sense of humor.  The existence of the breed of dog, pug, with the flat expressive face and pigtail, confirms God has a sense of humor.  My pug was named Reagan, after President Ronald Reagan; I was fond of them both. The equally funny thought of a manager of manufacturing engineering writing a book on Jesus and His teaching makes me smile and chuckle periodically.

Let us return to the topic of testing. I have observed that there are a variety of categories of tests in life. I suggest the following categories of tests for consideration:

- Earthly naturally occurring events, including floods, tornados, and tsunamis.
- Repercussion to mankind due to God's response to the sin of Adam and Eve: human body will die, need to sweat and toil to survive, need for food.
- Interactions with God's other creatures, such as, animals and people.
- Direct tests from the Devil in an attempt to have us lose faith in God.
- Repercussions of earthly laws, gravity, momentum, and force.
- Direct and overt tests by God Himself.

Earthly events, such as floods, tornados, and tsunamis occur naturally and may cause death and loss of property.

Genesis 3.3-6 records that when man disobeyed God, work, hunger, toil, and death were instituted. We humans are hungry and must be fed periodically or we will become sick and die.

Cain killed his brother Able, as recorded in Genesis 4.8. God chose not to stop Cain from killing Able. Evil people can disrupt our lives.

God established many laws of physics and biology. A childhood friend of my wife and I grew up and had a son named Lenny; Lenny was the same age as my son. Tragically, when Lenny was a teenager, a car Lenny was riding in crashed into a highway divider. The car impacted the highway divider on Lenny's side and Lenny was crushed and killed. The laws of physics fall on the just and the unjust: kinetic energy equals one half mass multiplied by the velocity squared. Regardless if the occupants of a vehicle are just or unjust, if a car traveling at a high speed hits an immovable object, the car will stop and the energy will be dissipated through crumpled metal and shattered lives. My daughter destroyed her car when she lost traction on ice and side swiped a highway divider. My daughter was unhurt because she was wearing her seat belt and the car bounced off the wall and continued in the same direction. The physics of automobile crashes can decide life and death.

As a younger man, I read scripture regarding tests, but did not understand the meaning. In the book of Job, God allowed the devil to test Job with suffering. In 2 Chronicles 32.31, God tested Hezekiah by leaving him for a time. In 2 Corinthians 12.10, God allowed the apostle Paul to suffer with a thorn in the flesh. The book of Jonah records that God sent a storm to impede Jonah from fleeing by boat to Tarshish, rather than going to Nineveh as God commanded. God commanded Jonah to preach to the people of Nineveh, but Jonah did not want to save the people in Nineveh. Jonah was thrown off the ship by the crew and transported by a great fish to Nineveh. God used His almighty power to overtly influence Jonah's life.

I falsely thought that I could pray to God for blessings and God would say yes or no to my request; my self-centered concept is contradicted by these specific scripture passages. I had mentally limited God to the Supreme Being that I talk to when I want something or when I thank Him for His gifts. I never thought or accepted that God may initiate talk, command us to do something, or test us.

God is in charge, not us. Personal interactions occur from man to God, but also from God to man. To my surprise, both the Old and New Testaments of the Bible clearly state that God tests us individually. We humans use testing to establish one's academic or professional competency and to note where improvement is needed. God gives tests to determine if we will endure suffering and keep the faith in Christ. We are tested to drive an automobile, pass high school and college, and certify our competency in our profession. Our tests regarding earthly activities pertain to earthly temporary things. God tests our faith with eternal results. Living and believing in God determines where we will spend eternity. Understanding that tests we endure in life may be orchestrated and proctored by God Himself illuminates the importance of remaining a child of God.

Several years ago, my body's immune system became overactive and started attacking my own body. My wife drove me to the emergency room; I had swollen legs and I was aching all over. Doctors determined my heart was not beating properly. I spent a week in the hospital and received intravenous antibiotics. The physicians diagnosed my condition as Sarcoidosis. My lungs and airways were damaged by the inflammation. Tests showed my breathing was not providing sufficient oxygen. My breathing worsened over the next few months. At my worst point, I could not walk across the room without stopping to take a break and breathe deeply. My minister at that time asked me what were the possible outcomes. I explained my Sarcoidosis could remedy itself, I could quickly die from the disease, or I could need supplemental oxygen and breathing apparatus to live. The pastor asked me what was my order of preference of the outcomes. I replied, "I first hope the disease will go into full remission, secondly I hope I die quickly with minimal pain, lastly, I live in pain and need supplemental oxygen and medical equipment to function."

After a few months of living with Sarcoidosis, doctors did more lung tests and determined my breathing had declined. The specialist physicians determined I needed supplemental oxygen in conjunction with a CPAP (Continuous Positive Airway Pressure) machine while sleeping and whenever I felt I was suffocating. For the next five years, my chest ached severely because my chest muscles strained to breathe with inflamed lungs and restricted airways.

God heard my preference and prayers to be cured soon or die quickly, and not experience Sarcoidosis symptoms and need oxygen. After being sick with Sarcoidosis for several years, it became clear to my doctors and I that I did not have a fatal version of Sarcoidosis, but I had a chronic case of Sarcoidosis. I eventually began to appreciate staying alive by using the air pressure machine and supplemental oxygen to reduce the constant pain in my chest. On bad days, I used my breathing equipment when I was awake. I never smoked cigarettes; I ate healthy foods, and exercised with karate. However, my immune system malfunctioned and was too aggressive toward my own body. I could have been angry with God, thought God betrayed me, and been enraged with being alive and short of breath. I chose to acknowledge God is in charge and I am not in charge. I acknowledged God did not allow me to die. I am thankful that several doctors stabilized my disease and eased my breathing problem with medical equipment. Rejecting reality and being angry does not have any benefit.

The apostle Paul's interaction with God teaches that God may not grant all of our requests.

"My grace is sufficient for you, for power is made perfect in weakness." 2 Corinthians 12.10

Thankfully, God did not answer my initial pompous prayer to cure me or kill me quickly. The Almighty did not fully cure my Sarcoidosis, nor did He allow the Sarcoidosis to quickly kill me. I suffered with the sense of suffocating and the fatigue, confusion, and lightheadedness associated with low oxygenation for over five years. I truly did not want to fight a disease that lasts many years. I did fight the good fight for many years and outlasted my most painful period of Sarcoidosis. Eventually my breathing became less of a struggle. I became able to ride a bicycle again, and mildly exercise. I consider each day of my life a gift from God. I am glad I did not die of

Sarcoidosis years ago. I enjoy my family and writing this book. With God's grace, life, with its rain and pain, is still enjoyable. Life moves on whether we enjoy life with its imperfections or grumble.

God allows disease to exist and God allows some of us humans to develop serious illnesses. I cannot say that my lung disease was an overt test of my faith or just a medical malfunction. The Holy Bible does indeed state that Satan did afflict Job with painful sores over his entire body. Job was angry with God after God permitted Satan to inflict suffering on him. Job still trusted in God, but wanted the world to be different. Job was disappointed in God that suffering occurred in his life. God spoke directly to Job and asked Job if he designed the wings of the hawk to allow it to fly or designed the brain of the hawk to cause it to fly south. God asked Job if he designed eagles to fly and nest at high altitudes and have keen eyesight to identify its prey. We humans are created beings, created in the image of God, by God Himself. All that the human eye can see belongs to God. We are visitors to the planet earth for perhaps seven to eight decades, then our bodies return to dust. God holds the life and breath of every living being in His hand. Every day we wake up and breathe is a gift from God. Regardless if Satan routinely afflicts specific people with specific diseases or if disease is a byproduct of the sin of Adam and Eve, pain will test humans to choose to curse God or keep faith in God and keep His commandments. Job made a profound short statement of faith:

Though he slay me, yet will I hope in him. Job 13.15a NIV

"For my thoughts are not your thoughts, neither are your ways my ways," declares the LORD. "As the heavens are higher than the earth, so are my ways higher than your ways and my thoughts than your thoughts." Isaiah 55.8-9 NIV

God knows and tells us that we humans will not understand God's world; we will not understand why we suffer, and why events in life are sometimes painful.

I could be considered a hypocrite by writing this book **Jesus is Our Friend**. Readers of this book may suppose I have great faith, but I clearly confess I had little faith for many years; therefore I am not a hypocrite. I am not preaching I have faith. The journey of life this side of the grave seems very long to me at times. Jesus Christ did indeed die on the cross for our eternal life in Heaven. However, living in the carnal world as a follower of

Jesus Christ is occasionally difficult. We may perceive the evil in the world that others do not see or others may find acceptable. We may experience unwelcomed tests. We may prefer God to intervene and spare us troubles. Perhaps life itself is truly a test; perhaps life is an obstacle course. Physicians in training are often required to work thirty consecutive hours in hospitals. Physicians in training in emergency rooms work without eating the entire shift. The ancient physician's code and training includes infusing super-human endurance into doctors. Perhaps life is an endurance test for Heaven. As I passed tests in life and survived, my spiritual strength grew.

I have fought the good fight, I have finished the race, I have kept the faith. 2 Timothy 4.7

These words dramatize that life can be long and contain struggles, but we must finish the race.

The road to eternal life is difficult and narrow; the path to destruction is wide and easy. However, surrendering to the temptations of the carnal man does not bring joy and peace. Our choice in life is simple:

- Follow God's commandments, keep the faith, then spend eternity in paradise with Jesus in Heaven.

Or

- Follow the devil, the father of lies, be filled with greed, self-centeredness, self-indulgence and wickedness, curse God, then spend eternity in Hell.

My wife declared, "We cannot choose our tests; we can only choose our response to life's tests." We choose whom we follow and where we want to spend eternity.

Therefore, since Christ has suffered in the flesh, arm yourselves also with the same purpose, because he who has suffered in the flesh has ceased from sin, so as to live the rest of the time in the flesh no longer for the lusts of men, but for the will of God. 1 Peter 4.1-2 NASB

This brief, yet powerful statement of scripture that indicates enduring suffering reduces our tendency to sin. My Pastor, Dan, shared these verses at our Thursday night men's Bible study and friendship night. The concept was so new to me and complex, I was truly surprised. I was surprised because my suffering with my breathing and other physical issues has supernaturally brought me closer to God. I am still a man in the flesh and tempted, but suffering has clarified that life is temporary. Strangely, when I am breathing better after a day of suffocating, my primary emotion is contentment with what is, rather than buying more luxurious treasures. Suffering illuminates what is important in life.

When I awake each morning I thank God for waking up another day and thank him for my loving wife. When driving to work I see the beautiful sunrise over a forested valley and I praise God for creating the trees and our beautiful earth. We do not see God directly in this life, but we see him through his creation.

When I arrive at work as an engineering manager, my conscious mind focuses on designing products and manufacturing. I feel God's presence throughout the day as I work and use the talents God gave me. My ride home takes me through a park system around northeast Ohio called the "emerald necklace". I often see deer, groundhogs, birds, and occasionally a snapping turtle in the park. A smile comes to my face as God's creation is unveiled. God makes everything! We must pause from the activities our daily lives and appreciate the awesome power of God. God made our bodies, our minds, and our soul to long for God like a deer longs for flowing streams.

As a middle aged engineer who worked for over thirty-five years, I do not want for material things that moth and rust destroy; I have my needs met. I have a wife, two children, a home, and a car. Different than my poor childhood, my wife and I have a dishwasher and I no longer wear patched pants; by the worldwide standard my family is very blessed. However, regardless of my material blessings, I am an incomplete creature without God. Humans, blessed with superior intelligence, glance into the night sky and view stars everywhere. We have no excuse to deny that God is the wonderful creator. As I view more of the world's oceans, forests, and deserts, humility overcomes me and I thank God for creating me. Jesus calls his people by name and leads us.

"I tell you the truth, whoever hears my word and believes him who sent me has eternal life and will not be condemned; he has crossed over from death to life." John 5.24 NIV

The war has been won, our life will continue for ETERNITY after death through faith in God. The tests in life we endure are eclipsed by eternity in

Heaven. Enjoy the time we have in this life, it is short and the best is yet to come!

Let us close this chapter in prayer, Holy Father, the world You created is good. Please provide us with Your grace to make us strong when we are weak.

We also boast in our sufferings, knowing that suffering produces endurance, and endurance produces character, and character produces hope, and hope does not disappoint us, because God's love has been poured into our hearts through the Holy Spirit that has been given to us.
Romans 5.3b-5.

# CHAPTER 8

# Do Not Worry, Have Faith and Trust in God

"Therefore I tell you, do not worry about your life, what you will eat or drink; or about your body, what you will wear. Is not life more important than food, and the body more important than clothes? Look at the birds of the air; they do not sow or reap or store away in barns, and yet your heavenly Father feeds them. Are you not much more valuable than they? Who of you by worrying can add a single hour to his life?" "And why do you worry about clothes? See how the lilies of the field grow. They do not labor or spin. Yet I tell you that not even Solomon in all his splendor was dressed like one of these. If that is how God clothes the grass of the field, which is here today and tomorrow is thrown into the fire, will he not much more clothe you, O you of little faith? So do not worry, saying, 'What shall we eat?' or 'What shall we drink?' or 'What shall we wear?' For the pagans run after all these things, and your heavenly Father knows that you need them. But seek first His kingdom and His righteousness, and all these things will be given to you as well. Therefore do not worry about tomorrow, for tomorrow will worry about itself. Each day has enough trouble of its own." Matthew 6.25-34 NIV

Do not fear those who kill the body but cannot kill the soul; rather fear him who can destroy both soul and body in hell. Are not two sparrows sold for a penny? Yet not one of them will fall to the ground apart from your Father. And even the hairs of your head are all counted. So do not be afraid; you are of more value than many sparrows. Matthew 10.28-31

He sat down opposite the treasury, and watched the crowd putting money into the treasury. Many rich people put in large sums. A poor widow came and put in two small copper coins, which are worth a penny. Then he called his disciples and said to them, "Truly I tell you, this poor widow has put in more than all those who are contributing to the treasury. For all of them have contributed out of their abundance; but she out of her poverty has put in everything she had, all she had to live on." Mark 12. 41-44 (The speaker in this passage is Jesus.)

So we are always confident; even though we know that while we are at home in the body we are away from the Lord--for we walk by faith, not by sight. 2 Corinthians 5.6-7

You are from God, little children, and have overcome them; because greater is He who is in you than he who is in the world. I John 4.4 NASB

Trust in the LORD with all your heart,
and do not rely on your own insight.
In all your ways acknowledge him,
and he will make straight your paths.
Do not be wise in your own eyes;
fear the LORD, and turn away from evil. Proverbs 3.5-7

The aforementioned scripture selections are profound and clearly stated, but I confess I personally had insufficient faith to believe for many years. When I finally surrendered and admitted that God is in charge, I felt a peace and patience that I would have preferred to have had all along in my life.

In my professional journey as an engineer, I upgraded jobs a few times to gain a diverse knowledge of engineering. I stayed at one company for ten years. In those ten years, I had the opportunity to improve the safety conditions for employees. I eventually plateaued at the company in terms of responsibility and pay. I began looking for a better job and prayed to God for His assistance. I patiently interviewed at a few companies. I told a company who was interested in me that I did not want the job because I would be required to work every Sunday morning to supervise preventive maintenance and consequently miss church. I prayed to God and asked God's help in finding a new job. I could not find a job with better pay anywhere. I told God that perhaps my pay is appropriate for the current job market and I would change jobs when God presents the opportunity.

A Christian friend and coworker, Pete, stopped in my office one day and handed me a paper with an executive recruiter's name on it. Pete explained that the recruiter called him looking for a corporate engineer with experience in plastics, chemical compatibility, and manufacturing systems, exactly my experience. Pete told the recruiter he would pass the information to me. I thanked Pete and bought him lunch.

I called the recruiter and had an interview with the company the next day. The company offered me the job that evening, with a pay offer greater than I estimated. I was working at my new job in a few weeks. It was very clear to me that God can make events occur at the precisely correct time through his planning. The job was perfect and I did not even search to find the job; God sent one of His ambassadors on earth to deliver the job message to me. I simply listened to God's message delivered by my friend.

The senior management at my new employer was very kind and appreciated the many improvements to the manufacturing process I made. I was promoted to engineering manager.

After working ten years at this great company, the senior management was suddenly replaced. My history of many improvements to manufacturing and cost savings projects was suddenly erased. The new management team needed to be impressed as if I was a new employee. Suddenly, my rewarding and fun job was transformed into a workplace filled with tension and mistrust. I had changed jobs before and thought I would simply search a few months and find another engineering manager job. However, finding a new engineering manager job in an era where manufacturing jobs were leaving Ohio would not be easy. I sent my resume to several recruiters and various companies. I was not offered a job at a promising company. One company announced a lay off the exact day I was being interviewed for a job that would soon be eliminated by budget cuts!

While I continued to go to work at my current job, the vice president was creating much stress in the company. I started getting stomachaches and a tightness in my chest from the unnecessary tension. Multiple people were being assigned the same projects and conflict management was the new culture. While the turmoil at work was occurring, I had been meeting with four men from church for a weekly Bible study and prayer breakfast at one of our homes. The five of us would follow a Bible study guide, read scripture, and discuss the Bible lesson. In addition, we would each ask for prayers or share celebrations in our life. My prayer at the weekly men's breakfast was "God, please help me find a new job and escape the pain at work."

After nine months of praying for a new job with my men's group, one of the four men mentioned, "Carl, perhaps God does not want to give you a new job, or He would have. Maybe God wants you to be a light of Christ at your work." At that point in my religious journey I was quite stubborn; I thought that was the most ridiculous comment my prayer buddy could have said. I did not want to hear that God was in charge, not me! I gave God my request, like a groom gives a bandleader a song request at his wedding; it is a request, but really it is an order.

When I wanted a new job the first time, my job was not unpleasant, it just paid poorly. God sent me a new job and all was well. This time, ten years later, my job was extremely stressful and I wanted out now! I had a house payment, a car payment, and a family to care for. I needed a new job and I prayed to God to help me find a new job. However, after a year of mental abuse at work, I was still in the same job and God was not providing an exit. Was God not hearing me? Was I being punished? Well, my Bible study friend was correct. I started ministering to people at work and my coworkers were in pain too. I soon discovered many of my coworkers were followers of Jesus and we supported one another through the challenging times. We changed our approach with the unpleasant boss and tried to ease the pain.

Within a year, the unpleasant boss resigned. The management changed several more times in the next several years. Eventually the senior management stabilized. My job became enjoyable once again. My coworkers and I still discuss the Bible and have bonded through surviving the unpleasant manager. The company placed me in a performance based bonus program and I am now blessed with more money than before and am blessed with an enjoyable job. God knew the future and wanted me to endure the short term suffering for a long-term good job. I am glad I did not change jobs and perhaps work for a less stable company. God does hear our prayers. God knows the future. Looking back, it was best that I endured a brief period of turmoil and did not change jobs at that time.

God provided well and I was too stubborn and narrow-sighted to understand that I needed patience. God may block something from happening when it is for the better good. I learned that if I pray for something and God does not provide what I want, perhaps God is saying NO! I would not let my son or daughter cross the street if a speeding car is coming. Likewise, God may protect us from an undesirable path in life. I stubbornly learned to walk by faith, not by sight. Life is a long journey that requires faith in God. Life is a marathon, not a short sprint.

A clear understanding that life is finite and relatively short in duration is very helpful in understanding NOT TO WORRY. There will be rough times occasionally. Jesus specifically tells us to not worry about our life.

Trust in the LORD with all your heart, and do not rely on your own insight. Proverbs 3.5

The above verse is engraved on a boulder in my backyard to continually remind me I do not know the future, God does. Do not worry about life; use the talents God gave you and do your best.

**Worry can be scientifically analyzed as the fear of events that have not occurred.** On a personal level, I disclose I was a worrier until God gave me the gift of wisdom gained through experience. I failed every test of worry I experienced in life until I was thirty-nine years old. At thirty-nine years old, doctors discovered that I had a tumor in my large intestine (colon). The first physician and then a second physician indicated my tumor would advance into cancer without surgery. The doctors indicated that they would need to remove one third of my colon. This was my first powerful test of worry that I finally passed. The surgeon indicated it was important that I have the surgery within two weeks to limit the spread of the ailment. I prayed to God to survive this ordeal. However, I did not worry! This decision to not worry was easy for me. The outcomes were limited:

1. Surgery is a success and I recover.
2. I die during the five-hour surgery.
3. I eventually die of colon cancer if I ignored the problem.

The morning of the surgery, the medical staff mentioned I was one of the calmest patents they had seen entering major surgery. I replied, "I am in God's hands and I have nothing to do with the outcome." A supernatural peace enveloped me. If I died during surgery of a colon tumor, I would be with God, just a little sooner than I expected. If I recovered from the colon tumor, I would be with God and my family on earth. Either outcome was a win-win.

After successfully surviving colon surgery, I had other tests of worry and I failed a few more. I worried about my job, investments, and things that moth and rust destroy. Slowly, the gift of wisdom provided the insight that worry is rooted in telling God what to do and worry is in opposition to the Lord's Prayer. In worrying, we are experiencing anxiety regarding the outcome of a future event; we have a specific goal for the outcome. I have worried that I would not be hired at a certain company, but perhaps God has a better employer for me. Worrying is the consequence of thinking we are in control of life, not God. God controls the wind and the waves; we do not have control. God controls everything.

Daniel 3 records that Shadrach, Meshach and Abednego refused to worship Nebuchadnezzar. Nebuchadnezzar had the three followers of God thrown into a blazing furnace to kill them because they would not worship him. The Godly men were willing to give up their lives rather than worship a false god. God protected the three men and they exited the furnace alive and had no smell of smoke on them. We demonstrate our faith when we have sufficient dedication to God to be thrown into the blazing furnace without worry.

Living in righteousness may expose us to being hated by society. Our false friends may reject us, a corrupt company may terminate our employment, and wicked family members may disown us for following Jesus. Do not worry. God knows the numbers of hairs on our head. Followers of Jesus must not worry, but acknowledge outcomes in life are often outside our control and move forward. The Lord's Prayer states, "Thy will be done." Joseph of the Old Testament was sold into slavery by his brothers, but eventually became powerful in Egypt. It is easier when we review our past to understand God's workings in our life. When we trust in God, we live life with a unique peace and are receptive to God's will, not our will.

But seek ye first the kingdom of God, and his righteousness; and all these things shall be added unto you.  Matthew 6.33 KJV

Let us pray. Jesus, thank you for proclaiming that we are to seek first your kingdom and His righteousness and you will provide our necessities. We humans are inclined to worry, but you Jesus, specifically command us not to worry. We listen to your command Jesus, and trust in the LORD with all our heart and not rely on our own understanding. We will persevere in our trials, keep the faith, and finish the race. Amen.

# CHAPTER 9

# Prayer: Talking with God

Be still and know that I am God. Psalm 46.10a   KJV

"And whenever you pray, do not be like the hypocrites; for they love to stand and pray in the synagogues and at the street corners, so that they may be seen by others. Truly I tell you, they have received their reward. But whenever you pray, go into your room and shut the door and pray to your Father who is in secret; and your Father who sees in secret will reward you." Matthew 6.5-6

"And when you are praying, do not use meaningless repetition as the Gentiles do, for they suppose that they will be heard for their many words. So do not be like them; for your Father knows what you need before you ask Him." Matthew 6.7-8 NASB

Our Father which art in heaven, Hallowed be thy name.
Thy kingdom come, Thy will be done
in earth, as it is in heaven.
Give us this day our daily bread.
And forgive us our debts, as we forgive our debtors.
And lead us not into temptation, but deliver us from evil:
For thine is the kingdom, and the power, and the glory, for ever. Amen.
Matthew 6.9b-13 KJV

"Ask, and it will be given to you; seek, and you will find; knock, and it will be opened to you. For everyone who asks receives, and he who seeks finds, and to him who knocks it will be opened. Or what man is there among you who, when his son asks for a loaf, will give him a stone? Or if he asks for a fish, he will not give him a snake, will he? If you then, being evil, know how to give good gifts to your children, how much more will your Father who is in heaven give what is good to those who ask Him!" Matthew 7.7-11 NASB

"Very, truly, I tell you, anyone who does not enter the sheepfold by the door but climbs in by another way is a thief and a bandit; but he who enters by the door is the shepherd of the sheep. The gatekeeper opens the gate for him, and the sheep hear his voice. He calls his own sheep by name and leads them out. When he has brought out all his own, he goes before them, and the sheep follow him, for they know his voice. They will not follow a stranger, but they will run from him, because they do not know the voice of strangers." John 10.1-5

As a deer longs for flowing streams, so my soul longs for You, O God. Psalm 42.1

Communication from God to humans and from humans to God occurred throughout the Bible and still occurs today. The communication between God and His people is specifically referred to by Jesus himself. We know Jesus' voice when He speaks to us!

God spoke to me when I was in my early twenties. My father's suicide in my childhood and the resulting turmoil minimized my self-confidence and instilled a sense of worthlessness, vulnerability and insecurity. Regardless if the cause was predisposition and trauma or trauma alone, I began to stutter after my father's suicide and sudden abandonment when I was eleven years old. My speech slowly improved through years of speech therapy in public schools and speech therapy in my freshman year in college. I still stuttered occasionally after I was married and twenty-four years old. For some reason, I was fearful of talking on the telephone and was prone to stutter during telephone conversations. As I was gaining more responsibility as a design engineer, it became important that I spoke clearly on the telephone. I began praying continually to God to cure me of my stuttering. I talked to God and explained that He was my creator and He was smart enough to make my brain communicate properly with my tongue, lips, and mouth to speak without stuttering. I told God I knew He existed and I wanted His help.

One evening, I was sitting and praying quietly with my eyes closed. I gently sensed a burning bush image and sensed the presence of heat; I knew this was somehow a vision in my mind. God spoke to me and said, "Carl, I love you as you are." I replied through a thought, "God, I have been praying to you to heal me of my stuttering." God replied, "Carl, I love you as you are." I replied again, "God, I have been praying to you to heal me of my stuttering." The burning bush vision gently left, I was looking at my closed eyelids and was very confused by God's strange communication to my request to stop stuttering. I was frustrated that I had been praying to God for several months to have fluent speech and when the Almighty finally talks to me, he did not ask me to perform some outward sign and then say you are healed. This conversation with God was approximately twenty seconds long; it appears God can be very efficient. I opened my eyes and returned to my daily life as a husband and father of my two-year-old son.

My wife approached me a few days later when I was washing our car and asked me, "Have you been talking with God?" I replied, "Yes." My wife then said, "God told me to tell you that you were given your answer. What was your question?" It is humorous God sent my wife to explain to me what I could not understand myself. My wife is a good angel. I told my wife that I was praying to God to cure me of my stuttering. My wife then asked, "What was God's answer?" I responded that God told me, "Carl, I love you as you are." My wife then explained to me that God did answer my prayer to stop stuttering; God loving me is the answer to resolving my stuttering. The conversation with my wife was so complex and extraordinary that I was more stunned than enlightened.

I prayed more over the next few weeks and God guided me to understand that He loves me, Carl, unconditionally. I was shocked to understand that God Almighty, the creator of the universe, actually knows me by name and loves ME! I felt I must be a wicked person and somehow deserved to be abandoned by my father as a child; I felt undeserving of God's love. God conveyed that bad things happen in life, and I was not at fault. God really loved me regardless of my childhood and I was not being punished. Even with my sins, God loves me unconditionally. Understanding that God loves me personally and I love God remedied my feelings of worthlessness, vulnerability and insecurity. With the confidence as a child of God himself, and the end of my life journey being heaven, I slowly became filled with peace. The worrisome thoughts of worthlessness, vulnerability and insecurity swirling just below my conscious mind were replaced with supernatural peace. With the guidance of God to instill peace and calm my worried mind, my stuttering gently subsided. Whenever I began to sense inner panic and become vulnerable to stutter, I remember to be still and know He is God and He is in charge. This twenty-second visit with God is as clear in my mind thirty years later as the day it occurred.

When our daughter was seventeen years old, while my wife was shopping, my daughter asked me if she could go to a nearby city on a Friday evening with two of her girlfriends. I gave my permission to go to a nearby city and be back by eleven o'clock. When my wife returned home at eight o'clock, I told my wife that our daughter was out with her friends. When my wife asked me specifically where our daughter was, I immediately realized I approved her to travel to a city, but had no idea what was her actual destination. I confessed to my wife that I approved our daughter going out for an evening without knowing the destination or the activity. My wife called our daughter on the cell phone that I let her borrow for safety that evening. My wife asked our daughter where she went and she indicated she was not where she had permission to go. My daughter's friend drove her and the two other girls two hours away to a lake; my daughter's friend wanted to visit a boy she had met. We thanked our daughter for being honest, but told her they must drive home immediately. My daughter indicated they would leave and be home in two hours. After eleven o'clock came and went, our daughter was not home. When my wife called our daughter on my cell phone at eleven thirty, our daughter told us the girl who drove refused to leave. My wife asked our daughter to pass the cell phone to the girl who drove the car and is refusing to leave. My wife calmly directed the girl to begin driving home safely immediately. The battery in my cell phone lost its charge as the phone conversation ended. The three girls entered the car and began the two-hour drive home at midnight. At one o'clock in the morning, my wife had a sense that the girls were in danger. My wife dropped to her knees and prayed to God, "Dear God, our daughter is in trouble, please keep her safe. Please protect her, give her peace, and tell her You are with her."

At one-thirty in the morning, our daughter called home on a cellular telephone with an unfamiliar number. Our daughter explained to my wife that the girl was driving too fast and our daughter became afraid they would crash. Our daughter continued and explained that she prayed to God for help. While she was praying to God, a state police officer had detected the girl was driving ninety miles per hour on a sixty mile per hour road. The state police officer illuminated his warning lights and directed the girls to pull over to the side of the road. The state police officer told the seventeen-year-old driver she was driving ninety miles per hour.

The officer then looked directly at my terrified daughter in the back seat and said, "Your mother is worried about you. Use my cell phone to call your mother and tell her you are safe." My daughter asked my wife if she had called the police to locate and rescue her. My wife replied that she called on God to save her.

My wife's prayer to protect our daughter was truly answered by God. My wife and I did not call the police because we did not have a description of the car, and did not know the location of the car. It is clear to my wife, my daughter, and I that God sent the police officer to assist the girls. My wife and I rejoiced that God answered my wife's and daughter's prayer for divine protection.

As for me and my house, we will serve the LORD. Joshua 24.15e KJV

I am a low maintenance servant of God and do not frequently request God to perform miracles in my life. As I previously mentioned, I had a lung problem called Sarcoidosis. On a Sunday morning in the early spring of 2008 my chest was aching from the chronic Sarcoidosis. While driving to church with my wife, I mentioned to her that I had severe chest pain and was suffocating. My breathing seemed worse on rainy cold days. We arrived at church and read the church program; there was a healing service that Sunday. Suffocating and having chest pain for years was becoming frustrating for me. Being healed from Sarcoidosis would be great.

It then occurred to me in church that I had never prayed to God to be healed of my Sarcoidosis lung problem. Sarcoidosis is a somewhat rare disease where the body's immune system attacks itself. Sarcoidosis may go into remission, linger for a long time, or be fatal. My minister and I had a casual chat after I was released from the hospital stay when my Sarcoidosis developed. I remembered I told my minister years ago I prefer to be healed quickly, die quickly, or least preferred, life with a chronic painful illness.

After my day dream before church service started, I asked my wife if she thought it would be imposing on God to request that I be healed of my Sarcoidosis. My wife replied "no, we are to ask God for help when we are in need." When the healing portion of the church service arrived, I walked to the front of the church and prayed to God with the minister and the congregation that my lungs be healed. I prayed to the Almighty God of Creation and humbly requested that He heal me. I felt a sense of peace and would love God if He cured me or if my lung problem remained. I was not miraculously and not instantaneously healed of my lung problem. It is critical to understand that God hears all prayers, but it is His choice in how He responds. God's grace was sufficient to keep me strong when I am weak. Over time, it seemed I became acclimated to the living with chest pain and being short of breath. With God's grace, I focused on living and being content.

In 2010, two years after the healing service, I went to my lung physician for a checkup. The physician ordered various tests of my lung functions.

The medical tests revealed the Sarcoidosis was healed. God did answer my prayers, but six years elapsed in my life. God answered my prayer in His time. We need patience, faith, and peace, the fruits of the Holy Spirit, to gain insight into prayer and God's response. God will answer our prayer requests in His manner and in His time. I still have some residual breathing issues, but I am grateful to God for the improvement in my life.

When praying to God, ask God for patience, faith, and peace also.

- We need **patience** to accept God's timing with regard to our prayer.
- We need **faith** to know that God hears our prayer and knows the number of hairs on our head and loves us so much, He gave up His life for us, His friends.
- We need **peace** through laying our heavy burden at the feet of the risen Jesus and accept Jesus' peace and rest.

God knows each and every one of His people by name. God does listen to each of our prayers. God will respond to our prayers in His time. God may talk to us directly or He may send someone to act on His behalf. Communication from humans to God and communication from God to humans is real. We all need God's help to survive life. God designed us to need Him.

As I matured in my faith with God, my prayers became more frequent and of many different types. While I was writing *Jesus is Our Friend*, my relationship with Jesus became more personal. I prayed for wisdom while writing the words for this book. I began to ponder God's message while I was driving my car to and from work. I then prayed when I had an available moment in my day or when I was on my lunch break at work. After the first year of writing this book, I perceived I was in almost constant contact with Jesus. The more I prayed to God for wisdom and understanding about the message of truth in the Holy Bible, the more peace I experienced. Prayer is the way we can talk with our heavenly Father, God. We are never alone on this big planet earth; God is always available to communicate with through prayer.

Let us pray. Thank you God for giving us the gift of prayer. Jesus, you tore the curtain of the temple from top to bottom and allow us to approach the throne of God! We can pray to you anytime we want, twenty-four hours a day, from any location. Our souls long to talk to You, oh God.

# CHAPTER 10

# Commandments

I am the LORD your God, who brought you out of the land of Egypt, out of the house of slavery; you shall have no other gods before me.

You shall not make for yourself an idol. You shall not bow down to them or worship them; for I the LORD your God am a jealous God.

You shall not make wrongful use of the name of the LORD your God, for the LORD will not acquit anyone who misuses his name.

Remember the Sabbath day, and keep it holy.

Honor your father and your mother.

You shall not murder.

You shall not commit adultery.

You shall not steal.

You shall not bear false witness against your neighbor.

You shall not covet your neighbor's house; you shall not covet your neighbor's wife, or male or female slave, or ox, or donkey, or anything that belongs to your neighbor. Exodus 20.2, 3, 4a, 5a, 7, 8, 12a, 13, 14, 15, 16, 17

The Holy Spirit also testifies to us, for after saying,
"This is the covenant that I will make with them
after those days, says the Lord.
I will put my laws in their hearts,
and I will write them on their minds." Hebrews 10. 15-16

Pray for us; for we are sure that we have a clear conscience, desiring to act honorably in all things. Hebrews 13.18

He said to him, "You shall love the Lord your God with all your heart, and with all your soul, and with all your mind. This is the greatest and first commandment. And a second is like it: You shall love your neighbor as yourself. On these two commandments hang all the law and the prophets." Matthew 22.37-40

Jesus said to him, "Again it is written, 'Do not put the Lord your God to the test.'"  Matthew 4.7

Treat others the same way you want them to treat you.  Luke 6.31 NASB

But I tell you, do not swear at all: either by heaven, for it is God's throne; or by the earth, for it is his footstool; or by Jerusalem, for it is the city of the Great King. And do not swear by your head, for you cannot make even one hair white or black.  Simply let your 'Yes' be 'Yes,' and your 'No,' 'No'; anything beyond this comes from the evil one.  Matthew 5.34-37 NIV

The precision of the Ten Commandments reflects the sovereignty of God.  No human being could have conceived the Ten Commandments, not thousands of years ago, not today.  The brevity of the Ten Commandments permits memorization.  In addition, God wrote the Ten Commandments in our hearts and minds.

We are created beings that exist only by the kindness of the Creator. As our Creator, God gave us four commandments regarding the relationship between humans and God.  God commands us to acknowledge He is the Almighty and we are to have no gods other than Him.  If we attain a comfortable lifestyle, it is tempting to sin and think we control and sustain our life and disregard God. I did commit the sin of thinking I was a "powerful" businessman and thought I did not need God.  When my alleged power vanished like the morning dew one day, the clarity of God's gifts and my frailty became evident. When my alleged "power" to conduct international business and make decisions with wide scale impact returned with a management change, I stayed humble and knew all power rests with God.

Worshipping idols, such as a golden calf, is an overt literal disobedience of the second commandment.  False gods may include oneself. The source of peace and love is not inside oneself, but rather being born again as a child of God.  The original sin of Adam and Eve was the desire to be equal to God. God is perfect; we are created beings.  In addition to elevating oneself as a Supreme Being, money, hobbies, education, work, other people, or pagan gods may cause us to sin by replacing God as the most important entity in our lives.

It is frightening when one ponders that one of the ten things God ordered us NOT to do is misuse his name. I cringe when I hear people casually speak the name of Jesus Christ when they are disgusted with something. Spending eternity in hell is a good reason to not misuse God's name.

God commands us to honor the Sabbath and keeping it holy. Worshipping God and allocating time exclusively for Him in a church service helps keep my daily challenges in perspective. Worshiping God is not a task for me; it rejuvenates and strengthens me. If I do not attend church for a few weeks, day-to-day problems seem bigger and my stress level increases. Being still and acknowledging He is God is comforting.

The other six commandments involve interaction between others.

Honoring our parents brings peace. It is easy to honor our parents if they are wonderful people. If our parents' actions are not good for us, it is best to minimize the frequency of instances where our parents can hurt us.

Murder is often committed in concert with other sins, such as cheating people in unethical business practices or committing adultery. A life of sin involving illegal drug trafficking, stealing and selling stolen property, cheating people, or adultery invites murderous behavior. Avoiding sinful choices can reduce the occurrence of murder in life.

Someone irritating another can also incite murder. A human, who does not control one's carnal animal instincts, may murder a driver who merged without a sufficient distance or did some other inappropriate maneuver. This is murder by road rage. Life is a short journey from birth to eternity. We cannot take our money with us to heaven or hell. If someone gets in front of us, we will arrive at our destination at approximately the same time. Rage is a reaction that we can control. Previously, I would become angry if a self-centered driver drove into my path inappropriately. Over many years of driving, I now **expect** most people to merge inappropriately, not permit me to merge on the freeway, and in general, drive poorly. When someone drives crazy, I am no longer surprised, and am not angered. Avoid rage by conditioning yourself to expect the worst from people and be pleased when courtesy is extended.

I would like to share my thoughts on a covert cause of murder. A covert cause of murder meandering into the world is stress. Humans have a natural instinct for self-preservation. If we fell into water, we would try to swim to shore any way we can. If we were hungry, we would search for food. If we were in danger of falling off a cliff, we would back up. If we touched a hot surface, our hand would recoil from the pain immediately to minimize the damage to our fingers. If we were in a very cold and snowy storm, we would seek warm shelter. If an animal attacked a human, we would fight or run away. If a warring tribe of humans attacked, we would fight for our life and freedom.

Murder may be a choice to eliminate ongoing extreme stress. The schoolmate who murders abusive bullies, an employee who murders abusive supervisors, and any victim of abuse who murders the abuser is responding to an instinct to survive and minimize pain. However, the outcome of murder may include prison, execution, and eternity in hell! My recommendations to prevent murder in response to abuse are not easy, but are necessary:

- Command the abuser to stop immediately
- Reject abuse
- Ask loved ones and the authorities for help
- Do not let abuse continue.

Murder in response to ongoing stress can be caused by inaction by the abused. Humans cannot tolerate indefinite stress without damaging results. God commands us not to murder people. To be and remain a child of God, it is prudent to curtail abuse toward us and control our anger.

God's seventh commandment is that men and women not commit adultery. Obeying this commandment can be compared to obeying a command to not walk in front of a speeding truck. As walking into the path of a speeding truck may kill the body, committing adultery may kill a marriage. Adultery destroys trust, marriages, and families. The people I have known who committed adultery have both destroyed their marriage and their nuclear family. Avoiding the situations for extra-marital romance is the best method to prevent adultery.

The eight, ninth, and tenth commandments, prohibiting stealing, lying, and coveting respectively, advise against acts that bring self-destruction. Taking an item that someone else worked for involves laziness in conjunction with stealing. Stealing an item risks prison and a criminal record. It is most efficient to work for and purchase an item, rather than stealing it.

Lying is a sin that is typically discovered. Lying is exposed when the parties lied to confer with other people or search for facts. If a person lies at work and declares they finished an engineering drawing when they actually did not, their lie is short lived. The boss will simply review the drawing and determine if it is complete. Lying may result in being terminated from employment. Telling the truth, such as disclosing one made a mistake, is righteous and appropriate.

Coveting is an emotional cancer that consumes its host. God can bless people with wealth or beauty. My mother and I were relatively poor folks in inner city Cleveland after my father died. As I explored the world outside my poor inner-city neighborhood, I set a personal goal of a good family, nice house in the suburbs, and an executive job. Due to my childhood environment, I was not particularly groomed or prepared for studying engineering. College was difficult for me and I did drop a few classes before I failed them. I considered dropping out of college completely when the school put me on academic probation for a few bad grades; I was embarrassed and felt incompetent. I met my future wife at the end of my worst semester in college. My girlfriend and future wife gave me the faith to endure and taught me how to study. Working together, I learned to learn and earned A's and B's in college courses. It took me five years to earn a bachelor's degree in engineering, but I succeeded. God did not give me my goals instantly; success comes as a result of work, and work is hard.

Coveting involves an entitlement attitude that one deserves goods that belong to one's neighbor. Coveting is a waste of time and energy. Cain killed his brother Abel because Cain was jealous God favored Abel's offering. Per Genesis 4, Cain willfully did not give God the best of his produce; Abel gave God the firstlings of his flock.

God said,

"I will be gracious to whom I will be gracious, and will show compassion on whom I will show compassion." Exodus 33.19b NASB

Coveting at its extreme can be evil; let me explain. My wife and I have been married for many years, have a son and a daughter, and try to live life in accordance with God's word. Our children both graduated from college through dedicated study and sacrifice. The marriage between my wife and I is strong because we are joined by God. Keeping marriage joyful through many years involves adapting to the personal growth of one's spouse. I dated my wife as a high school person. I have been married to my wife though many stages: a stay at home mom, a college student, a college graduate, an occupational therapist, a director, and an owner of a company. My wife has dated me as a college student. She has been married to an engineer, a workaholic senior engineer, an engineering manager, and an engineering manager writing a book on Jesus. In addition to the numerous evolutions of our attitudes and occupations in our lives, I have had various serious illnesses in my life. After numerous hospital stays and operations, God has allowed me to continue living.

Several years ago, while my son was earning his bachelor's degree, he experienced emotional pain over the ending of a romantic college relationship. While driving preoccupied and distracted, my son hit the car in front of him at a stoplight and a minor accident resulted. My wife and I paid the five hundred dollar deductible and arranged to have the car repaired and returned the car to my son. My son became upset he was involved in an accident in addition to the ending of his college romance. Within three weeks, while driving preoccupied and distracted, my son hit another car in front of him at another stoplight and a second minor accident resulted. My son drove his damaged car home and needed comforting from mom and dad for his misfortunes. We hugged our son and said all would be fine in time. After comforting our son all weekend, we drove him back to his college several hours away. My wife and I paid the second five hundred dollar deductible and had the car repaired. After the second accident and the subsequent repair, we kept our son's car in our driveway for three months. Since our son lived on campus and walked to classes, we felt we should keep our son safe and he not drive until he was done grieving and he was at peace. Since my wife and I were paying for his car insurance, we needed time to find another insurance company, as our current insurance company dropped his coverage.

One of our family friends of many years came by to visit and saw our son's car in our driveway. The friend asked if our son was home sick or on vacation from college. My wife explained that our son had been in two minor automobile accidents within a month after his college romance ended and we were keeping the car temporarily. The friend made a wicked smile and said, "It is about time your kids did something wrong; you guys are so perfect it is unreal!" My wife and I were stunned and very hurt by our friend's comment! Our alleged "friend" had evidently coveted our marriage, our well-behaved children, and our Godly lifestyle. Our friend had been divorced for years and raised her two children alone. Her two children were not as academically inclined as my children, but we never compared and never judged. Our friend's comment indicated she **coveted with malice**.

To want something that another possesses is to covet. To want something that another possesses and simultaneously desire that person to lose what they have is to **covet with malice**.

When Cain killed Abel, Cain coveted God's favor of Abel and wanted to deny Abel of God's blessing by killing Abel; this is another example of coveting with malice. To covet is a sin. To covet what one's neighbor has and wish evil on the neighbor involves wickedness with sin. Our "friend" has wished evil on my family in addition to coveting our life.

Coveting is a sin that usually implies laziness. Blessings often are based on choices and consequences. An enduring marriage is not usually based on luck. A marriage endures because the husband and wife are committed to one another for better and worse, in sickness and in health, till death. People change and grow throughout their marriage and constant quality communication is essential. Good children are typically the fruits of good upbringing. It is easier to let one's children become spoiled and unruly. Teaching children the commandments of God involves teaching by example and nurturing. A peaceful and happy family life is the result of hard work. Coveting someone for a happy life indicates they want the reward without the work. Those who covet are often lazy and feel an entitlement without doing the work.

Wealth is typically gained by hard work or at times by evil endeavors. If people we know are living in a mansion, they may have worked hard for the money and may afford the mansion. People in mansions may be very deep in debt and have a painful mortgage. Other people living in luxury may have attained their wealth through unrighteous activities. I have known people in all three of the examples mentioned. All things in life involve choices. I want an affordable house payment, so my wife and I purchased a middle class home. I did not want to work two jobs, so we purchased what we could afford. Life is made of choices and consequences. Those who covet do not align their choices and their desired outcome.

The Ten Commandments are not punishing restrictions, but rather instructions for life. Obeying the Ten Commandments brings joy and peace to our lives.

Jesus condensed the Ten Commandments into two:

* Love God
* Love your neighbor as yourself.

Loving God and keeping him in your daily life puts our daily life into perspective and reduces stress. Loving your neighbor as yourself is a brief statement with major implications. Loving your neighbor as yourself precludes being condescending or treating your neighbor poorly.

The commandments from God are written in the Bible and also in our minds.

The Holy Spirit communicates to us through our conscience. "Conscience" is a word we seldom hear discussed, yet I think is very important. The apostle Paul referred to having a "clear conscience" in his letter to the Hebrews. Our conscience is the voice of the Holy Spirit advising us if we have sinned or if we are following God's laws. May the Holy Spirit dwell within us to guide us to be righteous, faithful, and have eternal life. Amen.

Let us pray. Thank you God for authoring the Ten Commandments. The Ten Commandments do not imprison us, but rather set us free. Your laws, God, guide us to peace, love, and life. You put your laws in our heart and wrote them on our minds. We do not disobey your laws out of ignorance; every sin is disobedience to God. Jesus, you told us to treat others the same way we want them to treat us. We humans know in our hearts the principle of fairness. When anyone is treated unfairly, the person is aware of the unrighteousness. Let us remember to treat others with the same righteous indignation we feel when we are mistreated. Let us worship you alone God, for you are the living God who gives us everything. Amen.

# CHAPTER 11

# Joy and Contentment

This is the day which the LORD hath made; we will rejoice and be glad in it. Psalm 118.24 KJV

For all of us make many mistakes. James 3.2a

Do all things without grumbling or disputing; so that you will prove yourselves to be blameless and innocent, children of God above reproach in the midst of a crooked and perverse generation, among whom you appear as lights in the world. Philippians 2. 14, 15 NASB

Keep your lives free from the love of money, and be content with what you have; for he has said, "I will never leave you or forsake you." Hebrews 13.5

"My grace is sufficient for you, for power is made perfect in weakness." So, I will boast all the more gladly of my weaknesses, so that the power of Christ may dwell in me. Therefore I am content with weaknesses, insults, hardships, persecutions, and calamities for the sake of Christ; for whenever I am weak, then I am strong. 2 Corinthians 12.9b-10

And he said to them, "Take care! Be on your guard against all kinds of greed; for one's life does not consist in the abundance of possessions." Luke 12.15

Peace I leave with you; my peace I give you. I do not give to you as the world gives. Do not let your hearts be troubled and do not be afraid. John 14.27 NIV

"Beware of practicing your righteousness before men to be noticed by them; otherwise you have no reward with your Father who is in heaven." Matthew 6.1 NASB

Contentment is very much related to one's view of life and reaction to life's events. Contentment is a learned state of mind that can be achieved by understanding God's word.

My dog had five cute puppies. She had plenty of milk for four weeks and all was well. Suddenly, her milk stopped flowing. My wife and I did not immediately conceive there was no milk because the puppies were quiet and still nursing. Suddenly, the smallest of her puppies seemed to stagger when he walked and did not hold his head up properly. We rushed the pup to the veterinarian at one o'clock in the morning. The veterinarian said the pup was dehydrated and gave it sugar water to drink and an intravenous saline solution. When we returned home, the mom dog developed a severe twitch in her right eye. She was very stressed she had no milk and her babies could die. I purchased many cans of substitute dog milk and saved the litter. My dog's eye did not stop twitching until the puppies were ten weeks old and eating solid dog food. When we creatures, or our children, do not have our basic physical needs met, including, food, water, shelter, and companionship, we are stressed. I never knew dogs could feel the emotion of stress, nearly identical to us humans.

Contentment supersedes our environment and allows us to feel joy when things are not "perfect." If we needed all to be perfect before we were content and filled with joy, all of us would be unhappy. Joy, peace, and contentment are gifts from God through the Holy Spirit that occur regardless of our immediate transient earthly situation.

The news media for the masses, with its tendencies for sensationalism, typically reports every murder in the area on the daily news. It appears the news media has a preoccupation with frightening the public with being murdered. Various states in the United States have legalized carrying a concealed weapon. Perhaps this effort to carry guns to protect oneself is based on the murders that are reported on the nightly news. Paying careful attention to the news may reveal that the person murdered was not in your neighborhood, city, metropolitan area, state, or within one thousand miles. The bad news sellers may have reported a murder in a far away state because no one was killed near you. However, what you may not hear on the news programs is that the SUICIDE RATE IS 173% OF THE MURDER RATE! MORE PEOPLE IN THE WEALTHY UNITED STATES KILL THEMSELVES THAN ARE MURDERED. 5.6 per 100,000 people are murdered and 9.7 per 100,000 people kill themselves. The Center for Disease Control 2003[9] records are alarming to me. Suicide is the ultimate statement and action that one is not content with their life.

I am not an expert in suicide, nor a physician; I am just a humble engineer presenting God's pearls of wisdom. If you or anyone you know considers suicide, seek treatment by a physician.

Let us move to the Bible for insight on contentment. If Bible verses and the words in this chapter help at least one person increase their level of contentment, I am grateful to God to be of service to His glory.

Psalm 118.24 teaches that we are to rejoice and be glad each day we are alive. There is no pre-existing reason to be sad, so rejoice in being alive. Jesus frequently gave thanks to God the Father. It is good for us to give thanks to God for the opportunity to be born and to live. We are blessed to be able to listen to birds sing, view a beautiful sunrise, and love one another. God does not owe us anything; any graciousness God bestows onto us is an undeserved gift. Being in a thankful mindset primes us to be content.

Hebrews 13.5 directs us to not love money and be content with our possessions. Luke 12.15 warns us not to covet our neighbors' goods and that our life is not based on our possessions. Much unhappiness is based on choices regarding money and possessions.

Enjoying the possessions we have and not coveting our neighbor's status symbols can enhance contentment. Making our happiness contingent on owning a certain brand name of clothing or certain make of car may make us unhappy if we do not obtain it.

Expect people to act rude and selfishly; if they act kindly, be pleasantly surprised. Jesus commands us to treat others as we want to be treated. It appears many people like to be treated well while they treat others badly. Human babies begin life as self-centered and demanding beings. Babies scream when they want to be fed, entertained, or have their clothes changed. Being self-centered and demanding is the natural state of humans. Acknowledging that people may be rude and self-absorbed reduces stress by eliminating our false expectations. People are kind to one another only if they choose to be kind and place the needs of others over theirs.

Inappropriate expectations from one's spouse can cause marital problems. Expecting a spouse to always be perfect, meet all our needs, and never age will prevent contentment. Loved ones must communicate with each other to understand each other's desires and agree on what is realistic. Expressing thanks to one another for acts of kindness and expressing thanks for being a good spouse are critical to the success of a marriage. I clearly remember a comment a young man made to a few of his acquaintances, including me, many years ago. He said, "My wife told me she is moving out and divorcing me because I did not appreciate her and I never said 'thank you' to her." Jesus teaches we are to give thanks for acts of kindness.

The story of the ten lepers in Luke 17.12-19 explains that Jesus cured ten lepers, but only one came back to thank Him. Jesus commented that he cured ten lepers, but only one was grateful and expressed thanks. This story in Luke teaches that Jesus finds it appropriate we express thanks to those who show us kindness. Another lesson from Luke 17 is that nine out of ten people may not express appreciation. If we show kindness, do a good deed, or perform extraordinarily well at our job, perhaps ninety percent of the time we will not be thanked! For our own tranquility, understand that those who do acts of kindness and show the love of Jesus may be thanked only ten percent of the time.

The need for praise from fellow people is an internal desire that can escalate to discontentment. As schoolchildren, we are conditioned to seek a gold star from our grade school teacher when we do well. As an adult, we may still want the gold star from someone when we do well. **If we live to fulfill others' expectations and obtain their approval, we are controlled and destined for defeat.** Jesus specifically states in Matthew 6.1 that we are not to expect praise from others for doing God's work. We are not to be taken advantage of by others. It is prudent our spouse, children, and other family members give thanks to one another for kind acts. However, in the world outside our home, appreciation may not be received, but we are to persevere.

The writer James declared that all of us make many mistakes. As humans, we are not perfect.

I would like to make an aside here regarding the writer James. Acts 12.2 records that King Herod killed the apostle James with a sword. In Galatians 1.18-20, the apostle Paul shared that he met with Jesus' brother James. In Galatians 2.8-9, Paul explained that Jesus' brother James taught the good news of Jesus to the gentiles. I am not a Bible scholar, but I personally think the book of James was written by the half brother of Jesus. I enjoy the book of James and I hope you enjoy the writings of James also. The clarity and kindness of James' writing gives me the impression that he was indeed the half brother of Jesus. James initially did not believe that his half brother Jesus was the Son of the living God. Later, James taught the good news of Jesus to the gentiles. Perhaps James acknowledged he made a mistake in not believing he was the half brother of the Son of God. Perhaps James declared that all of us make mistakes based on his personal life. James is correct; all of us make mistakes. The book of James gives me a special comfort when I read it; may you also be comforted.

When decisions become more complex, it is difficult to make a perfect decision. We can make the best decision with the information available at that time. Expecting ourselves to be perfect will decrease our effectiveness. When my wife and I purchased our second home when we moved to Ohio, my requirement for my personal perfection bit me like a snake. The home was large, well built, and in a pleasant rural setting. The first January in the house was unusually cold and the heating costs were expensive. I panicked and was outraged at myself that I had underestimated the operating cost of the inefficient heating system in the home. The utility bills were indeed elevated for January and February, but I wasted those two months of my life obsessing how I underestimated the heating costs. My sins were not trusting God and not acknowledging that only God is perfect. I disrupted my joy and contentment by false expectations of perfection. We humans do not know the future. We can only base our decisions on the facts available. We are to do our best and trust God with the rest.

Our response regarding attaining or not attaining our goals and requests, has a major impact on our contentment. When Jesus prayed the Lord's prayer in Matthew 6.9-13 KJV, the words included "Thy will be done." The Lord's Prayer does not include Carl Butcher's will be done or our will be done. "Thy will be done" means God has the ultimate authority in His creation. We can be content knowing that God has our life, death, and eternity under His control. God loves us and will not abandon us.

The Holy Bible is an instruction manual of life. When we obey the commandments and the principles explained in the Holy Bible, we are more likely to be content. Loving God and loving our neighbor as ourselves will illuminate the path to contentment. Those who comit adultry, steal, love money, and hate God and hate their neighbor are seldom content and joyful people. Obeying the commandments will not exempt us from experiencing bad events, but breaking the laws of God greatly increases the likelihood of causing bad events in our lives. Bad randon events may happen to anyone. Poor life choices may result in bad events in addition to naturally occurring bad events.

Let us pray. God please fill us with peace that exceeds our understanding. Let us be content with what You provide us. We as humans must do our best and then accept reality. We cannot force events in life to occur that are outside of your plan, God. Help us remember that we are to rejoice in each day that You provide, God. Please teach us to not worry, but have faith in You God. We are not all-knowing beings. Humans journey through life and often learn by trial and error. Wisdom is attained through experience. Please teach us to graciously accept our blessings and not expect more. Amen.

# CHAPTER 12

# Family

Then the LORD God said, "It is not good for the man to be alone; I will make him a helper suitable for him." Genesis 2.18 NASB

"But from the beginning of creation, "God made them male and female." "For this reason a man shall leave his father and mother and be joined to his wife, and the two shall become one flesh." So they are no longer two, but one flesh. Therefore what God has joined together, let no one separate." Mark 10.6-9

A wise son makes a father glad, but a foolish son is a grief to his mother. Proverbs 10.1b NASB

"And I say to you, whoever divorces his wife, except for unchastity, and marries another woman commits adultery." Matthew 19.9

Be on your guard! If your brother sins, rebuke him; and if he repents, forgive him. "And if he sins against you seven times a day, and returns to you seven times, saying, 'I repent,' forgive him." Luke 17.3-4 NASB

But if they are not practicing self-control, they should marry. For it is better to marry than to be aflame with passion. 1 Corinthians 7.9

An excellent wife, who can find? For her worth is far above jewels. Proverbs 31.10 NASB

"Do not suppose that I have come to bring peace to the earth. I did not come to bring peace, but a sword. For I have come to turn a man against his father, a daughter against her mother, a daughter-in-law against her mother-in-law — a man's enemies will be the members of his own household. Anyone who loves his father or mother more than me is not worthy of me; anyone who loves his son or daughter more than me is not worthy of me; and anyone who does not take his cross and follow me is not worthy of me. Whoever finds his life will lose it, and whoever loses his life for my sake will find it." Matthew 10.34-39 NIV

The men of Israel said, "Have you seen this man who is coming up? Surely he is coming up to defy Israel. And it will be that the king will enrich the man who kills him with great riches and will give him his daughter and make his father's house free in Israel." Then David spoke to the men who were standing by him, saying, "What will be done for the man who kills this Philistine and takes away the reproach from Israel? For who is this uncircumcised Philistine, that he should taunt the armies of the living God?" The people answered him in accord with this word, saying, "Thus it will be done for the man who kills him." Now Eliab his oldest brother heard when he spoke to the men; and Eliab's anger burned against David and he said, "Why have you come down? And with whom have you left those few sheep in the wilderness? I know your insolence and the wickedness of your heart; for you have come down in order to see the battle." But David said, "What have I done now? Was it not just a question?" I Samuel 17.25-29 NASB

If I speak in the tongues of mortals and of angels, but do not have love, I am a noisy gong or a clanging cymbal. And if I have prophetic powers, and understand all mysteries and all knowledge, and if I have all faith, so as to remove mountains, but do not have love, I am nothing. If I give away all my possessions, and if I hand over my body so that I may boast, but do not have love, I gain nothing. Love is patient; love is kind; love is not envious or boastful or arrogant or rude. It does not insist on its own way; it is not irritable or resentful; it does not rejoice in wrongdoing, but rejoices in the truth. It bears all things, believes all things, hopes all things, endures all things. I Corinthians 13.1-7

And whoever does not provide for relatives, and especially for family members, has denied the faith and is worse than an unbeliever. I Timothy 5.8

So then, whenever we have an opportunity, let us work for the good of all, and especially for those of the family of faith. Galatians 6.10

"Fathers, do not exasperate your children; instead, bring them up in the training and instruction of the Lord." Ephesians 6.4 NIV

Train up a child in the way he should go: and when he is old he will not depart from it. Proverbs 22.6 KJV

God made Adam and said it is not good for him to be alone. God indicated that man is a social creature and needs human company. God created Eve. God created them male and female. God told Adam and Eve to be fruitful and multiply. Humans have an instinct to gather with other humans.

Mark 10.6-9 records Jesus preached that God Himself joins husband and wife together. This single statement from Jesus, the Son of God, and who is one with the Father, brings a seriousness, sacredness, and permanence to marriage.

I met my future wife when I was a twenty-year-old college student and she was a seventeen-year-old-high school senior. Prior to meeting my wife, I prayed to God to guide me to find my future spouse. I had an inner guidance from God to find my wife. My wife and I got married within a month of my college graduation. As I am finishing this book, my wife and I have been married over thirty years. Marriage is a commitment to one another. The commitment to each other will involve adapting to one another on life's journey. I married my wife when she was a twenty-years-old. My wife and I were adventurous young adults when we were first married. We had moved directly from Ohio to Texas for my first engineering job and our first apartment. We explored Dallas, various other parts of Texas, and vacationed in Oklahoma. Life was fun as newlyweds. We purchased our first new car. My first engineering job did not involve the work that was promised and I located to another position in Pennsylvania. My wife and I purchased our first home in Pennsylvania and had a good life. My wife was laid off from her bookkeeping job for a while and we often paid for food at the grocery store by counting out our collected change. Drying clothes for us entailed hanging wet clothes on hangers in the bathroom; we could afford a washer, but not a dryer too.

On March 28, 1979, my wife and I drove home from work, greeted each other at home, and began to make dinner. As we listened to the television while making dinner, the newscaster announced that the Three Mile Island nuclear power plant, near Middletown, Pennsylvania, was overheating and in danger of releasing massive amounts of radioactivity into the air.[10] Coincidently, my wife and I lived very close to Middletown, Pennsylvania!

We drove back to Ohio for the weekend. Although half of the nuclear fuel did melt down, the walls of the containment building remained intact and massive quantities of radiation were not released into the atmosphere. My wife and I returned home the next week and went to work. We enjoyed living in Lancaster County, Pennsylvania for a couple of years. My wife and I decided to have children. We wanted grandparents in our children's lives and decided to move back to Ohio.

My wife and I sold our Pennsylvania house, moved back to Ohio, and were blessed with a son and a daughter. When we returned to Ohio, we rented, saved as much money as we could, and then purchased a home in the country. Becoming parents added a responsibility to take care of our children. I coached our son's and daughter's ball teams in alternate years. We enjoyed traveling with our children to special places in the United States and took them with us to visit England. My wife went back to college and earned a bachelor's degree in Occupational Therapy.

We enjoyed watching our son perform in the marching band at football games. We attended every meet that our daughter ran in cross-country during high school and college. It seemed quickly that our children grew up, earned their doctorate and master's degrees, moved away and started their careers.

My fiancée and then wife, and I have been high school students, college students, parents of babies, toddlers, and college students, and now empty nesters. We have been poor, and not struggling. We have been healthy and my body has malfunctioned. My wife and I have been ideal weight, overweight, and weights in between. The two people who get married do not remain the same people for long.

I share some details of my life to provide insight that marriage is not a static condition. The wrinkle free, carefree, and young person we marry will change. Understand and embrace the person we marry will change; we will change. Although each member of a couple has different talents and interests, the young couple is primarily focused on one another when together. The members of the marriage continue to grow personally. A husband and wife will each change as life experiences and education cause each member to gain a more diversified understanding of life. The interests and hobbies of each spouse may change in time. Children simultaneously are growing up from infants and toddlers, and then attend preschool, grade school, middle school, and high school. The time that the members of the family allocate to one another changes constantly. I started learning the piano at forty-nine years old after my children graduated from high school. My wife and I hosted a Japanese high school exchange student at forty-seven and fifty-years-old, respectively. As the perception of life changes for each spouse, the interaction between the spouses will change. Like work is necessary to keep a home clean and a lawn manicured; marriage compatibility requires work. To keep a marriage happy with two people growing intellectually and changing, good communication is necessary.

I knew a man who indicated he was divorcing his wife after being married for only a few years and having a child. I suggested that his wife seemed to be a kind and loving person and they should see a marriage counselor. The man insisted his marriage was "no longer exciting" and that they had different interests. The man divorced his wife. I am not an expert on marriage, but I have observed several patterns common to the destruction of marriage. Humans seem to derive a pleasure and excitement associated with new possessions, such as new cars, new clothes, and new furniture or appliances. Marketing experts have reinforced the concept that new is better. Perhaps the drive for newness and excitement has migrated into marriage. It is critical to remember that God Himself joins a husband and wife.

Marriage joins the couple in their physical and spiritual aspects. Marriage is different than buying car and subsequently trading the old car in for a newer model. When considering marriage, we acknowledge that physical life is finite, our human bodies will become less defined over time, heal slower, and our skin will not be as smooth as a baby's indefinitely. The newness of marriage will not last; however, the enjoyment and appreciation of one's spouse is to endure. We marry the spirit of our spouse, which transcends personal growth, aging, and changing interests. Spouses are to work to keep their marriage enjoyable. Hunting for a new spouse is not the way to induce excitement. Instant gratification is an addiction that does not cease. When I talk to men who have divorced their wife to find excitement with a new woman, the same unique needs of men and women reoccur. Wives want to be appreciated, romanced, and have their spouse involved in the care of the home.

Marriage can be damaged by the misguided urge to escape. Life is often a difficult journey. Raising children, addressing illnesses, and other responsibilities cause stress. Spending more money than we earn and going deeper in debt causes much stress. When family life becomes stressful, the simplistic instinct is to escape. When life becomes stressful, the blame may be misdirected. Excessive bills or committing to too many responsibilities may be the root cause of stress. God's love for the couple and the couple's love for one another may be overshadowed by stress. It is critical to escape the stress for a weekend and recommit to the marriage. Couples need time to evaluate the source of the stress and realize the marriage may not be the problem. An occasional weekend vacation to relax and gain clarity of thought is good for a married couple.

Training children properly is the responsibility of the family. Children remember the values their parents displayed. Genesis 8.21 initially surprised me when I read it; every inclination of a human heart is evil from childhood. God Himself indicated children have the propensity for evil in their heart. It is crucial parents understand innocent children may tell lies and break other laws of God. Parents must teach children the laws of God. Evil is a part of the natural carnal human being. Righteousness and holiness can prevail over evil when the carnal nature of man is acknowledged and goodness is chosen, not evil. Parents are to treat their children with kindness and guide them. Micromanaging a child and giving them no freedom to choose may cause a child to rebel. My wife and I have children with very different personalities; we must treat each of them in a manner that brings harmony.

Parents have the challenging job of training their children in a manner that the children choose righteousness. God created all humans with the ability to choose right or wrong and good or evil. God taught humans right from wrong by praising them when they did good and rebuking them when they did evil. Although God is the perfect parent, His children, humans, may choose to resist proper guidance. As human parents, we can emulate God and praise our children when they are righteous and rebuke them when our children act improperly.

The words of Jesus from Matthew 10, that indicate members of one's own household may become foes, can be troubling. I Samuel 17.25-29 explains that Eliab became angry at his brother David when David inquired about killing the giant Philistine warrior. Ironically, it was indeed David who would kill the giant Philistine Goliath and become king of Israel. When Eliab saw David, Eliab told David he should be home watching the family sheep. Eliab continued insulting David by telling him that he was arrogant and wicked and that he only came to observe the battle and not fight. The Bible teaches that members of our own family may be against us. David wrote these words in response to his brother's attempts to steal, kill, and destroy his self-confidence and service to God:

For You are my hope; O Lord GOD, You are my confidence from my youth. Psalm 71.5 NASB

I did not fully grasp the significance of these Bible verses regarding family conflict over God until I gained better understanding of Christianity and acknowledged the family interactions with clarity. As a young person, I tried to be accepted and liked by all family members. Some members of my family did not enjoy my company, or accept me as I was. I felt hurt for many years that I was never the popular family member, nor the most exciting. I was a beacon of light shining for Jesus in the darkness and was disliked because of it. One family member shared that he did not like being with me because I was a conservative and a Christian. I was shocked because I seldom talked politics or religion with this person. A person living the life of a Christian, a forgiven sinner trying to obey the commandments, is obvious to others. The body is truly a temple of the Holy Spirit. When you are a Christian, others can perceive you are an ambassador of Jesus. Various family members disliked me because I was a Christian. Only when I truly understood that I was disliked and rejected because I was a Christian did Matthew 10.34-39 make sense to me! Once one understands that your family rejects you because you are a Christian, a choice becomes painfully clear: do you love Jesus or your family more? The second question is similar: do you want to spend your time on earth with your non-believing family members and an eternity in hell or do you want to live for Jesus on earth and spend eternity in Heaven? I made the decision to believe in Jesus and spend eternity in Heaven.

We are to love all and love Jesus. However, as we become a little bit more like Jesus, we will likely be rejected and avoided by family members who are children of darkness. Over my lifetime, I have noted that people who live as committed Christians tend to have a Godly and pleasant life. Obeying the commandments of God brings peace and a gentle lifestyle. People who reject God and do not obey His commandments may have more chaos in their life. Jealousy between cousins and other family members tends to make those who do not follow God dislike those who follow God. For my first forty-five years, I did not understand Jesus' commentary that a man's enemies will be the members of his own household, as recorded in Matthew 10.34-39. As I move toward the autumn of my life, I have observed a pattern that those who do not follow Jesus tend to not associate with committed Christians. Children of darkness in families stay together and children of the light are drawn to the light. I have witnessed some family members control their envy regarding strangers, but unleash their jealousy toward fellow family members. It is unfortunate some family members target their jealously toward their own family. It is natural to minimize association with those who do not like us for loving and obeying God. Jesus provides clear guidance regarding family relationships. Luke 17.3 records that we are to rebuke our brother if he sins. It is important to advise others if they speak hurtful or untrue words. Jesus tells us we are to forgive our brothers seven times a day if he repents. Many families have interpersonal tensions. Establishing boundaries and explaining expectations in communication is critical to gaining peace within families. However, we must minimize our stress from unkind family members.

All have sinned and fall short of the glory of God; they are now justified by his grace as a gift, through the redemption that is in Christ Jesus, whom God put forward as a sacrifice of atonement by his blood, effective through faith. Romans 3.23-25a

Let us pray. Heavenly Father, thank You for family. Life is too hard and too long and too lonely to live without the love of a family. Thank you for sending those who love us into the world. Of equal importance, send us out to love those who need love. Amen.

# CHAPTER 13

# Work and Creativity

Then God said, "Behold, I have given you every plant yielding seed that is on the surface of all the earth, and every tree which has fruit yielding seed; it shall be food for you. Genesis 1.29 NASB

Then the LORD God took the man and put him into the Garden of Eden to cultivate it and keep it. Genesis 2.15 NASB

"By the sweat of your face shall you eat bread until you return to the ground, for out of it you were taken; you are dust and to dust you will return." Genesis 3.19

The LORD spoke to Moses: See, I have called by name Bezalel son of Uri son of Hur, of the tribe of Judah: and I have filled him with divine spirit, with ability, intelligence, and knowledge in every kind of craft, to devise artistic designs, to work in gold, silver, and bronze, in cutting stones for setting, and in carving wood, in every kind of craft. Exodus 31.1-5

When the Sabbath came, He began to teach in the synagogue; and the many listeners were astonished, saying, "Where did this man get these things, and what is this wisdom given to Him, and such miracles as these performed by His hands?" "Is not this the carpenter, the son of Mary, and brother of James and Joses and Judas and Simon? Are not His sisters here with us?" Mark 6.2-3a, b NASB

"Again, it will be like a man going on a journey, who called his servants and entrusted his property to them. To one he gave five talents of money, to another two talents, and to another one talent, each according to his ability. Then he went on his journey. The man who had received the five talents went at once and put his money to work and gained five more. So also, the one with the two talents gained two more. But the man who had received the one talent went off, dug a hole in the ground and hid his master's money." "After a long time the master of those servants returned and settled accounts with them. The man who had received the five talents brought the other five. 'Master,' he said, 'you entrusted me with five talents. See, I have gained five more.'" "His master replied, 'Well done, good and faithful servant! You have been faithful with a few things; I will put you in charge of many things. Come and share your master's happiness!' The man with the two talents also came. 'Master,' he said, 'you entrusted me with two talents; see, I have gained two more.'" "His master replied, 'Well done, good and faithful servant! You have been faithful with a few things; I will put you in charge of many things. Come and share your master's happiness!' "Then the man who had received the one talent came. 'Master,' he said, 'I knew that you are a hard man, harvesting where you have not sown and gathering where you have not scattered seed. So I was afraid and went out and hid your talent in the ground. See, here is what belongs to you.' "His master replied, 'You wicked, lazy servant! So you knew that I harvest where I have not sown and gather where I have not scattered seed? Well then, you should have put my money on deposit with the bankers, so that when I returned I would have received it back with interest. 'Take the talent from him and give it to the one who has the ten talents. For everyone who has will be given more, and he will have an abundance. Whoever does not have, even what he has will be taken from him. And throw that worthless servant outside, into the darkness, where there will be weeping and gnashing of teeth.'" Matthew 25.14-30 NIV

Who plants a vineyard and does not eat the fruit of it? Or who tends a flock and does not use the milk of the flock? I am not speaking these things according to human judgment, am I? Or does not the Law also say these things? For it is written in the Law of Moses, "YOU SHALL NOT MUZZLE THE OX WHILE HE IS THRESHING." God is not concerned about oxen, is He? Or is He speaking altogether for our sake? Yes, for our sake it was written, because the plowman ought to plow in hope, and the thresher to thresh in hope of sharing the crops. I Corinthians 9.7b-10 NASB

Your wealth has rotted, and moths have eaten your clothes. Your gold and silver are corroded. Their corrosion will testify against you and eat your flesh like fire. You have hoarded wealth in the last days. Look! The wages you failed to pay the workmen who mowed your fields are crying out against you. The cries of the harvesters have reached the ears of the Lord Almighty.

You have lived on earth in luxury and self-indulgence. You have fattened yourselves in the day of slaughter. James 5.2-5 NIV

Whatever your task, put yourselves into it, as done for the Lord and not for your masters, since you know that from the Lord you will receive the inheritance as your reward; you serve the Lord Christ. Colossians 3.23-24

For you yourselves know how you ought to imitate us; we were not idle when we were with you, and we did not eat anyone's bread without paying for it; but with toil and labor we worked night and day, so that we might not burden any of you. This was not because we do not have that right, but in order to give you an example to imitate. For even when we were with you, we gave you this command: Anyone unwilling to work should not eat. For we hear that some of you are living in idleness, mere busybodies, not doing any work. 2 Thessalonians 3.7-11

Genesis 1.27 indicates that God created humans, both male and female, in His image. God Himself is very talented and creative. God instilled creativity in the human brain. Humans have the ability to create art, music, buildings, tools, and other items to make our lives easier and more efficient.

Somewhat surprising to me, Genesis 2.15 teaches that even prior to the sin and the fall of Adam and Eve, God placed Adam in the Garden of Eden to cultivate the land and grow crops. I mistakenly thought that Adam and Eve did not work in the Garden of Eden; I thought they ate fruit from the trees and lounged all day. God instituted work in the beginning.

And on the seventh day God ended his work which he had made; and he rested on the seventh day from all his work which he had made. Genesis 2. 2 KJV

It is logical that humans work because God Himself created work. God did not create work as a punishment. God was in the beginning and was self-sustaining. God Himself chose to utilize His creative talents and work to create the world. Being made in God's image, humans are to utilize our talents also. God bestowed work and creativity as gifts. Adam and Eve worked in the Garden of Eden prior to the fall of man. After Adam's and Eve's sin, God sent them out of the Garden of Eden to till cursed soil with thorns and thistles (see Genesis 3.17-19). Human beings are still creative and need to work, but we must toil to survive.

God filled Bezalel with His spirit, including ability, intelligence, knowledge, craftsmanship, and the creativity to design. Understanding that the ability, intelligence, knowledge, and craftsmanship we possess are gifts from God realigns our perspective.

I took piano lessons to develop my musical skills. I am not a good piano player, but I enjoy trying to use the musical talent God gave me. People participate in hobbies to utilize their talents. Work and creativity are integral to the functioning of all creatures on earth, including us. Birds work to find seeds to eat, build nests, and feed their young. I have watched robins build a sturdy nest in my pine trees to house their babies. The adult robins hunt for food and feed their hatched babies throughout the day.

Humans must work to provide food, a home, and take care of their children for a long time. It is interesting that all of God's creatures have the requirement to work to survive and provide for their offspring. Humans are extraordinary in comparison with God's other creatures. Unlike birds and animals, humans do not need to devote their entire day, every day, to hunting and gathering food. We each have a role using our God-given intelligence and skills to work for our livelihood. Humans have a natural system of specialized skills. We ultimately work to provide goods or services to our neighbor for pay. Humans have specialized talents that enable farmers to grow sufficient vegetables and grains, ranchers to raise cattle, and craftspeople to make tools and perform other jobs. I have no idea how to manufacture eyeglasses, but I pay an optician to make them for me. Without eyeglasses, I could not perform my job as an engineer. Humans depend on one another to live in a society. We must work for our daily bread. The LORD'S prayer includes the line "give us this day our daily bread." God gives us the ability to earn our daily bread and to honor Him in our daily jobs.

Colossians 3.23 indicates we are to do our jobs as if we are working for the LORD. By performing our jobs well, we are beacons of light in a fallen world. We are to be kind to our customers and joyous in our work. The guidance to work as if you are working for Jesus is beneficial in another way. Many bosses do not thank or even appreciate the excellent work an employee may provide. However, the desire for praise regarding a job well done, to be appreciated, and to be part of a team seems to be an instinct in the human mind. Excellent managers acknowledge that people work to get paid, but people do an excellent job when they are motivated. Thanking a worker for a job well done, and perhaps providing a dinner or other reward for an excellent accomplishment will motivate people. If we expect to hear a "thank you for that fine job" from our boss, many of us will be frequently discouraged. To remain motivated when working, regardless if our boss is appreciative or not, utilize your talents and do your best to honor Jesus.

The parable of the talents in Matthew 25 is very profound. Jesus tells us in that story that we are to utilize the gifts God has given us. The very detailed parable discloses many things about God's interactions with human achievement, life, work, and human effort. God chooses to give each of us varying levels of human <u>ability</u> and <u>money</u>. God gave people in the parable five, two, or one talent and different human abilities. The master left the people and went on his journey. In my opinion, when Jesus states in Matthew 25.15 that the master went on his journey, perhaps that indicates that God entrusts us with His gifts and allows us the free will to use our talents. The person who received five talents earned five more talents. The person who received two talents earned two more. The servant who received one talent buried it in the ground earned no money.

The master was pleased with both servants who used their talents and earned more. The master was pleased they were faithful with a few talents and would put them in charge of many things! The master was displeased with the servant who buried the one talent. The worthless servant who did not utilize his talent was thrown into the darkness where he would weep and gnash his teeth. We are to use the talents God gave us.

Mark 6 indicated Jesus Himself worked as a carpenter prior to beginning His full time ministry. Jesus obviously did what He preached and earned money. Even the Son of God worked while on earth to provide service to his fellow man and earn money to eat. Jesus demonstrated we are to use the talents God gave us to be productive. Working and doing a good job shows love for our fellow man. Our labor provides a service for our fellow man and provides pay for ourselves.

Scripture directs us to work to eat. If anyone is not willing to work, he is not to eat. In addition, work involves being God's representative on earth. We are to work at church, God's house. We also are to visit the sick and feed the hungry. My wife, our therapy dog, and I visit residents in a nursing home in our city. We have also delivered hot meals to the hungry in their neighborhood from an especially equipped church bus. God calls each of us to do a part of His work. I am writing **Jesus is Our Friend** in my spare time to spread the gospel of Jesus Christ. God is very patient; if one does not listen to God's urging to build His kingdom, He will remind us. God encourages me to finish the race He commanded.

I Corinthians 9.7b-10 metaphorically refers to a selfish businessperson who does not properly share the profits generated by his business. A businessperson who exploits his employees is like a person who uses his ox to make grain, but does not let the ox eat any of the grain it makes. The Holy Bible indicates that if a business is profitable, the profits are to be fairly shared with the employees. Perhaps the lesson in I Corinthians may prompt a question regarding the fairness of paying an executive tens of millions of dollars per year while paying those who generate the profits a meager wage.

James 5.2-5 contains a stern warning to those who cheat others in business. The warning is especially harsh to those who live in luxury and self-indulgence, but do not pay workmen and laborers. The metaphor about "fattened yourself for slaughter" made me laugh; I have an odd sense of humor. The Old Testament burnt offering involved a fattened calf. James' metaphor of a person living in luxury and self-indulgence fattening himself to be slaughtered by God is a very profound and humbling statement. The book of James makes another important statement that God hears the cries of the cheated workmen and harvesters. Self-indulgent and unethical businessmen may scoff at their workers during their life on earth, but the evil ones will be subject to the wrath of God upon death.

The scripture lessons in I Corinthians 9 and James 5 proclaim that God Himself is aware of abuses toward the working person. It is critical we treat all people under our authority with dignity and provide proper compensation. As a manager of fellow employees, it is my responsibility to check the pay of people hired in my department and ensure the newcomer is making at least the minimum wage for a pay grade in the engineering department. If an employee is paid too low, the manager is responsible to raise the person's pay to the appropriate level. Leaving a person underpaid in a department is very similar to muzzling an ox threshing grain. I do not want to displease God by mistreating any employees under my authority!

Let us end this chapter in prayer. Heavenly Father, thank you for giving us our own special talents in life. You have faith in us and entrust us with your planet and the talent in our mind and body. Let each of us perform our jobs to the best of our abilities, as if we were working directly for God. Lets us serve one another, so others will perceive the love of Jesus in us. Amen.

# CHAPTER 14

# Treasures, Abstract and Concrete

In the course of time Cain brought some of the fruits of the soil as an offering to the LORD.  But Abel brought fat portions from some of the firstborn of his flock. The LORD looked with favor on Abel and his offering, but on Cain and his offering he did not look with favor.  Genesis 4.3-5a NIV

There was a certain man without a dependent, having neither a son nor a brother, yet there was no end to all his labor. Indeed, his eyes were not satisfied with riches and he never asked, "And for whom am I laboring and depriving myself of pleasure?" This too is vanity and it is a grievous task. Ecclesiastes 4.8 NASB

Also, I collected for myself silver and gold and the treasure of kings and provinces. All that my eyes desired I did not refuse them I did not withhold my heart from any pleasure, for my heart was pleased because of all my labor and this was my reward for all my labor. Thus I considered all my activities which my hands had done and the labor which I had exerted, and behold all was vanity and striving after wind and there was no profit under the sun. Ecclesiastes 2.8a, 10-11 NASB

Do not store up for yourselves treasures on earth, where moth and rust destroy, and where thieves break in and steal.  But store up for yourselves treasures in heaven, where neither moth nor rust destroys, and where thieves do not break in or steal; for where your treasure is, there your heart will be also.  Matthew 6.19-21 NASB

"No servant can serve two masters. Either he will hate the one and love the other, or he will be devoted to the one and despise the other. You cannot serve both God and Money." Luke 16.13 NIV

Dishonest money dwindles away, but he who gathers money little by little makes it grow.  Proverbs 13.11 NIV

"Bring the whole tithe into the storehouse, that there may be food in my house. Test me in this," says the LORD Almighty, "and see if I will not throw open the floodgates of heaven and pour out so much blessing that you will not have room enough for it."  Malachi 3.10 NIV

For the love of money is a root of all kinds of evil, and in their eagerness to be rich some have wandered away from the faith and pierced themselves with many pains.  1 Timothy 6.10

"Woe to you, scribes and Pharisees, hypocrites!  For you tithe mint, dill, and cummin, and have neglected the weightier matters of the law: justice and mercy and faith.  It is these you ought to have practiced without neglecting the others."  Matthew 23.23

"When the Son of Man comes in his glory, and all the angels with him, then he will sit on the throne of his glory. All the nations will be gathered before him, and he will separate people one from another as a shepherd separates the sheep from the goats, and he will put the sheep at his right hand and the goats at the left. Then the king will say to those at his right hand, 'Come, you that are blessed by my Father, inherit the kingdom prepared for you from the foundation of the world; for I was hungry and you gave me food, I was thirsty and you gave me something to drink, I was a stranger and you welcomed me, I was naked and you gave me clothing, I was sick and you took care of me, I was in prison and you visited me.' Then the righteous will answer him, 'Lord, when was it that we saw you hungry and gave you food, or thirsty and gave you something to drink?  And when was it that we saw you a stranger and welcomed you, or naked and gave you clothing?  And when was it that we saw you sick or in prison and visited you?'  And the king will answer them, 'Truly I tell you, just as you did it to one of the least of these who are members of my family, you did it to me.'  Then he will say to those at his left hand, 'You that are accursed, depart from me into the eternal fire prepared for the devil and his angels; for I was hungry and you gave me no food, I was thirsty and you gave me nothing to drink, I was a stranger and you did not welcome me, naked and you did not give me clothing, sick and in prison and you did not visit me.'  Then they also will answer, 'Lord, when was it that we saw you hungry or thirsty or a stranger or naked or sick or in prison, and did not take care of you?' Then he will answer them, 'Truly I tell you, just as you did not do it to one of the least of these, you did not do it to me.' And these will go away into eternal punishment, but the righteous into eternal life." Matthew 25.31-46

From everyone who has been given much, much will be required. Luke 12.48b NASB

For whoever gives you a cup of water to drink because of your name as followers of Christ, truly I say to you, he will not lose his reward. Mark 9.41 NASB

He who loves money will not be satisfied with money, nor he who loves abundance with its income. This too is vanity. Ecclesiastes 5.10 NASB

"For what will it profit a man if he gains the whole world and forfeits his soul? Or what will a man give in exchange for his soul? Matthew 16.26 NASB

Better to be poor and walk in integrity than to be crooked in one's ways even though rich. Proverbs 28.6

Jesus' instruction to not store up treasures on earth, but store up your treasures in heaven, recorded in Matthew 6.19, contradicts what civilization relentlessly promotes and many follow. When I was a young boy in the 1950's and 1960's there was a popular expression "Keeping up with the Joneses." The phrase described a desire to have a social status or ownership of goods that were the status symbol of that era. In the 1950's and 1960's, keeping up with the Jones had a clear meaning. Perhaps some wealthy people were in a competition to own the newest or most extravagant earthly treasures. Jesus' warning to not focus on earthly treasures seemed most appropriate for the wealthy. As I am finishing this book in the twenty first century, "keeping up with the Joneses" is seldom heard as a goal for the rich. Through credit cards and other debt, many are buying treasures that moth and rust destroy, regardless of their income! Through peer pressure and marketing, society is encouraged to purchase costly name brand items and expensive accessories. Jesus' warning not to focus on earthly treasures, but store for yourselves treasures in heaven, has a broader applicability. In my travels, I have seen numerous poor people with expensive tennis shoes and expensive cell phones.

The motivation in storing treasures on earth may be to impress others, elevate oneself, or make one's life more luxurious. Being blessed by God, with earnings achieved honestly is good. Luke 12.48 indicates that God may bless someone with much wealth, but much will be required. Luke 16.13 records Jesus' words that we cannot serve God and money.

God's teaching on money can be understood after it is carefully examined. Jesus indicated we cannot love God and money. God must come first in our lives. Genesis 4.3-4 provides a profound insight into giving to God. Abel brought the best portions from the firstborn of his flock. Cain brought some of the fruits of the soil as an offering to the LORD. Cain's offering was not necessarily his best fruit. The LORD looked with favor on Abel and his offering. The LORD did not find favor with Cain's offering. The living word of God explains that we are to offer to God out of first, not the leftovers. For years, I was doing exactly the wrong thing by giving God my leftovers and not giving to God first! I did not want to be like Cain, Adam and Eve's wayward son! God looks with favor on us if we give God thanks first with the money He provides us. My wife and I are now allocating money for God's kingdom first out of our pay, rather than last. Setting money aside for God's kingdom first gives God the glory and clarifies God is first in our life and blessing come from God.

At times I have gave more money for the Lord's work and other years gave a small amount to the Lord. I can truly state that in the years when I gave more money to the Lord, I lived more abundantly. In years when I gave the least to the Lord, I was financially burdened and accidentally over-drafted my checking account numerous times. In the years when I gave less to God and tried to keep more for myself, I actually had LESS to spend. In the years when I gave more to God, I somehow had MORE to spend. The miracle of giving more to God and being blessed with more is explained in the Holy Bible.

Jesus Himself indicated in Matthew 23.23 that we should tithe, but not neglect weightier provisions in the laws of God, such as justice, mercy, and faithfulness. I confess I have been an immature Christian, had little faith, and never considered tithing. I grew up as a poor child from the inner city. I was never as good as the widow who had little, but gave all she had. As I matured in my Christian journey, God guided my wife and I to increase our giving with tithing as our goal. The Holy Spirit has perfect timing and asked us to begin tithing at the perfect time.

It is very difficult to begin tithing if one has not been giving to God first. After paying our monthly house mortgage, two car payments, insurance, food, taxes, and numerous utilities, my wife and I had little of our net pay remaining. God understands tithing is a commitment. At times, my wife and I considered skipping church on various Sundays because we had no money remaining. God wanted my wife and I at church every Sunday whether we had money to give or not! We were embarrassed, but we gave a small amount in the offering plate, but it was all we had. God wanted my wife and I to begin giving to Him first, then pay our bills.

The Holy Spirit of God nudges us when He wants us to tithe. As our faith grows in Jesus Christ and we hear the voice of God more clearly, God will talk to believers regarding tithing. After years of reducing our expenses, our contribution to God's work increased. We now have tithing as part of our goal in commitment to honoring God. Tithing is a commitment regarding what is precious to most of us: money. Tithing is a commitment that demonstrates a high level of trust in Jesus. Most important in tithing is placing God first in our life. In growing from someone born in sin to a born-again Christian, the commitment to giving often grows in steps. Regardless if we are able to tithe or give God something less than a tithe God loves us.

The Holy Spirit guides us in our giving to God's work, but we must listen. Tithing is a good goal in giving to God, but it takes work and planning. It is easier to tithe if one figures God's portion first, then spends accordingly. Giving time and money to God's work involves the Holy Spirit. God is patient.

God warned the hypocritical Pharisees that tithing financially to God is good, but we are not to neglect more important laws, such as justice and mercy and faith. We are not to neglect tithing; we are not to neglect justice, mercy, and faith.

The subject of financial giving to church may turn people away from attending church. I know people who do not attend church because they do not want to give away any money. My wife and I volunteered one year to visit church members who had not attended church recently and asked them to fill out an estimate of church financial giving for the following year. My wife and I knocked on the door of a church member who lived in a mobile home. The woman had not attended church in a year and no one from the church had checked on her. A lady answered the door and I said we were from her church; she was initially glad we stopped by. I then presented her with an estimate of giving card and asked if she would complete the card and mail it to the church. The woman's reply is clear in my mind over twenty years later. She explained that her husband had been very ill for the past year and died two months ago. No one called from the church in a year to ask if she and her husband were well and tell her she was valued and missed. No one called from the church when her husband's death was listed in the obituary section of the newspaper. No one from church came to comfort her when her husband died. No one from the church attended her husband's funeral. My wife and I visited the widow, and apologized no one visited her from the church. I left the woman enlightened that we should be like Jesus and find the lost sheep to bring them back. I am sure if my wife and I visited the woman out of concern for her and not asked her to estimate her giving to the church next year, she may have returned to church and donated money. Asking lost people to give money to church may drive them away from Jesus; bringing lost people to Jesus is more likely to cause them to give willingly. Worshiping God and saving souls is the function of the church. Monetary support for the church will come when people attend.

King Solomon wrote several profound concepts regarding treasures in the book of Ecclesiastes. In chapter two, King Solomon indicated he collected silver, gold, and king's treasures. He partook of all the pleasures his eyes desired. After experiencing earthly pleasures and accumulating treasures, he declared them meaningless. In chapter four of Ecclesiastes, King Solomon commented on a man with no family who worked endlessly. He worked for the purpose of work and riches, but never asked why. Working for no purpose is meaningless. In chapter five of Ecclesiastes, King Solomon declared that those who love money would never be satisfied with money. Loving money is the cause of much evil. The sins of stealing, making false statements, and murder can come out from a love of money. Coveting is a sin that can result in committing various other sins.

The journey of life permits us to grow in wisdom if we are aware of our surroundings. When I was in my thirties, I purchased my most luxurious car with many options. To afford the payments, I took out a five-year car loan. At ten years old, the car was rusting severely and had numerous mechanical problems. I sold my ten-year-old car to a car dealer and purchased a new car. Jesus' command in Matthew 6.19 to not store up treasures on earth that moth and rust destroy came into my mind as I traded in my car. In ten short years my luxurious new automobile became rusted, obsolete, and inoperative. To store items permanently, we must store up items for heaven.

Abstract treasures of social status are equally meaningless with respect to heaven. In addition to observing my automobile rust and decay over the course of ten years, I have seen people's careers come and go. Whether we achieve the rank of senior person, manager, director, or vice president in a company, it will come to an end. We will each lose our job, retire, or die while working. The only status worth keeping is our citizenship of heaven.

Contrary to the worldview, joy is not attained though earthly treasures and earthly status. The Preacher in Ecclesiastes indicated treasures are vanity and will not bring joy. Jesus specifically answered the question of joy with respect to possessions in the following scripture:

"Take care! Be on your guard against all kinds of greed; for one's life does not consist in the abundance of possessions." Luke 12.15b

Joy is not based on treasures. Joy and contentment come from loving God and trusting in God.

The parable from Jesus in Matthew 25.31-46 explains storing treasures in heaven verses storing treasures on earth. Lavishing treasures on yourself for your own selfish use builds earthly treasures. Loving God and loving one's neighbor builds treasures for God's kingdom.

Nothing is wrong with earthly treasures. We, who work, deserve to buy treasures for our family and ourselves. However, Jesus taught that we are to share our treasures and our time with those in need to enter the kingdom of heaven. Jesus commands we share our food and water with the hungry and thirsty. Jesus commands we love our neighbor by welcoming strangers. Jesus commands us to clothe the naked, take care of the sick, and visit the imprisoned.

We humans cannot gain entrance to heaven by our good deeds. Jesus loved us first and died as an atoning sacrifice for our sins. We store treasures in heaven by believing and living in Jesus. Eternal life in heaven is a gift from God.

Let us pray. Dear Jesus, fill us with the Holy Spirit and teach us that earthly treasures are meaningless with respect to eternity in Heaven. Let us prioritize our use of money to serve the kingdom of God first and then meet our needs. For where our treasure is, there will our heart be.

# CHAPTER 15

# Humility

All who exalt themselves will be humbled, and those who humble themselves will be exalted.  Luke 14.11b

A wise son hears his father's instruction, but a scoffer does not listen to rebuke. Proverbs 13.1

For all that is in the world -- the desire of the flesh and the desire of the eyes, the pride in riches -- comes not of the Father but from the world.  1 John 2.16

"Do not judge by appearances, but judge with right judgment."  John 7.24

We know that we are God's children, and that the whole world lies under the power of the evil one.  1 John 5.19

"If you belonged to the world, the world would love you as its own.  Because you do not belong to the world, but I have chosen you out of the world - therefore the world hates you."  John 15.19

Thus says the LORD: Do not let the wise boast in their wisdom, do not let the mighty boast in their might, do not let the wealthy boast in their wealth; but let those who boast, boast in this, that they understand and know me, that I am the LORD; I act with steadfast love, justice, and righteousness in the earth, for in these things I delight, says the LORD.  Jeremiah 9.23-24

Humility is an attribute that is not valued much in worldly society.  Contrary to John 7.24, those of the world often judge by appearances, not with right

judgment. I cringe when I hear someone say, "Perception is reality." I reply with a quote:

"Do not judge by appearances, but judge with right judgment." John 7.24

The perception of status and belonging to the elite crowd motivates many of this world. It is easy to be lured into exalting oneself; I did.

After several years of doing engineering projects up to one million dollars in cost, I was asked to serve as the project manager for a multi-million dollar production line. I assumed that when I completed the line, my company would reward me for the great work I did.

My boss never designed a complete high-speed automated production line before and did not understand the extensive amount of work involved. My boss did not free me of my day-to-day job of designing new products, designing machine parts, and managing the engineering department. Researching the equipment and finalizing the technical details for the chemical processing line involved many trips to machine builders. I was designing and examining equipment during the day, then discussing business in restaurants at night with the sales staff. The sales staff knew I was the guy with the big budget and treated me with the dignity of a visiting king. I developed the delusion I was a powerful celebrity. Slowly, I thought I did not need God; I was all-powerful myself.

I specified how every machine should be built and I awarded all the contracts. Next, I flew to numerous cities throughout the United States to approve the equipment designs. Oh, I forgot to mention my wife. While I was flying around the country specifying and selecting machines, and doing my normal job, I was quite busy. For a year, I worked sixty hours per week to do my normal job and my project. No problem, I was a celebrity. I told my wife I was going places and she could come along, but I did not need her or God.

I had to visit a machine builder on the south coast, so I took my wife and two children along. Living the good life was a new experience. I discussed engineering details during the day, and then my wife, children, and I did fine dining at night that week. Then my wife received a telephone call that her father died. I felt my father-in-law's death was very inconvenient and of poor timing. My wife made all the funeral arrangements and we drove to the funeral parlor. Upon arrival, I asked the funeral director for an office to work in. While my father-in-law's body was at the funeral home, I worked in a nearby office. Rather than comforting my wife regarding her father's death,

I spent several hours a day on the telephone finalizing the equipment design. I did take time to visit my wife occasionally.

After the funeral, we drove home and I went back to the office the next day. I continued to travel extensively to approve each piece of equipment. Within a few months of the funeral, the fabrication of each of the individual machines was completed. Next, all the equipment was sent to one location to be assembled into one huge automated production line. I continued to work sixty hours per week during the installation of the machinery. When the production line was assembled and tested, very few problems occurred. When the line was started, it operated beautifully and produced much more product per shift than I had conservatively estimated because the production line seldom jammed up. The company's business management enjoyed the profit the manufacturing line generated; the production workers enjoyed the flawless and continuous operation of the production line. My reputation as a skilled project manager and design engineer was becoming wide spread in the company. A few months later, the annual performance review time came. I had always received an excellent rating in my performance reviews in the past. After working sixty hours a week for a year and devoting myself fully to the company, I was expecting an excellent performance rating, a promotion, and a large raise. To my shock, my engineering boss gave me poor grades in most categories of my performance review.

Perhaps my boss decided to destroy the competition, in this case me. When an employee performs extraordinarily well, an insecure and selfish boss may attempt to destroy the reputation of a high performing subordinate to maintain his status as the boss; it is quite common for an insecure and self-centered boss to suppress good employees.

Perhaps my boss had such unrealistic expectations that he assumed I could work one full time job designing new products and establishing the related manufacturing systems, while simultaneously designing the largest production line the company ever had by myself. Maybe the boss expected me to work eighty hours and perform two full time jobs.

Perhaps the boss did not think at all. Maybe the boss did not care if he worked me to exhaustion and I forsook my family life.

Regardless if my boss rated me poorly out of malice or ignorance, my work profile and my annual raise would be adversely impacted. I told my boss the production line I designed had the highest productivity of any line in all the company's North American facilities. I became angry, complained to upper management, and was re-assigned to a pleasant boss.

I worked sixty hours per week for a year, compromised a year of my life and no one really cared. The company expected me to design a perfectly functioning production line; I completed the job the company expected me to accomplish. The company paid me my same salary, regardless if I worked fifty percent more with no more pay. I received no promotion, no bonus, no award dinner, not even an engraved pen. Shortly after the installation was complete, another company purchased the company that employed me. Next, the automated production line, and the entire associated business unit, was divested to another company. The new owners retained me, but, ironically, few of the executives I worked to impress were employed by the same company. All history of my extraordinary overtime and impressive design skills vanished like the morning mist on a hot day.

I can personally confirm that pride goes before destruction.

Pride goes before destruction, and a haughty spirit before a fall. Proverbs 16.18

I worked relentlessly in an attempt to earn the praise of men for my engineering expertise and therefore prove my worth as a human being. Instead of thanking God for a great job and the exciting travel, I thought I did not need God at all. I became selfish with my wife and even trivialized the death of my father-in-law for work. With my false conceit, I thought I did not need my wife. Lucky for me, my two best friends, Jesus and my wife, forgave me for losing my humility. I felt God's presence in humbling me at that early part of my career. I mistakenly thought hard work and sacrificing one's family life would bring reward by man. If my boss would have said great job, gave me a raise and gave me a promotion, I could have been seduced by the world for a long time. I could have worked sixty-hour weeks until I destroyed my family life. Praise by men and titles bestowed by men are meaningless with respect to eternity.

The experience of being rejected by man taught me that God is the only consistently righteous judge. The sale of the production line I designed served as a metaphor of death in this life. All of our hard work and accomplishments will stay behind when we die. Our material possessions will not travel with us when we die, so do not store up our treasures on earth. An expensive status symbol automobile will likely be an old rusty car in less than twelve years. We are not to boast in our earthly power or in our earthly treasures. Let us humbly acknowledge that our entrance into heaven is a gift from the grace of God and we are saved through faith, so that none can boast.

Humility is important between humans and between humans and God. My first lapse in humility was in exalting myself. I did not realize God is in charge and everything we receive is a gift. I evolved into thinking I did not need God. When completely filled with delusion, I thought I was superior to my life partner, my wife.

The world does love its own, especially when you have money. There is nothing wrong with business travel and lunches, but it is critical to know it is the temporary possession of money that may give the false perception of power.

Humility can be more easily diminished when one is healthy, wealthy, and wise. This is when the temptations of this world may easily lure us. Worshiping money and power leads to destruction. Understanding God gives and can take away wealth may keep us humble. Death or serious illness may humble us. Understanding that we are mortal and that we will die keeps arrogance in perspective.

Let us pray. Heavenly Father, kindly remind us that you are God and we are not. You are in charge and we are not. Please teach us not to boast in our wisdom. Please teach us not to boast in any accomplishments we may achieve. Please guide us to not expect praise by men; only You, God are the righteous judge. Please remind us that the pompous will be humbled and the humble will be exalted by You, God. Amen.

# CHAPTER 16

# Anger

After they went up to the Valley of Eshcol and viewed the land, they discouraged the Israelites from entering the land the LORD had given them. The LORD's anger was aroused that day and he swore this oath: 'Because they have not followed me wholeheartedly, not one of the men twenty years old or more who came up out of Egypt will see the land I promised on oath to Abraham, Isaac and Jacob not one except Caleb son of Jephunneh the Kenizzite and Joshua son of Nun, for they followed the LORD wholeheartedly.' The LORD's anger burned against Israel and he made them wander in the desert forty years, until the whole generation of those who had done evil in his sight was gone. Numbers 32.9-13 NIV

A man of knowledge uses words with restraint, and a man of understanding is even-tempered. Proverbs 17.27 NIV

In the temple he found people selling cattle, sheep, and doves, and the money changers seated at their tables. Making a whip of cords, he drove all of them out of the temple, both the sheep and the cattle. He also poured out the coins of the money changers and overturned their tables. He told those who were selling the doves, "Take these things out of here! Stop making my Father's house a marketplace!" John 2.14-16

Anger is very complex. I have written this chapter on anger, not as a master of anger, but as a humbled servant of Jesus Christ who has struggled with anger issues for many years. God created us as emotional and sensitive creatures. When we converse with another, we perceive the inflection and tone of the voice, body language, and the words chosen.

I was a broken young person. As a youth, I was unable to express anger. As I grew into a college student, my self-confidence emerged and my ability to validate righteous anger also emerged. When I was a young adult, my girlfriend and future wife entered my life and I experienced joy for the first time in a long time. Love taught me life could be good again. When a person was unkind to my girlfriend, I became angry and defensive on her behalf. The love of my girlfriend awoke my instinct for self-preservation for both her and I. From that day onward, I would allow my anger to surface when a loved one or I were being mistreated. My self-confidence increased through college graduation and beyond.

My son was shy in grade school and my wife and I enrolled our son and daughter in martial arts school. I joined the martial arts class with my children to help train them. Time seemed to pass quickly and soon we had taken six years of training in martial arts. Nearing the completion of our training, I could shatter two-inch thick boards with the two striking knuckles in my tight fist in concert with a fierce yell. In the martial arts, one develops and refines the ability to instantly activate one's self-defense skills; bringing out the fierce animal within is quite similar to acting on anger. After six years of martial arts training, my fighting skills and physical fitness were in peak form. The ability to initiate my self-defense emotions and respond was quite developed. A martial artist must be able to harness his fighting ability and act peacefully when appropriate, even when being mistreated.

My years of martial arts training developed my ability to instantly invoke my carnal self-defense animal instincts. After a childhood of suppressing anger, I needed to identify when I should allow myself to experience anger and act on the knowledge that I was being mistreated. As a child, I consciously suppressed my anger and any response when I knew I was being mistreated. As a young man, I could experience anger, but was not confident my anger was warranted.

After I opened myself to experience anger, my response to anger needed improvement. I will explain intricate issues regarding my anger issues in this chapter because my problems are not unique; mastering anger takes work. When I talk with people and share our respective challenges in life, the problems in life are very common. It is unfortunate that unless we take time and deliberately talk to one another, we each can feel isolated and uniquely bad, when we are actually experiencing many common situations in life. It is my goal here to clearly tell readers many problems with family, parents, work, faith, organized religion, and friends are NOT unique. Many problems in life that isolate us occur in many people's lives. Talking with people about emotional issues can ease our pain and provide remedies to life's challenges.

Anger is a survival instinct bestowed on us by our creator, God. My wise friend and anger management advisor, Sharon, taught me **anger is a natural response when one is being mistreated or treated unfairly.** Anger is an emotion based on our senses we utilize including sight, hearing, and touch. Anger is an animal carnal instinct that is necessary for survival. Perhaps God created us humans with the anger instinct to help us survive. To properly utilize anger, two conditions must be satisfied:

1. Determine if the anger response is righteous, or wrong (rooted in sin or misdirected).

and

2. Respond to the situation causing anger in a right, healthy, and constructive manner, not a wrong, unhealthy and destructive manner.

Righteous or justified anger is prompted by a situation where we are being mistreated or treated unfairly. Numbers 32.9-13 indicates God was angry at the evil ones who disobeyed Him and would not enter the land God gave to His people. God caused His people to wander in the desert for forty years.

John 2.14-16 documents that Jesus made a whip and drove the sheep and cattle out of God's temple and overturned the tables of the moneychangers.

If in doubt if our anger is righteous, a short phrase is helpful: **reciprocity is the test of fairness.** If you treated the person in the manner they were treating you, how would they react? A thief finds nothing wrong with stealing unless his goods are stolen. A bully is content with tormenting people unless he is the one being mistreated.

Righteous anger with righteous action is appropriate; correctly perceiving reality and reacting appropriately are difficult and takes wisdom. My wife had the wisdom to correctly identify and correctly respond to anger issues since childhood; God gave my wife the gift of wisdom. I am still refining my response to anger at fifty years old; I am a slow learner.

There are four ways to respond to anger; three ways to respond to anger are wrong and only one is correct. Following are four examples of situations involving anger from the Holy Bible.

## **Wrong anger with a wrong response**

In the course of time Cain brought some of the fruits of the soil as an offering to the LORD. But Abel brought fat portions from some of the firstborn of his flock. The LORD looked with favor on Abel and his offering, but on Cain and his offering he did not look with favor. So Cain was very angry, and his face was downcast. Then the LORD said to Cain, "Why are you angry? Why is your face downcast? If you do what is right, will you not be accepted? But if you do not do what is right, sin is crouching at your door; it desires to have you, but you must master it." Now Cain said to his brother Abel, "Let's go out to the field." And while they were in the field, Cain attacked his brother Abel and killed him. Genesis 4.3-8 NIV

Then he said to them, "Is it lawful to do good or to do harm on the Sabbath, to save life or to kill?" But they were silent. He looked around at them with anger; he was grieved at their hardness of heart and said to the man, "Stretch out your hand." He stretched it out, and his hand was restored. The Pharisees went out and immediately conspired with the Herodians against him, how to destroy him. Mark 3.4-6

Then the chief priests and the Pharisees called a meeting of the Sanhedrin. "What are we accomplishing?" "Here is this man performing many miraculous signs. If we let him go on like this, everyone will believe in him, and then the Romans will come and take away both our place and our nation." Then one of them, named Caiaphas, who was high priest that year, spoke up, "You know nothing at all! You do not realize that it is better for you that one man die for the people than that the whole nation perish." John 11.47-49 NIV

The story of Cain and Abel is profound as a historical event. Cain was jealous of Abel because God looked with favor on Abel's generous offering of his best. Cain coveted Abel's status with God. God told Cain he could do what is right and he too would be favored. Cain did not want to offer his best to God. Cain responded to his jealous anger by murdering Abel. Cain did not steal God's blessing from Abel. Cain murdered Abel so neither he nor Abel would live with God's blessing. This tragic story is an example of wrongful anger with a wrong response.

A second story of wrongful anger with a wrong response is the murder of Jesus Christ. The Pharisees did not murder Jesus because they thought he was a fraud; the Pharisees murdered Jesus because He was performing miracles and "everyone" would believe in Him! Pontius Pilot may have been the politician of the day, but the established religious community murdered Jesus out of jealousy, anger, and greed. When Jesus taught, He gathered more crowds than the Pharisees.

Anger associated with jealously, greed, revenge, coveting, and wickedness is wrong. Lets us run from anger when it is prompted by sin. Heavenly Father, please fill our hearts with love for God and love for our neighbor and purge any anger rooted in evil. Amen.

## **Wrong anger with the right response**

While he was still speaking, another messenger came and said, "The Chaldeans formed three raiding parties and swept down on your camels and carried them off. They put the servants to the sword, and I am the only one who has escaped to tell you!" While he was still speaking, yet another messenger came and said, "Your sons and daughters were feasting and drinking wine at the oldest brother's house, when suddenly a mighty wind swept in from the desert and struck the four corners of the house. It collapsed on them and they are dead, and I am the only one who has escaped to tell you!" Job 1.17-19 NIV

So Satan went out from the presence of the LORD and afflicted Job with painful sores from the soles of his feet to the top of his head. Then Job took a piece of broken pottery and scraped himself with it as he sat among the ashes. Job 2.7, 8 NIV

"Although I am blameless, have no concern for myself; I despise my own life. It is all the same; that is why I say, 'He destroys both the blameless and the wicked.' When a scourge brings sudden death, he mocks the despair of the innocent. Job 9.21-23 NIV.

The LORD said to Job: "Will the one who contends with the Almighty correct him? Let him who accuses God answer him!" Then Job answered the LORD: "I am unworthy -- how can I reply to you? I put my hand over my mouth." Job 40.1-4 NIV

Then Job replied to the LORD: "I know that you can do all things; no plan of yours can be thwarted. You asked, 'Who is this that obscures my counsel without knowledge?' Surely I spoke of things I did not understand, things too wonderful for me to know. Therefore I despise myself and repent in dust and ashes." Job 42.1-3, 6 NIV

The story of Job is a clear example of wrong anger with the right response. Job accuses God of mocking the despair of the innocent. Job also accuses God of ruthlessly turning on him and attacking him. Job's apparent anger at God was wrong, it was misdirected. The Chaldeans killed Job's servants and stole his camels. A great wind exceeded the wind resistance of Job's eldest son's house, causing it to fall and killed all of Job's children. Satan inflicted Job with painful sores. Job had a personal relationship with God and blamed God for his tragedies. God did not cause Job's tragedies. God did not perform a miracle and prevent Job's tragedies, but God did not cause Job's tragedies.

God asked Job if he would correct the Almighty. Job declared himself unworthy and put his hand over his mouth. Job acknowledged God's ways are too wonderful and beyond understanding. Job responded rightly to his wrong anger by acknowledging his anger was directed to the wrong person. Job was angry with God, but God did not harm Job or his family. Job asked God to forgive him for his false accusation.

The story of Job is very profound. Job's questioning God is repeated in the lives of those who believe in God. We may become angry with God when bad things happen to us. Being angry with God is a complex paradox. To be angry with God, one must believe that God exists, is all-powerful and all knowing, but did not perform a miracle to alter an event that happened in one's life. I became angry with God when my father committed suicide while I was in grade school. I was angry with God for permitting my happy childhood to be shattered into chaos. My mother grieved her husband's suicide until she died of old age nearly forty years later. Anger is an emotion relating to displeasure with reality of being mistreated or treated unfairly. The paradox with anger toward God is He perhaps chose not to perform a miracle to change or prevent an event from occurring. I am quite certain God knew my father's suicide would be unpleasant for me, a child in grade school. Anger is a normal part of grief, but healing can occur only when we accept reality and move beyond anger. Bitterness is the rejection of reality and prevents healing. My bitterness was based on my false preconception that a horrible event could never enter my life! Believing in Christ means He will never abandon us, even when horrible events occur. Romans 8.28 NIV states: in all things God works for the good of those who love him, who have been called according to his purpose. With help from my friend, Sharon, I embraced my life and chose to accept reality and move on. I accepted reality. My father's suicide in my life journey has prompted me to be sensitive to people, know the pain of others, to view life as a brief and precious gift and to know God. I know God understands the pain we feel; God designed us to experience emotional pain when a loved one dies. I do not understand why life is painful at times. God is the designer of the world, the designer of us human beings, and He is in charge. Anger at God is misdirected. The choice to any and all circumstances we encounter in life's journeys is bitterness and darkness or hope, joy, and light. Let us choose hope, joy and light.

God is not the distributor of tragedy. The insurance business phrase to refuse payment for a claim involving a tragedy, "Acts of God" is incorrect. Tragedies are not "Acts of God" and God is not to be blamed. Tragedies are the result of evil in the world, man's sin against man, and man's fall from grace due to original sin. Let us remember God loves us and not be angry with God.

## Righteous anger with the wrong response

There the angel of the LORD appeared to him in flames of fire from within a bush. Moses saw that though the bush was on fire it did not burn up. Exodus 3.2 NIV

When the LORD finished speaking to Moses on Mount Sinai, he gave him the two tablets of the Testimony, the tablets of stone inscribed by the finger of God. Exodus 31.18 NIV

Aaron answered them, "Take off the gold earrings that your wives, your sons and your daughters are wearing, and bring them to me." So all the people took off their earrings and brought them to Aaron. He took what they handed him and made it into an idol cast in the shape of a calf, fashioning it with a tool. Then they said, "These are your gods, O Israel, who brought you up out of Egypt." Exodus 32.2-4 NIV

Moses turned and went down the mountain with the two tablets of the Testimony in his hands. They were inscribed on both sides, front and back. Exodus 32.15 NIV

When Moses approached the camp and saw the calf and the dancing, his anger burned and he threw the tablets out of his hands, breaking them to pieces at the foot of the mountain. Exodus 32.19 NIV

Moses breaking the tablets inscribed with the Ten Commandments is a clear case of righteous anger with the wrong response. God entrusted Moses to deliver the Ten Commandments. When Moses came down from Mt. Sinai, he saw the people worshipping a pagan idol in the form of a golden calf. Moses became very angry. In his anger, Moses threw the tablets and broke them into pieces.

Although Moses had righteous anger, breaking the precious tablets inscribed with the Ten Commandments was a wrong and destructive response. People continue to have righteous anger and a wrong response thousands of years later, including me. I have learned to properly respond to righteous anger in many situations. In situations where my family or I am not directly impacted by unrighteousness, I can typically calmly and clearly state what is appropriate. If the opposing views could not be reconciled, we could agree to disagree. If the disagreement was important to me, parting ways may be appropriate. I minimize my exposure to situations that cause me righteous anger. If a retailer sells me something that is defective, I return it with my anger under control. It is best to not associate with organizations or people that mistreat others.

Controlling my anger when I was personally disrespected was difficult for me. Like Moses smashing the commandments, a person attempting to manipulate me or providing unsolicited advice tested my self-control. Others disrespecting my property or disrespecting my family tested my self-control. When I became angry, I have found it best to pause for a moment and try to relax. My anger management therapist told me, "Whoever angers you owns you." Sharon is correct. If someone can prompt an automatic response in me, they control me. With help, I can usually calmly state what provoked my anger and briefly suggest a remedy.

If I am not sufficiently calm or if I cannot speak in private, I might say, "that is really inappropriate and I am hurt, but I can not talk about it right now." Identifying what action you want the person to avoid and forgiving them is critical. A most profound thought from my advisor, Sharon, "View life in the context that everyone has his or her respective flaws or idiosyncrasies." If one understands that many people view life from a self-centered perspective, responding to the anger provocation is easier by avoiding being on the defensive."

Common triggers that anger me and perhaps others include:

- demanding attention when I am doing something
- disrespecting my property
- demanding money when money is needed elsewhere
- devaluing or humiliating speech or actions toward me
- exerting control
- demanding another's problem be remedied
- exploiting rather than loving
- intimidating through anger
- building oneself up by tearing others down
- unfair treatment.

I openly confess I am still not able to totally control my response to anger all the time. There is hope for us; the fruit of the Holy Spirit of God includes kindness and self-control. Lets us pray to God when confronted with a situation that causes righteous anger. Pray for guidance to assertively remedy the situation with kindness and self-control. Express how that person mistreated us, how we feel, and determine how to avoid repeating our incurrence of pain.

## Righteous anger with the right response

Now Israel loved Joseph more than any other of his children, because he was the son of his old age; and he had made him a long robe with sleeves. But when his brothers saw that their father loved him more than all his brothers, they hated him, and could not speak peaceably to him. Genesis 37.3-4

So when Joseph came to his brothers, they stripped him of his robe, the long robe with sleeves that he wore; and they took him and threw him into a pit. The pit was empty; there was no water in it. Genesis 37.23-24

When some Midianite traders passed by, they drew Joseph up, lifting him out of the pit, and sold him to the Ishmaelites for twenty pieces of silver. And they took Joseph to Egypt. Genesis 37.28

Then they took Joseph's robe, slaughtered a goat, and dipped the robe in the blood. They had the long robe with sleeves taken to their father, and they said, "This we have found; see now whether it is your son's robe or not." Genesis 37.31-32

Meanwhile the Midianites had sold him in Egypt to Potiphar, one of Pharaoh's officials, the captain of the guard. Genesis 37.36

But the LORD was with Joseph and showed him steadfast love; he gave him favor in the sight of the chief jailer. Genesis 39.21

And Pharaoh said to Joseph, "See, I have set you over all the land of Egypt." Removing his signet ring from his hand, Pharaoh put it on Joseph's hand; he arrayed him in garments of fine linen, and put a gold chain around his neck. He had him ride in the chariot of his second-in-command; and they cried out in front of him, "Bow the knee!" Thus he set him over all the land of Egypt. Genesis 41.41-43

When Jacob learned that there was grain in Egypt, he said to his sons, "Why do you keep looking at one another? I have heard," he said, "that there is grain in Egypt; go down and buy grain for us there, that we may live and not die." Genesis 42.1-2

Now Joseph was governor over the land; it was he who sold to all the people of the land. And Joseph's brothers came and bowed themselves before him with their faces to the ground. When Joseph saw his brothers, he recognized them, but he treated them like strangers and spoke harshly to them. "Where do you come from?" he said. They said, "From the land of Canaan, to buy food." Although Joseph had recognized his brothers, they did not recognize him. "Let one of you go and bring your brother, while the rest of you remain in prison, in order that your words may be tested, whether there is truth in you; or else, as Pharaoh lives, surely you are spies." And he put them all together in prison for three days. Genesis 42.6-8, 16-17

Then Joseph said to his brothers, "Come closer to me." And they came closer. He said, "I am your brother, Joseph, whom you sold into Egypt. And now do not be distressed, or angry with yourselves, because you sold me here; for God sent me before you to preserve life. For the famine has been in the land these two years; and there are five more years in which there will be neither plowing nor harvest." Genesis 45.4-6

The experiences of Joseph, son of Jacob, are profound regarding faith and forgiveness. Joseph was the favored son of Jacob. Jacob gave Joseph a decorated robe. The brothers of Joseph resented that he was favored by their father and coveted him with malice. The brothers wanted Joseph's status and wanted Joseph to lose his status. The brothers sold Joseph into slavery. The Book of Genesis details that Potiphar found favor with Joseph and made Joseph overseer of his home. Potiphar's wife wanted to commit adultery with Joseph, but Joseph fled. Potiphar's wife falsely accused Joseph of insulting her and Joseph was imprisoned. After two years in prison, Joseph interpreted Pharaoh's dream of seven years of plenty and seven years of famine. Eventually Pharaoh made Joseph ruler over Egypt. It is critical to note that God was with Joseph in his pain and in his triumphs. The LORD was with Joseph when his brothers sold him into slavery. The LORD was with Joseph when he was in prison for two years. The LORD was with Joseph when he ruled all of Egypt.

Joseph clearly had righteous anger associated with his brothers selling him as a slave. When Joseph met his brothers years later, he put them in jail for three days. Ultimately, Joseph then forgave his brothers and gave them food and land. The story of Joseph and his brothers illustrates people are capable of doing bad acts, but we can choose to forgive them. Joseph did punish his brothers, but he did forgive them. Joseph's righteous response to righteous anger included acknowledging the wrong act, telling his brothers to forgive themselves, and Joseph forgiving his brothers.

Joseph also chose a righteous response to God. Joseph did not get bitter or angry with God when his brothers sold him into slavery or Potiphar's wife had him imprisoned. God did not immediately end Joseph's slavery or imprisonment, but Joseph remained faithful to God. God's grace was sufficient for Joseph to endure. We do not understand God's ways, but we are to persevere and remain faithful to God.

I was challenged to learn the right response to righteous anger in my life. I confess it took me several decades to learn the right response for the suicide of my father. My father's suicide during my childhood left me wounded; my nuclear family was broken. As a child I was an outcast at family functions and the fatherless one who was easily ridiculed. Living in a haze of learned helplessness, my childhood response to ridicule and intimidation was silence. As a child, any response of anger was crushed by my fear of escalated retaliatory unkindness. Suicide is very difficult for the ones left behind. My feelings of abandonment, betrayal, and sadness paralyzed me for several years. Eventually I acknowledged the bad dream I was experiencing was my reality.

The reality of my father's suicide hit me like being showered by a bucket of freezing cold water. Although I was unprepared, I was still alive and had to resume life. Unfortunately, I became the man of the house responsible for home repairs. At fourteen, I replaced the rear entrance door on our home. Thankfully, my friend Paul's dad helped me by drilling the holes for the lockset because I did not own a hole saw. When I began to make incremental accomplishments in my life, I became increasingly angry with my dad for placing me in this position. I recall taking a bus to apply for college by myself and had no idea what I was doing. Somehow the college application staff managed to enroll a broken kid with no parental guidance. In a paradox, the more I accomplished on my own, the angrier I became with my father. I was hurt and angry with my dad because he could not attend the wedding of my wife and I. I was angry with my dad for not being present at our children's birthday parties.

Anger with my dad did not fill me with joy. In my spiritual journey through the Holy Bible, Jesus told us we are to forgive those who sin against us seven times seventy times.

For if you forgive men when they sin against you, your heavenly Father will also forgive you. But if you do not forgive men their sins, your Father will not forgive your sins. Matthew 6.14, 15 NIV

Jesus commands us to forgive those who sin against us; I was commanded to forgive my father. I scheduled time to talk with Sharon, my anger management therapist, about forgiving my father. After I explained my childhood to Sharon, she made me laugh by indicating I was quite well adjusted in life considering my childhood. Sharon told me that holding onto anger may cause physical and emotional problems. I told Sharon the Bible indicates I must forgive my father and the therapy community indicates I must forgive; therefore, it is prudent I forgive my father. With Sharon's guidance, I typed a letter to my father. In my letter, I told my dad it was wrong to have killed himself and he destroyed my childhood and damaged me for many years. I read the letter out loud and forgave my father.

We cannot control other humans; each of us has the ability to make good or bad choices. All of us have sinned and fallen short of the glory of

God. Forgiving is a win-win decision. When we forgive, we are freed of the damaging effects of anger, can think more clearly, and God is pleased.

We each wander through our wilderness in life and experience suffering and triumphs. God is always with His people. God's grace is sufficient for us; God's power gives us strength when we are weak. Our suffering humbles us and gives us endurance. Endurance gives us hope and reminds us that Jesus conquered death and won the war over evil.

Let us close this chapter on anger in prayer. Heavenly Father, when our anger is founded in evil, please guide us to choose goodness. When our anger is misdirected, please guide us to the truth. When our anger is righteous, please guide us to kindness, gentleness, self-control, resolution, and forgiveness. Please fill us with your grace when we suffer to make us strong when we are weak. Amen.

# CHAPTER 17

# Tongue

Even a fool is thought wise if he keeps silent, and discerning if he holds his tongue. Proverbs 17.28 NIV

I tell you, on the Day of Judgment you will have to give an account for every careless word you utter; for by your words you will be justified, and by your words you will be condemned.
Matthew 12.36-37

A truthful witness saves lives, But he who utters lies is treacherous. Proverbs 14.25 NASB

You shall not make wrongful use of the name of the LORD your God, for the LORD will not acquit anyone who misuses his name. Exodus 20.7

You shall not bear false witness against your neighbor. Exodus 20.16 NASB

The heart of the righteous ponders how to answer, but the mouth of the wicked pours out evil things. Proverbs 15.28 NASB

If any think they are religious, and do not bridle their tongues but deceive their hearts, their religion is worthless. James 1.26

The LORD hates a man who stirs up dissension among brothers. Proverbs 6.16b, 19b NIV

So also the tongue is a little member and boasts of great exploits. How great a forest is set ablaze by a small fire! And the tongue is a fire. The tongue is placed among our members as a world of iniquity; it stains the whole body, sets on fire the cycle of nature, and is itself set on fire by hell. James 3.5-6

Do not let any unwholesome talk come out of your mouths, but only what is helpful for building others up according to their needs, that it may benefit those who listen. Ephesians 4.29 NIV

Your lips have spoken falsehood, Your tongue mutters wickedness. Isaiah 59.3b NASB

The tongue that brings healing is a tree of life, but a deceitful tongue crushes the spirit. Proverbs 15.4 NIV

Don't have anything to do with foolish and stupid arguments, because you know they produce quarrels. And the Lord's servant must not quarrel; instead, he must be kind to everyone, able to teach, not resentful. Those who oppose him he must gently instruct, in the hope that God will grant them repentance leading them to a knowledge of the truth, and that they will come to their senses and escape from the trap of the devil, who has taken them captive to do his will. 2 Timothy 2.23-26 NIV

Beware then of useless grumbling, and keep your tongue from slander; because no secret word is without result and a lying mouth destroys the soul. Wisdom of Solomon 1.11

May the words of my mouth and the meditation of my heart be pleasing in your sight, O LORD, my Rock and my Redeemer. Psalm 19.14 NIV

I have written this chapter on the tongue from the perspective of someone who has not mastered his tongue. I am someone who struggles to control his tongue. As I mentioned previously, the Center for Disease Control indicated that 6.18 people per 100,000 are murdered annually. One's chance of being murdered can be reduced below the national average by obeying the law, associating with law-abiding citizens and staying out of dangerous situations. It would be great if keeping people's tongues from getting into trouble was that easy, but it is not. Unfortunately, unless we are isolated from humanity, all of us will fall victim to someone's evil tongue. Also, nearly everyone will injure someone's feelings, either intentionally or accidentally. Jesus specifically cautioned us in Matthew 12.36-37 that we each would be held accountable for careless words. The words we have spoken during our lifetime will cause our condemnation or justification on our judgment day. Jesus stating that our words are an important consideration in determining where we spend eternity makes speaking a very serious part of life and our relationship with others. Similar to a physical attack or murder, a vicious verbal attack can severely injure someone.

In the 1970's, I attended a lecture that included the topic of "Targeted Humor" given by a psychology professor. I confess I forgot the professor's name and the exact wording of the lecture. I apologize to the professor for not being able to remember his name. I have pondered the topic of targeted humor with respect to loving your neighbor for many years. Targeted humor is humor directed toward someone. Females may direct their humor at themselves to build friendship with other women. When a female compliments another female's clothing, the one receiving the compliment may joke about the clothes rather than accept the compliment at face value. If I compliment my wife, she may joke about the compliment, rather than say "thank you." Targeted humor directed at oneself is a personal communication choice to disarm others and gain friendship through humility. For simplicity, I will discard self-directed targeted humor in this context. The targeted humor I will elaborate on in a Christian context involves mankind's carnal instincts.

Targeted humor is a modern day version of fighting for status in a group of people. Pack animals, including dogs, and monkeys may physically fight to determine who is the alpha leader. I have seen monkeys at the zoo and my own dogs fight for rank. Pack animals will align themselves in a rank of order in the group. The carnal instincts of humans are similar to that of pack animals, including the quest to dominate others and establish a rank higher than one's neighbor. Humans have been killing each other, starting with Cain murdering Abel, to establish rank amongst other humans. As mankind established laws, law enforcement, and punishment, killing one's neighbor to establish a higher rank seems to be less common. Targeted humor is humor directed at another intended to emotionally injure, degrade, tear down, and defeat another human. Targeted humor's goal is to crush the spirit of another to build oneself up; Ephesians 4.29 commands us that our speech is to build others up. Targeted humor is rooted in wickedness. Jesus was not timid and He demonstrated that we are to rebuke the spiritual forces of wickedness. We are to love and build up our neighbors, never torment them with hurtful targeted humor. If we are ever the recipients of targeted humor and we are hurt, rebuke the wicked. I prefer to quote Isaiah 59.3

when I am attacked: "Your tongue mutters wickedness" or say "You have a wicked tongue."

The most vicious verbal attack with the tongue involves words spoken to degrade or humiliate the person as a human being. I clearly remember the words spoken to me by a chemistry instructor during my first semester at college. I was majoring in Industrial Engineering and the college required me to take two chemistry classes. I had taken many physics, electrical, and math classes in high school, but no chemistry courses. The college chemistry class was entry level and I knew I would need to be attentive in class to be successful. On the first day of the hands-on portion of the class in the lab, the instructor told the class to use litmus paper to determine if the liquid in the beakers on each of our tables was an acid or a base. Being the poor kid from the inner city, I politely asked the instructor, "How should I use the blue and red litmus paper strips to dip into the solution to check for pH?" Her answer to the poor kid trying to get an education was so cruel, I clearly remember her vicious words decades later. The chemistry instructor said to me: "If you do not even know how to use litmus paper, you have no chance of passing this class. You should drop this class and you do not belong here." I repeated the question and the instructor repeated her vicious statement.

The vicious statement from the chemistry instructor actually felt like a kick to my stomach; I was instantly nauseated and felt I was being attacked. First, my face was flushed with embarrassment and I thought maybe I am too stupid for college. As a poor young man who grew up in the inner city, I knew I had lacked the exposure to a premier preparatory school; the instructor told me nothing I had not already told myself. The instructor confirmed the thoughts in my head that my life was dysfunctional and I would be a failure. Secondly, the vicious attack on someone trying to rise above poverty demonstrated that evil exists in everyday life.

The chemistry instructor's verbal attack could have caused me to simply quit school. I felt like a foreigner in college and was already unsure of myself without her belittling me. I had nowhere else to go, but intuitively knew my calling was engineering. The instructor did not stab me with a knife and murder me; she attempted to murder my spirit, self-confidence, and my career with her tongue. Jesus indicated, in Matthew 12.36-37, that on the Day of Judgment, our words would justify or condemn us; words can be as lethal and destructive as murder!

This is a good time to comment on evil. In all situations in life, from Adam and Eve deciding whether or not to eat the fruit of the knowledge of good and evil, to our daily lives, our wandering in life causes us to constantly choose the path of good or evil. The authority people have in life determines how their evil can be manifested, but evil can be chosen at any socioeconomic level in society.

Jesus' command regarding relationships is very clear:

He said to him, "'You shall love the Lord your God with all your heart, and with all your soul, and with all your mind.' This is the greatest and first commandment. And a second is like it: 'You shall love your neighbor as yourself.' On these two commandments hang all the law and the prophets." Matthew 22.37b-40

Not loving one's neighbor as oneself may involve evil acts, such as attempting to destroy the body, spirit, or life of a student or a neighbor. The evil may be done to materially benefit the evildoer or perhaps cause another to suffer for wicked pleasure. People may attempt to destroy others to exalt themselves; this is wickedness.

Perhaps the chemistry instructor told me to drop out of her class and drop out of college because she did not want to teach a student who did not already learn chemistry in high school. That is, she was lazy and did not want to actually teach someone. Perhaps the instructor saw a poor kid from the inner city and wanted to keep him poor and uneducated. Perhaps she wanted to prevent me from ever reaching her social status to keep herself on her imaginary pedestal. Perhaps the chemistry instructor sensed I was vulnerable and wanted to destroy my dreams of college for her enjoyment. I cannot state what was the instructor's motive. I can truly state the instructor chose not to treat me as she would want to be treated. The instructor earned her degree, but did not want me to earn a degree. Her wicked tongue could have caused me to drop out of school or commit suicide like my father. The instructor abused her authority to try to crush a student.

I had successfully survived a challenging childhood, and I was not going to be intimidated by a college instructor. Obviously, the instructor had no intention of teaching me chemistry, so I walked to my lab table and asked my lab partner about litmus paper. My lab partner kindly told me the technical answer in less time than the instructor spent humiliating me: "blue litmus paper turns red with acids, red litmus paper turns blue with bases."

I was repulsed by the wicked nature of the instructor. God gave us an instinct to perceive evil and to flee from it. I respected my instinct to avoid the instructor as much as possible for the remainder of the semester.

I studied with fellow students and passed chemistry 201 and subsequently chemistry 202.

Ironically, I have worked as an engineering manager in the chemical manufacturing industry for over thirty years after graduating from college. Litmus paper is seldom used in the chemical industry; it is too inaccurate for most applications. I have purchased pH meters several times in my career to determine the acid or base level of chemicals. The instructor's wicked tongue could have destroyed a poor kid from the inner city. Remembering the teacher's vicious attack years later, I know God showered me with His grace to give me strength when I was weak.

A vicious tongue can do much damage to another's life. Lies can prompt people to make the wrong decision. I have seen people use a wicked tongue solely to control and hurt others; there was no satisfaction to the person with the wicked tongue other than inflicting pain on someone. I have learned to rebuke evil people when they attack me. I pray that God grants each reader of this book the courage to rebuke the wicked ones with evil tongues.

Proverbs 6.16-19 lists six things the LORD hates, including a man who stirs up dissension among brothers. When I was a young husband and father, my wife and I were becoming active in a church. My wife and I attended a seminar for church leaders pertaining to the Bible Book of Acts. Primarily ordained ministers, and a few Sunday school teachers, attended the seminar. The person leading the seminar on the Book of Acts started his talk by saying that various people observing the same event may each have a unique perspective on the event. The lecturer then stated that many people observed the landing on the moon by American astronauts, but people around the world each had a unique perception and personal significance of the lunar landing. A person in the audience immediately raised his hand and interrupted the lecturer with a question. As soon as the first question was answered, the audience badgered the speaker with stupid argumentative questions regarding televised events versus live events. An hour passed and we learned nothing about the Book of Acts. The vicious people in the audience sinned by stirring up dissension, creating stupid arguments, and by not treating others the same way you want them to treat you. The class was dismissed and the dissension resulting in a total waste of time and emotional injury to the speaker. The tongue can be a vicious weapon.

Useless grumbling is another abuse of the tongue. Solomon 1.11 directs us to not grumble, that is, complain and whine. The Old Testament story of the Children of Israel escaping bondage in Egypt is an excellent story of grumbling. God sends twelve plagues to Egypt to persuade Pharaoh to free the Jews. God has the people freed and they travel to the Red Sea. When the Jews were traveling from Egypt and approached the Red Sea, they saw Pharaoh's army approaching to attack them. The people had little faith and began to grumble toward God and Moses.

They said to Moses, "Was it because there were no graves in Egypt that you have taken us away to die in the wilderness? What have you done to us, bringing us out of Egypt? Is this not the very thing we told you in Egypt, "Let us alone and let us serve the Egyptians"? For it would have been better for us to serve the Egyptians than to die in the wilderness." Exodus 14.11-12

Exodus 14.21 documents that God parted the Red Sea so Pharaoh's army would not kill the Children of Israel. God works in his time and not our time. Understanding that we are part of God's plan is humbling. We will not understand the complexity of life this side of Heaven.

Grumbling is complaining about the current situation, but with no plans to improve the outcome. God gave us talent to do good. Let us do our best and acknowledge what is out of our control. Grumbling about what could have been or the way things should be brings unhappiness. Joy is basking in God's love and being content with the fruits of our best effort. Grumbling is the opposite of praising God's world.

The heart of the righteous weighs its answers, but the mouth of the wicked gushes evil. Proverbs 15.28 NIV

Thinking before we speak allows us to filter out unkind words and select words that best convey our thoughts with kindness and love. An evil tongue exposes wicked intensions.

One of the Ten Commandments is not to bear false witness, that is, lie. Lies can prompt people to make wrong decisions. In the twenty-first century the word lying seems to be seldom used. However, a lie is still a lie. People may overtly lie, lie by stating half-truths, or spin the truth. However, the devil is the father of lies and Jesus is the Truth. We should be careful when we speak and know our speech advances the cause of the devil or Jesus.

A wise man's heart guides his mouth, and his lips promote instruction. Proverbs 16.23 NIV

It is not good to be overbearing and give people unsolicited advise. However, there is a time to share wisdom to those who appreciate additional knowledge. I shared with a coworker that I always negotiate the interest on my car loans. He was shocked that interest was negotiable and achieved an interest rate much lower than the rate initially proposed by the dealership. My suggestion saved my colleague several thousands of dollars in interest on a car loan. I typically ask my adult children and others before I share information, "would you like some information on that subject?" If the answer is "no, I know all about it", I may reply, "Great, all is well." Intentionally being secretive to hurt someone is unkindness by omission. God knows our heart and our motives. Let us be beacons of light and kindness.

Psalm 19.14 clarifies how we are to speak. The words of our mouths and the meditation of our hearts are to please God. This verse from the book of Psalms humbles me to embarrassment. Over the years, I have conditioned my speech to not lie. Jesus warned us that by careless words we will be condemned. Perhaps my words were seldom bad enough to condemn me; however, my words too frequently are not pleasing to God. Scripture teaches us that our words are to be pleasing to God places a higher demand on us. I am very humbled.

Kind people are more likely to be able to have speech pleasing to God when all is going well. The risk of normally kind people saying words displeasing to God occurs in times of displeasure, stress, or when they are under attack. When we are verbally attacked, our natural animal instinct is to attack back harshly. Out of animal instinct, when a wolf growls and shows his fangs, the wolf being challenged will growl louder and show his fangs more viciously. The carnal, animal part within kind people is dormant in the heart, but there is an instinct within us to defend ourselves when provoked.

When attacked, our defensive self-preservation instinct of flight or fight reacts quickly. I confess I have difficulty controlling my tongue and mouth when attacked. I apologize for the unkind words I have ever spoken. We are to rebuke the wicked, but not sin in the process.

The human tongue may speak words that share and convey love, joy, peace, patience, kindness, goodness, gentleness, wisdom, knowledge, healing, holinesses, and God's scripture. A disciplined and Godly person may have a tongue that is pleasing to God Himself! Preachers share the word of God and a lesson with their congregation in a church. We sing praises to God and give Him glory.

In our daily activities, we have the ability to share our knowledge and love. The tone of one's voice and the words we say are very important to families and all interpersonal communication. Loving kindness between people brings friendship and love. Kind and appreciative words between husband and wife make a marriage strong. Saying please and thank you costs nothing, but the results are very valuable in terms of human benefits! Jesus commands us to thank others when they show us kindness.

Last week at work I had a conference telephone call with people in Ohio, Connecticut, Germany, and Ireland. We had a detailed discussion regarding manufacturing of chemical products consumed in numerous countries. If used properly, the tongue can be very helpful in business. People have the ability to be rude or kind in business meetings. Kindness in business improves productivity. When people are intimidated, they focus on surviving and fighting, and disengage from other activities.

Let us pray. Dear God, fill us with your love and let us be beacons of light in a fallen world. Thank you for the gifts you give us and we praise you God. Let us speak kindly to all. Let us share our knowledge with those who do not know; let us teach the gospel to those who live in darkness. On our day of judgment, may the words we have spoken be pleasing to You. Amen.

# CHAPTER 18

# Hypocrisy

"Woe to you, teachers of the law and Pharisees, you hypocrites! You give a tenth of your spices - mint, dill and cummin. But you have neglected the more important matters of the law - justice, mercy and faithfulness. You should have practiced the latter, without neglecting the former. You blind guides! You strain out a gnat but swallow a camel. Matthew 23.23-24 NIV

"Woe to you, teachers of the law and Pharisees, you hypocrites! You clean the outside of the cup and dish, but inside they are full of greed and self-indulgence. Blind Pharisee! First clean the inside of the cup and dish, and then the outside also will be clean. Matthew 23.25-26 NIV

"Woe to you, teachers of the law and Pharisees, you hypocrites! You are like whitewashed tombs, which look beautiful on the outside but on the inside are full of dead men's bones and everything unclean. In the same way, on the outside you appear to people as righteous but on the inside you are full of hypocrisy and wickedness. You snakes, you brood of vipers! How will you escape being condemned to hell? Therefore I am sending you prophets and wise men and teachers. Some of them you will kill and crucify; others you will flog in your synagogues and pursue from town to town. Matthew 23.27, 28, 33, 34 NIV

He said to them "Isaiah prophesied rightly about you hypocrites, as it is written, 'This people honor me with their lips, but their hearts are far from me; in vain do they worship me, teaching human precepts as doctrines.' You abandon the commandment of God and hold to human tradition." Mark 7.6-8

Now one of the Pharisees was requesting Him to dine with him, and He entered the Pharisee's house and reclined at the table. And there was a woman in the city who was a sinner; and when she learned that He was reclining at the table in the Pharisee's house, she brought an alabaster vial of perfume, and standing behind Him at His feet, weeping, she began to wet His feet with her tears, and kept wiping them with the hair of her head, and kissing His feet and anointing them with the perfume. Now when the Pharisee who had invited Him saw this, he said to himself, "If this man were a prophet He would know who and what sort of person this woman is who is touching Him, that she is a sinner." Luke 7.36-39 NASB

Turning toward the woman, He said to Simon, "Do you see this woman? I entered your house; you gave Me no water for My feet, but she has wet My feet with her tears and wiped them with her hair. "You gave Me no kiss; but she, since the time I came in, has not ceased to kiss My feet. You did not anoint My head with oil, but she anointed My feet with perfume. "For this reason I say to you, her sins, which are many, have been forgiven, for she loved much; but he who is forgiven little, loves little." Then He said to her, "Your sins have been forgiven." Those who were reclining at the table with Him began to say to themselves, "Who is this man who even forgives sins?" And He said to the woman, "Your faith has saved you; go in peace." Luke 7.44-50 NASB

Now he was teaching in one of the synagogues on the Sabbath. And just then there appeared a woman with a spirit that had crippled her for eighteen years. She was bent over and was quite unable to stand up straight. When Jesus saw her, he called her over and said, "Woman, you are set free from your ailment." When he laid his hands on her, immediately she stood up straight and began praising God. But the leader of the synagogue, indignant because Jesus had cured on the Sabbath, kept saying to the crowd, "There are six days on which work ought to be done; come on those days and be cured, and not on the Sabbath day." But the Lord answered him and said, "You hypocrites! Does not each of you on the Sabbath untie his ox or his donkey from the manger, and lead it away to give it water? And ought not this woman, a daughter of Abraham whom Satan bound for eighteen long years, be set free from this bondage on the Sabbath day?" When he said this, all his opponents were put to shame; and the entire crowd was rejoicing at all the wonderful things that he was doing. Luke 13.10-17

Why do you see the speck in your neighbor's eye, but do not notice the log in your own eye? Or how can you say to your neighbor, Let me take the speck out of your eye, while the log is in your own eye? You hypocrite, first take the log out of your own eye, and then you will see clearly to take the speck out of your neighbor's eye. Matthew 7.3-5

To some who were confident of their own righteousness and looked down on everybody else, Jesus told this parable: "Two men went up to the temple to pray, one a Pharisee and the other a tax collector. The Pharisee stood up and prayed about himself: 'God, I thank you that I am not like other men - robbers, evildoers, adulterers - or even like this tax collector. I fast twice a week and give a tenth of all I get.' "But the tax collector stood at a distance. He would not even look up to heaven, but beat his breast and said, 'God, have mercy on me, a sinner.' "I tell you that this man, rather than the other, went home justified before God. For everyone who exalts himself will be humbled, and he who humbles himself will be exalted." Luke 18.9-14 NIV

"Be careful not to do your 'acts of righteousness' before men, to be seen by them. If you do, you will have no reward from your Father in heaven. So when you give to the needy, do not announce it with trumpets, as the hypocrites do in the synagogues and on the streets, to be honored by men. I tell you the truth, they have received their reward in full. But when you give to the needy, do not let your left hand know what your right hand is doing, so that your giving may be in secret. Then your Father, who sees what is done in secret, will reward you. And when you pray, do not be like the hypocrites, for they love to pray standing in the synagogues and on the street corners to be seen by men. I tell you the truth, they have received their reward in full." Matthew 6.1-5 NIV

As he began the settlement, a man who owed him ten thousand talents was brought to him. Since he was not able to pay, the master ordered that he and his wife and his children and all that he had be sold to repay the debt. "The servant fell on his knees before him. 'Be patient with me,' he begged, 'and I will pay back everything.' The servant's master took pity on him, canceled the debt and let him go. "But when that servant went out, he found one of his fellow servants who owed him a hundred denarii. He grabbed him and began to choke him. 'Pay back what you owe me!' he demanded. His fellow servant fell to his knees and begged him, 'Be patient with me, and I will pay you back.' "But he refused. Instead, he went off and had the man thrown into prison until he could pay the debt. When the other servants saw what had happened, they were greatly distressed and went and told their master everything that had happened. "Then the master called the servant in. 'You wicked servant,' he said, 'I canceled all that debt of yours because you begged me to. Shouldn't you have had mercy on your fellow servant just as I had on you?' In anger his master turned him over to the jailers to be tortured, until he should pay back all he owed. Matthew 18.24-34 NIV

Jesus' teachings regarding hypocrisy are very profound, and have provoked me to research His views of hypocrisy. How do we avoid being a hypocrite, and how should we react to hypocrisy in our personal life? The word "hypocrite" is not commonly used in the mainstream America, but hypocrisy is quite common.

Hypocrisy can be classically defined as attempting to create an image that would suggest one has qualities that he or she does not actually possess. This type of hypocrisy can be defined as **Hypocrisy of Image**. The teaching of Jesus in Matthew 23 illuminates this type of hypocrisy. The teachers of the law and Pharisees presented an image of righteousness, but were not righteous. Jesus declared, "Woe to you, teachers of the law and Pharisees, you hypocrites!" The leaders implied their dedication to God in some outward acts, but neglected justice, mercy and faithfulness. Jesus brilliantly uses metaphors to explain the hypocrisy of the blind guides by saying, "You strain out a gnat but swallow a camel." Jesus uses a second metaphor in calling the leaders a cup that is clean on the outside, but dirty on the inside with greed and self-indulgence. Jesus also uses a third metaphor by referring to them as whitewashed tombs that are beautiful on the outside, but contain dead men's bones and are unclean. Claiming to follow Jesus, but rejecting justice, mercy, and faithfulness to embrace greed, self-indulgence, and wickedness is hypocrisy. These teachings from Jesus concern me because I am not immune to the temptation to be a hypocrite myself; per Paul, all have sinned and fall short of the glory of God. The world around us promotes self-centeredness, boasting, greed, self-indulgence, and wickedness. Following Jesus and choosing kindness, love, humility, and generosity is a challenging effort. I pray to God frequently to keep me focused on treasures in Heaven, not earthly treasures. The temptation to choose self-centeredness and self-indulgence, as opposed to following Jesus and demonstrating righteousness confronts us daily in this fallen world. The downward spiral of desires for earthly treasures and greed is a dangerous trap that tempts us continually.

I remain a very humble Christian because I am aware of my human sinful nature; I am righteous because I consciously choose to be righteous.

People may claim to be pious Christians to elevate their perceived social status. If a businessperson brags that he or she is a Christian to imply they have ideal behavior, I am immediately suspicious of their intentions and ethics. True Christianity is demonstrated though action, not through hollow words. We demonstrate Christ-like behavior by loving God and loving our neighbor as ourselves. Christians are saved by faith, but we are saved sinners; all have sinned and fall short of the glory of God, so that no one can boast.

A second type of hypocrisy can pertain to proposing or endorsing that a particular accomplishment be achieved, but refusing to participate in doing any of the work necessary to accomplish the goal. This type of hypocrisy can be defined as **Hypocrisy by Personal Exemption.** The Gospel of Luke 7.36-39 and 44-47 explain the actions of a Pharisee who invited Jesus to his home for dinner. The host was inhospitable to Jesus during his visit. The hypocrisy of the Pharisee is very ironic. The unwelcoming host did not provide a washbasin with water or a towel, so Jesus could wash His feet. The host did not greet Jesus with a kiss or provide oil for Jesus' head. A woman, who had lived a sinful life, entered the home and approached Jesus to show her love for Him. The woman humbly washed Jesus' feet with her tears, dried His feet with her hair, and poured perfume on Jesus' feet. The Pharisee thought that Jesus should reject the woman because a prophet should have known she was a sinner.

Jesus told the pompous Pharisee Simon, that he neglected to perform the acts of hospitality for Him as his guest. Simon's preoccupation with thinking Jesus was not a prophet for accepting the woman and Simon finding fault with the woman was hypocrisy. Simon neglected his obligation to welcome a stranger and love his neighbor. Ironically, the repentant woman, who had lived a sinful life and wanted to be forgiven for her sins, demonstrated love. Simon did not show love.

A third type of hypocrisy involves endorsing or soliciting others to follow a law or achieve a goal, while secretly desiring a side benefit for personal reward. This can be referred to as the **Hypocrisy of Personal Benefit.** The events recorded in Luke 13.10-17 are an example of hypocrisy desiring a personal benefit. Jesus was teaching in a synagogue on the Sabbath and saw a woman who could not straighten up her back for eighteen years. Jesus laid His hands upon her and healed the woman's back. The woman praised God for healing her. The leader of the synagogue criticized Jesus publicly for healing the sick woman on the Sabbath. Jesus then called his accuser a hypocrite. Jesus inquired if his accuser untied his animals and gave them water on the Sabbath. The leader of the synagogue likely gives water to his animals on the Sabbath. The leader of the synagogue criticized Jesus for healing on the Sabbath to turn the crowd against Jesus. The leader criticized Jesus to attack and discredit Him. Since God is the ultimate source of miraculous healing, it is nonsense to criticize someone for dishonoring God on the Sabbath when God Himself was the healer of the woman's back. The leader of the synagogue was a hypocrite. The leader portrayed he was concerned about keeping the Sabbath holy, but his true intent was to discredit Jesus and falsely charge Jesus with breaking the law of God. Jesus indicated that cattle are given water on the Sabbath, and therefore a woman can be healed on the Sabbath. May our motives be honest and true.

A fourth type of hypocrisy involves implying one's superiority and another's inferiority by condemning others regarding a practice or isolated act that the instigator cannot achieve. This can be defined as **Hypocrisy by Deflecting Guilt**. Jesus uses a metaphor again in comparing sin to a speck and a log. Jesus asks:

Why do you see the speck in your neighbor's eye, but do not notice the log in your own eye? Or how can you say to your neighbor, 'Let me take the speck out of your eye,' while the log is in your own eye? You hypocrite, first take the log out of your own eye, and then you will see clearly to take the speck out of your neighbor's eye. Matthew 7.3-5

Jesus' parable recorded in Luke 18.9-14 cautions about self-righteousness and feeling superior to one's neighbor. A confident Pharisee was proud he was more righteous than a tax collector and looked down on him. The humble tax collector acknowledged he was a sinner and requested mercy from God. Jesus indicated upon death, the tax collector is justified by his faith in God's mercy. Jesus reiterated justification is by faith:

"For all who exalt themselves will be humbled, and those who humble themselves will be exalted." Luke 14.11

Perhaps delusions of grandeur can come more easily to those who were born privileged or insecure people overcompensating for their insecurity. To keep our faith in Jesus, remain humble, and keep the commandments, perhaps it is best to remember that our physical life on earth has a fairly short duration and eternal life in Heaven is for those who live and believe in Jesus.

John 8 records the story of Jesus and a woman who committed adultery. A crowd had gathered to stone the woman to death. The crowd was willing to punish someone who committed a sin, yet those in the crowd were not perfect themselves.

Jesus said:

"He that is without sin among you, let him first cast a stone at her." John 8.7b KJV

When Jesus told the crowd whoever is without sin might throw a stone at the woman, no one threw a stone. Since all have sinned and fall short of the glory of Jesus, we must be careful to not be a hypocrite in finding faults in others. We should be primarily concerned about our sins and improving ourselves, rather than trying to find fault with others.

A fifth type of hypocrisy involves the motive in giving money to individuals or a charity. **Hypocrisy in Giving** is an abstract concept that was clarified by Jesus. Jesus stated:

"So when you give to the poor, do not sound a trumpet before you, as the hypocrites do in the synagogues and in the streets, so that they may be honored by men. Truly I say to you, they have their reward in full." Matthew 6.2 NASB

Jesus is very aware of the motive when people give to the poor. Giving to the poor may generally indicate the person is performing an act of kindness to give glory to God. God wants us to give to the poor with unselfish, righteous intentions. This concept of humble giving is not encouraged in contemporary society. Individuals or companies that donate to the poor may want to be honored by men. Doing a good deed and wanting to be honored by men is not hypocrisy, provided the giver understands he can either be honored by man or be honored by God, but not both. **Hypocrisy in giving** occurs when someone wants to give to the poor with trumpets sounding to be honored by both man and God.

Carnal people may donate money to the poor with the motive of being praised by men. One may give to the poor to gain acceptance in an elite clique. One may give to the poor to enhance business relationships and to increase sales. Jesus teaches that if we give to poor to attain honor by man, God will not honor our gift as charity. Jesus' teaching of humble giving is not easy to follow. Perhaps the choice we are to make in giving is who we want to give us honor: God or man?

If we want to achieve notoriety, increased advertisement, and more profits for our bank account, then spend the money for charitable organizations with trumpets blasting and consider the funds an investment. Smart business investing is good. However, do not be like the hypocrites who pretend to be honoring God, but are actually investing in a business deal. God knows what is in our hearts and knows what we think before we speak.

Jesus declares the humble will be exalted and those who exalt themselves will be humbled. Jesus' declaration that the humble will be exalted prompts me to NEVER exalt myself and never think I am better than my neighbor before God.

A sixth type of hypocrisy involves fairness. **Hypocrisy Regarding Reciprocity and Fairness** is explained very well in Jesus' parable in Matthew 18.23-34 regarding the indebted servant. The parable from Jesus explains that a man had a large debt of 10,000 talents that he could not pay. The man and his family were going to be sold into slavery by his master. The indebted man begged to be forgiven and he was forgiven of his huge debt.

The forgiven man went out and saw a servant that owed him a meager 100 denarii. The forgiven man demanded his money, then had the servant placed in debtor's prison. The forgiven man's huge debt was cancelled, but he demonstrated no forgiveness to another. The forgiven man had the hypocritical audacity to imprison a servant who owed him a meager 100 denarii. The master of the self-indulgent hypocritical servant heard that he imprisoned a servant for a meager debt. The master reinstated the huge debt of the unfair man and had him imprisoned because he showed no mercy. The Lord's Prayer includes:

And forgive us our debts, as we forgive our debtors. Matthew 6.12 KJV

It is hypocrisy to expect our debts to be forgiven, but not forgive our debtors. If a friend buys us dinner or treats us to an event, let us say thank you and give our friend a gift the next time. Always expecting generosity from others, but being selfish in return, is displeasing to God. As mentioned in the chapter on anger, self-centered people, who treat others without fairness, will become indignant and enraged if they are treated unfairly. **Reciprocity is indeed the test of fairness.**

Let us close in prayer. Please guide us to walk in righteousness and not be hypocrites. Hypocrisy surrounds us in our daily life, but it is hidden in plain sight. Please help us to be aware of the sin of hypocrisy and not be like the world. Let us have the courage to speak the truth. Let us have the courage to analyze our own actions and not scrutinize others to accuse them of sin. Let us have the courage to not hide behind a mask of perfection, but share our faults and accomplishments with others. Holy Spirit, please guide us to keep us to be humble servants of God. Let us not seek to impress or demean others; let us never build ourselves up by tearing others down. Amen.

# CHAPTER 19

# Lawyers

Woe also to you lawyers! For you load people with burdens hard to bear, and you yourselves do not lift a finger to ease them. Woe to you! For you build the tombs of the prophets whom your ancestors killed. So you are witnesses and approve of the deeds of your ancestors; for they killed them, and you build their tombs. Therefore also the Wisdom of God said, 'I will send them prophets and apostles, some of whom they will kill and persecute.' Luke 11.46b-49

"And why do you not judge for yourselves what is right? Thus, when you go with your accuser before a magistrate, on the way make an effort to settle the case, or you may be dragged before the judge, and the judge hand you over to the officer, and the officer throw you in prison. I tell you, you will never get out until you have paid the very last penny." Luke 12.57-59

For our struggle is not against flesh and blood, but against the rulers, against the powers, against the world forces of this darkness, against the spiritual forces of wickedness in the heavenly places. Ephesians 6.12 NASB

They answered him, "If you will be a servant to this people today and serve them, and speak good words to them when you answer them, then they will be your servants forever." 1 Kings 12.7

When any of you has a grievance against another, do you dare to take it to court before the unrighteous, instead of taking it before the saints? 1 Corinthians 6.1

In the Gospel book Luke 7.36-48, a sinful woman visited Jesus and poured perfume on Jesus' feet while crying. Although the woman had led a sinful

life, Jesus forgave the woman of her sins because she demonstrated her love for Him.

In John 8.3-11, a woman was about to be stoned to death for committing adultery. Jesus told the crowd that anyone without sin may throw a stone at her. Jesus asked the woman if anyone condemned her and she respectfully replied "no one sir." Jesus indicated He did not condemn her and she should go and sin no more.

In dramatic contrast to forgiving repentant sinners, Jesus gave lawmakers a different message. Luke 11.46b-49 records that Jesus said woe to lawyers! Jesus declared that lawyers burden people, and do not ease their suffering. Jesus also indicated lawyers had approved the murder of prophets; woe to lawyers. As a young man reading the Holy Bible for the first time many years ago, I did not understand Jesus' warning to lawyers. I humbly recorded various scripture passages involving lawyers for future research. Only through prayer and many years of living and observing society did I come to understand why Jesus specifically warned lawyers and forgave so many others.

My wife and I vacationed in Savanna, Georgia in the summer of 2005. During a walking tour of downtown Savanna, the tour guide and historian mentioned that General James Oglethorpe founded the state of Georgia for English settlers relocating to a new land. General Oglethorpe observed that English lawyers had burdened the people of England. The original charter of Georgia forbade lawyers to practice in Savannah!

Trial lawyers serve a valuable function in criminal law. I served on a jury several years ago. The prosecuting attorney indicated a crime was committed and the person charged with the crime did the wrongful act. The defense attorney agreed that a crime was committed, but said his client did not participate in the crime. This interaction of the prosecuting and the defense attorneys generally facilitates a civilized society where wrong doers are punished and the innocent are set free. British and American civil laws have similarities to the Ten Commandments. Laws prohibiting murder, prohibiting stealing and guaranteeing the right to own property and have freedom seem necessary to have a flourishing civilization and avoid chaos. Even the residents of the state of Georgia changed the state charter to have laws and allow lawyers to practice.

Luke 12.57-59 documents that Jesus encouraged people to righteously settle disputes out of court. I know many people personally who have been sued and taken to court instead of resolving the issue between the people involved. People may sue another in court to perhaps receive a large settlement. Righteously resolving matters between one another may bring a fair settlement; dragging another before a judge may load one with undeserved financial gain.

Lawyers write civil code to promote order. Those who break the law and are convicted will experience negative consequences. Lawyers write tax law to generate revenue and also control the behavior of society. The ability of lawyers to write civil code and tax law gives them much power to burden and shape society. Careful reading of Luke 11.46 clarifies that Jesus said woe to lawyers who load people with burdens hard to bear. A law will have a direct and intentional impact on society. A law may also have secondary consequences; secondary consequences of law may be intentional or unintentional. Lawyers have the power to affect a civilization by both the direct and secondary impacts of a law. This chapter will present several laws with both a direct result and a secondary result. Jesus' warning is to lawyers who load people with burdens hard to bear.

In a monarchy or dictatorship, the king or dictator issues the laws. The Bible book of 1 Kings 12.1-20 records that the people of Israel requested King Rehoboam, son of King Solomon, to decrease taxes and stop slave labor. King Rehoboam refused to lighten the load on the people of Israel. King Rehoboam indicated he would increase his burden on the people. Consequently, ten of the twelve tribes of Israel succeeded from his rule. Two tribes, Benjamin and Judah, remained with Rehoboam and his repressive ways. Rehoboam used his authority to perpetuate and escalate laws that excessively burdened society. It is interesting that the elders of the chosen people advised King Rehoboam to be a servant of the people by reducing the burden and that the people would serve him in return. The direct result of Rehoboam's decrees was an increase in taxation on the people. The secondary result of Rehoboam's decrees was unintentional: ten tribes succeeded and formed Israel and the two tribes that remained with Rehoboam formed Judea. Legislators have the power to directly burden society; however, the secondary result may be of larger consequence than the primary impact. Abuse of power and over-taxation caused the chosen people to divide and form two nations. Abuse of power resulted in the destruction of a nation.

Another record of a dangerous legal decree is recorded in detail in the Old Testament book of Esther. Esther Chapter 2 teaches that Nebuchadnezzar, King of Babylon, arranged to have a man named Mordecai carried into exile from Jerusalem. Mordecai raised his orphaned cousin named Esther and she grew up to be beautiful. King Xerxes chose Esther to be his queen.

Mordecai became aware that two officers conspired to kill King Xerxes and informed Queen Esther. Esther warned King Xerxes that two of his officers planned to assassinate him and that Mordecai provided the information to protect the King. The two potential assassins were executed after an investigation. King Xerxes promoted Haman to rule over the King's servants.

When Haman saw that Mordecai would not kneel down or pay him honor, he was enraged. Yet having learned who Mordecai's people were, he scorned the idea of killing only Mordecai. Instead Haman looked for a way to destroy all Mordecai's people, the Jews, throughout the whole kingdom of Xerxes. Esther 3.5-6 NIV

Then Haman said to King Xerxes, "There is a certain people dispersed and scattered among the peoples in all the provinces of your kingdom whose customs are different from those of all other people and who do not obey the king's laws; it is not in the king's best interest to tolerate them. If it pleases the king, let a decree be issued to destroy them, and I will put ten thousand talents of silver into the royal treasury for the men who carry out this business." So the king took his signet ring from his finger and gave it to Haman son of Hammedatha, the Agagite, the enemy of the Jews. "Keep the money," the king said to Haman, "and do with the people as you please." Then on the thirteenth day of the first month the royal secretaries were summoned. They wrote out in the script of each province and in the language of each people all Haman's orders to the king's satraps, the governors of the various provinces and the nobles of the various peoples. These were written in the name of King Xerxes himself and sealed with his own ring. Dispatches were sent by couriers to all the king's provinces with the order to destroy, kill and annihilate all the Jews - young and old, women and little children - on a single day, the thirteenth day of the twelfth month, the month of Adar, and to plunder their goods. A copy of the text of the edict was to be issued as law in every province and made known to the people of every nationality so they would be ready for that day. Esther 3.8-14 NIV

Mordecai learned of the decree of annihilation and wore sackcloth as a sign of mourning. Esther sent her aide, Hathach, to determine why Mordecai was in mourning and learned of the order to destroy all Jews and plunder their goods.

So the king and Haman went to dine with Queen Esther, and as they were drinking wine on that second day, the king again asked, "Queen Esther, what is your petition? It will be given you. What is your request? Even up to half the kingdom, it will be granted." Then Queen Esther answered, "If I have found favor with you, O king, and if it pleases your majesty, grant me my life - this is my petition. And spare my people - this is my request. For I and my people have been sold for destruction and slaughter and annihilation. If we had merely been sold as male and female slaves, I would have kept quiet, because no such distress would justify disturbing the king." King Xerxes asked Queen Esther, "Who is he? Where is the man who has dared to do such a thing?" Esther said, "The adversary and enemy is this vile Haman." Esther 7.1-6 NIV

Then Harbona, one of the eunuchs attending the king, said, "A gallows seventy-five feet high stands by Haman's house. He had it made for Mordecai, who spoke up to help the king." The king said, "Hang him on it!" So they hanged Haman on the gallows he had prepared for Mordecai. Then the king's fury subsided. Esther 7.9-10 NIV

The account of Haman in the book of Esther details how a single law can be written with potentially devastating results. Haman's self-centered and revengeful abuse of power is startling. Haman became furious when Mordecai would not bow to him. Why would Haman become furious with Mordecai for not bowing? Haman's anger was likely prompted by his presumptions that his political rank made him superior to others as a human being and that superiority gave him the authority to control others. Both of these presumptions are false. Possessing a political rank is simply that, a title declared on a person by another person. Mordecai refused to kneel to Haman. Haman desired to humiliate Mordecai and make him be subservient; this level of control is contrary to Jesus' teachings. Jesus commands that we are to treat others in the manner that we would like to be treated. Possessing a rank established by man does not elevate a human to another level; humans came from dust and will return to dust. Mordecai's refusal to kneel to Haman perhaps angered Haman because his action declared Haman was just a man. Rather than acknowledge that Mordecai's refusal to kneel to Haman was a reminder of Haman's mortality and equality to his neighbor, Haman wanted Mordecai dead. Haman's lust for power and revenge grew in wickedness. Haman wanted to murder Mordecai and all Jews! Haman wanted to totally eliminate all Jewish people who may not be subservient to a royalty created by man. Haman gathered the royal law writers and made a decree to annihilate all the Jews and siege their goods. Governors and soldiers from Xerxes' kingdom would carry out the decree to kill the Jews. The authority to murder an entire civilization can be gathered by the ink on paper of a written law!

Queen Esther prevented the mass murder of the Jewish people by telling King Xerxes that she was a Jew herself. The execution of Haman, ordered by King Xerxes, made it clear that earthly power is fleeting.

An attempt to mass murder Jewish people was repeated in the twentieth century. Unlike the unsuccessful attempt to murder Jews by Haman, Jews were actually murdered in mass in the twentieth century. Documentaries and movies regarding the persecution of the Jews in the Holocaust, which occurred between 1939 and 1945, were common during my childhood. The fact that Jewish people were deported to ghettos, and then murdered saddened me that mankind could be so unkind. As a young man, I superficially and simplistically thought soldiers were solely responsible for killing the Jews. Watching documentaries regarding the holocaust on the public television network as an adult prompted me to do additional reading. Much to my surprise, a major catalyst in the mistreatment and eventual murder of Jews were laws issued by lawyers! Laws made of ink on paper almost prompted the annihilation of the Jewish people at the time of King Xerxes. Laws made of ink on paper did prompt the mass murder of many Jewish people during the Holocaust. Prior to the actions of lawyers, various Jews living in Germany were considered German citizens and were entitled to the rights of a German citizen.

Numerous laws, decrees, ordinances, and regulations were issued between 1933 and 1940, to restrict Jews. The Nuremberg Laws of 1935 included the Reich Citizenship Law and the Law for the Protection of German Blood and Honor. The Nuremberg Laws of 1935 and other laws produced the following impact on Jewish people:

- Restricted the compensation or activities of Jewish physicians and lawyers
- Revoked the license of Jewish tax professionals
- Prohibited marriage between a German and a Jew
- Excluded German Jews from citizenship
- Expelled Jewish officers from the military
- Transferred ownership from Jewish owned companies
- Banned Jews from public schools, universities, theater, and sporting events.

With carefully crafted wording by lawyers, ink on paper, the civil rights of Jews living in Germany were reduced. With the legal protection of Jewish people overturned, the political climate for mayhem and murder evolved. Jews were deported and then murdered in Chelmno, Treblinka, Auschwitz, Belzec, Sobibor, and Majdanek death camps.[11]

A subsequent question regarding the Holocaust is: why did people cooperate to murder Jews? The reasons why people may abuse or kill another may include: evil pleasure, peer pressure, or simply following orders.

The answer why the King Xerxes' military personnel were ready to slaughter the Jews and why the holocaust was actually accomplished is an unpleasant reality: people are inclined to be evil and people are like sheep.

Jesus went through all the towns and villages, teaching in their synagogues, preaching the good news of the kingdom and healing every disease and sickness. When he saw the crowds, he had compassion on them, because they were harassed and helpless, like sheep without a shepherd. Matthew 9.35, 36 NIV

Jesus is the good shepherd. Sheep generally are not self-motivated and not self-directed creatures; sheep obey a shepherd. Jesus made numerous comparisons between human beings and sheep during his ministry on earth.

Jesus said, "Take care of my sheep." John 21.16c NIV

Jesus used sheep as a metaphor for people. Perhaps the reference of people to sheep provides insight that people share behavioral similarities with sheep:

- Both sheep and people may not use their brain to formulate their own opinion or judgment, but may mindlessly follow an authority, such as a shepherd
- A shepherd may easily redirect both sheep and people
- Both may not consider the consequences of following a good or evil shepherd, they may follow blindly.

Professor Stanley Milgram conducted extensive research involving obedience and published his findings in his book *Obedience to Authority*. Professor Milgram conducted situational experiments to determine if test subjects would obey someone perceived as an authority, even if the action to be done was contrary to the subjects' moral values. Professor Milgram wanted to determine if test subjects would inflict supposedly severe electrical shocks on an innocent victim if commanded by someone in authority.[12]

The behavior of the subjects in Professor Milgram's test was frightening and enlightening. Experiment 1 and Experiment 18 provided profound insight into humankind's ability to harm one another. I recommend reading Professor Milgram's book in its entirety. The behavior of the people in the controlled test seemed to reflect the action of people throughout history, but the mental mechanics were clarified. When prompted by an authority, nearly everyone, who volunteered to participate in the experiment, found inflicting a tolerable shock on an innocent person to be acceptable. Surprising to me, over one half of the volunteers obeyed the authority to inflict the most severe shock.[12]

A vast majority of volunteers would assist the authority in inflicting the most severe electric shock. (See Experiment 18) Unknown by the test subjects, the electrical control panel was not connected to high voltage. No one was actually electrocuting the learning victim and the electric buzzing noise was intended to create an illusion of high voltage. Professor Milgram's experiment provided insight into human behavior and authority. Scripture tells us in Genesis Chapter 8 that the heart of man is inclined to evil.

Human behavior indicates that some people indeed submit to authority, even if the pending action is immoral. People can be easily manipulated to do evil acts when simply told to act in an evil manner. People may be inclined to do evil deeds if they are prompted by peer pressure, submit to authority, or when the accountability for the evil act is transferred to another.

Evil may flourish when people disregard righteousness and do not accept accountability for their actions. It is through personal weakness and passive agreement that the evil concepts of a few are accomplished by the masses. Perhaps the murder of Jewish people in the 1940's was accomplished through the instigation of a few and the cooperation of many. Perhaps some members of mankind are prepared to act in an evil manner when provided an opportunity to not be punished. Lawyers have the dangerous ability to unleash evil by removing the deterrent of punishment for doing evil. Professor Milgram's Experiment 18 illustrated mankind still has the propensity to be sheep. God tells us mankind is inclined to evil.

In this era of automobiles, those who drive a vehicle faster than the posted speed limit may receive a speeding ticket. The high cost of a speeding ticket is intended to be a punishment and deterrent to driving too fast. Punishing or rewarding members of society for performing certain acts controls the behavior of society; lawyers write the laws to control society.

The income tax law in the United States is configured to generate revenue and direct society's actions. Home mortgage interest is deductible and lowers the tax paid for those who own a mortgaged home. The United States wants people to buy homes with borrowed money. In the 1980's inflation was high and personal savings was low. The United States government issued a law that created "All Savers" certificates. The direct impact of the law provided citizens with tax-free interest on "All Savers" certificates. The secondary intentional impact was prompting citizens to save money and not spend it. People generally obey the authorities in government by doing actions where they are rewarded and avoiding actions where they will be financially punished.

In the spring of 2001, I was appalled as a citizen when calculating my United States Federal Income Tax for the tax year 2000. The United States government taxed me an additional $562 for being married. My wife was taxed an additional $562 for being married. An additional tax of $1,124 annually is approximately equivalent to the financial punishment of twelve speeding tickets. Married United States citizens are financially punished $93.67 monthly for following Jesus and being married! God joins husband and wife in Holy Matrimony; marriage is a religious practice.

Jesus stated:

"But at the beginning of creation God 'made them male and female.' 'For this reason a man will leave his father and mother and be united to his wife, and the two will become one flesh.' So they are no longer two, but one. Therefore what God has joined together, let man not separate." Mark 10.6-9 NIV

The United States government was financially punishing my religious practice of marriage through unequal taxation. With God's gentle, but firm, prompting I filed a civil rights lawsuit against the United States, Case Number 1:01CV1701. In my case, I stated that my first amendment right to free exercise of religion was being violated.

Before I filed my complaint, my research indicated the First Amendment in the Bill of Rights is not in the United States Legal Code. The official law is stated in US Code Title 42, chapter 21b, Section 2000bb-1[13]:

(a) In general

Government shall not substantially burden a person's exercise of religion even if the burden results from a rule of general applicability, except as provided in subsection (b) of this section.

(b) Exception

Government may substantially burden a person's exercise of religion only if it demonstrates that application of the burden to the person -

(1) is in furtherance of a compelling governmental interest;

and

(2) is the least restrictive means of furthering that compelling governmental interest.

The United States District Court dismissed my civil complaint on the basis of jurisdiction, not content. Although I lost my First Amendment complaint, I felt God was pleased that I did what He asked and exposed religious persecution in the United States. The judge's dismissal of my marriage tax complaint was well researched and included the following:

1. Declaratory Judgment Act deprives any federal court jurisdiction over federal taxes. 28USC 2201(a).
2. Anti-Injunction Act deprives anyone from filing a lawsuit regarding federal taxes. 26 USC 7421 (a).
3. The Sixteenth Amendment gave Congress the power to lay and collect taxes on incomes from whatever source derived. The key word "whatever" evidently implied Congress can tax citizens unequally, contingent on one's religious and moral beliefs; citizens have no authority to disagree.
4. The protection of life, liberty, property, and due process indicated by the Fourteenth Amendment specifically sites "states" and excludes the Federal Government. The actions of the Federal Government are beyond the scope of the Fourteenth Amendment. 42 USC 1983.

Let me clarify. The lawyers wrote the fourteenth amendment such that the states may not violate the life, liberty, and property of U. S. citizens. However, protection from the United States federal government violating the rights of citizens is not guaranteed under the fourteenth amendment. The fourteenth amendment does not protect the common people from the United States federal government enacting laws similar to the Nuremberg laws of 1935. Let us pray the United States government does not progress from financially persecuting married Christians to outlawing the worship of God, stripping us of our property, or murdering Christians.

After my case was dismissed in 2001, I wrote and requested every member of the Senate, the House of Representatives, and the President eliminate the additional federal tax on married citizens. Congress slightly reduced the marriage tax in the following years. In the 2008 tax year, a husband and wife will pay an additional $788 penalty for obeying God's command of Holy Marriage. When people are fined $100 for exceeding the speed limit in an automobile, people may tend to speed less. The direct impact of congress financially punishing citizens for being married is more taxes given to Caesar. The secondary result of the marriage tax perhaps is more couples living together unmarried and an escalating divorce rate. Laws do indeed influence society. It is obvious that marriage is under attack while I write this book. Christians and Jews being persecuted by government is not surprising and is not new.

Jesus said:

"If ye were of the world, the world would love his own: but because ye are not of the world, but I have chosen you out of the world, therefore the world hateth you." John 15.19 KJV

My wife and I will keep our marriage strong, and understand the United States government is persecuting us for being married before God and man. My wife and I will not sell our souls for $788.

God, please give us the strength to be as courageous as Mordecai and Esther to protest and change the laws of man that conflict with the laws of God.

Lawyers have the responsibility to create laws that comply with the Ten Commandments.

Jesus said to His disciples: "Things that cause people to sin are bound to come, but woe to that person through whom they come. It would be better for him to be thrown into the sea with a millstone tied around his neck than for him to cause one of these little ones to sin." Luke 17.1-2 NIV

Dear Jesus, let us pray. This chapter on lawyers was difficult to write, it is difficult to read, and it is discomforting when understood. Please fill the hearts and minds of lawmakers and lawyers to fully understand that their power comes with much responsibility. The actions of many are influenced by the decrees of the lawyers. Remind the lawyers that it is better they be thrown into the sea with a millstone tied around their neck than cause people to sin. When lawyers write laws that foster evil and defy God, events such as the Holocaust may occur. Please remind the lawyers of the Laws of God placed in their hearts and written on their minds. Also, let the voice of the common people be declared from the mountaintops such that lawyers cannot avoid the truth. Please open our minds to see laws that cause people to sin. If laws of man persecute us for following Jesus, please give us the strength to endure suffering, rather than to conform to the world.

Jesus' warning of woe to those who cause others to sin is applicable to us all. Anytime each of us has authority over another, we must bridle our lust for power, control, self-indulgence, and our nature to sin. May the Holy Spirit guide all those who have authority to influence others to act with kindness, love, and righteousness. Let us act like Jesus, the Servant King. Amen.

# CHAPTER 20

# Life in the Flesh is Temporary; Things Unseen are Eternal

I have seen all the works which have been done under the sun, and behold, all is vanity and striving after wind. Ecclesiastes 1.14 NASB

For our light and momentary troubles are achieving for us an eternal glory that far outweighs them all. So we fix our eyes not on what is seen, but on what is unseen. For what is seen is temporary, but what is unseen is eternal. 2 Corinthians 4.17-18 NIV

Also, I collected for myself silver and gold and the treasure of kings and provinces. All that my eyes desired I did not refuse them I did not withhold my heart from any pleasure, for my heart was pleased because of all my labor and this was my reward for all my labor. Thus I considered all my activities which my hands had done and the labor which I had exerted, and behold all was vanity and striving after wind and there was no profit under the sun. Ecclesiastes 2.8a, 10-11 NASB

He has made everything beautiful in its time. He has also set eternity in the hearts of men; yet they cannot fathom what God has done from beginning to end. Ecclesiastes 3.11 NIV

Thomas said to him, "My Lord and my God!" Then Jesus told him, "Because you have seen me, you have believed; blessed are those who have not seen and yet have believed." John 20.28-29 NIV

For those who want to save their life will lose it, and those who lose their life for my sake, and for the sake of the gospel, will save it. For what will it profit them to gain the whole world and forfeit their life?   Mark 8.35, 36

Do not work for the food that perishes, but for the food that endures for eternal life, which the Son of Man will give you. For it is on him that God the Father has set his seal." John 6.27

Do not love the world or anything in the world. If anyone loves the world, the love of the Father is not in him. For everything in the world—the cravings of sinful man, the lust of his eyes and the boasting of what he has and does—comes not from the Father but from the world. The world and its desires pass away, but the man who does the will of God lives forever. 1 John 2.15-17 NIV

For I am already being poured out like a drink offering, and the time has come for my departure. I have fought the good fight, I have finished the race, I have kept the faith. Now there is in store for me the crown of righteousness, which the Lord, the righteous Judge, will award to me on that day - and not only to me, but also to all who have longed for his appearing. 2 Timothy 4.6-8 NASB

Ever since the creation of the world his eternal power and divine nature, invisible though they are, have been understood and seen through the things he has made. So they are without excuse. Romans 1.20

For you are a mist that appears for a little while and then vanishes. James 4.14c

Even if we live a long life, perhaps 80 years, it is still very short and temporary in comparison to eternity. When my son was in college, he was pondering life and calculus at the same time. There is an expression in calculus called the limit. The value of the equation is approximated as the limit is approached. My son's equation is:

$$\lim_{X \to \infty} f(X) = \frac{\text{80 year earthly life}}{X}$$

In the equation, as X approaches infinity, the value of the equation approaches zero. My son's equation demonstrates a long life of 80 years divided by infinity or eternity approaches zero. The limit of a short lifespan of 30 years also approaches zero when divided by infinity. The mathematical equation illustrates that however long we live, where we spend eternity is most important and our brief earthly accomplishments of this life will become less significant with respect to eternal life. In a major contrast, how we live our life will determine where we spend eternity.

My wife and I enjoy our two pet dogs. Since our grown children are not home on a daily basis, our dogs have become more like children to my wife and I. Whenever my wife or I are sick, the dogs sense our pain and stay next to us to snuggle and express their love and concern. When my wife and I return home from being away, our dogs run to greet us with tails wagging. We took our dogs to obedience training. In the classes, we learned that promptly responding to a dog's action is very important. Praising and petting a dog when it sits teaches the dog sitting is good and is pleasing to the master. Turning away and ignoring a dog when it jumps up to be acknowledged teaches the dog that jumping up is bad and is displeasing to the master. Dog training will not instill a sense of morality of right and wrong in the dog. Dogs are creatures of instinct. A trained dog is still a pack animal, but it has learned to obey the leader of the pack. Dogs are carnal beings, living in the flesh, and appear to not have eternity written in their hearts. Isaiah 11.6 indicated the wolf will live with the lamb and the leopard will lie down with the young goat. Perhaps God has space in Heaven for animals, regardless if they understand eternity in their hearts.

I think humans are somewhat of a social pack animal also. God Himself indicated that it is not good for man to be alone in Genesis 2. Unlike other animals, we uniquely have the knowledge of good and evil. As recorded in Ecclesiastes 3.11, God gave mankind an awareness of eternity in our hearts.

From everyone who has been given much, much will be demanded. Luke 12.48b NIV

Humans are demanded by God to live a more Godly life than beasts because we know the laws of God in our mind and have an awareness of eternity. The principle of God demanding more from those who have been given more is repeated throughout the Holy Bible.

James, the earthly half brother of Jesus, compared us to a mist that appears for a short time and then disappears. We humans have the unique knowledge that we will live for only a short time with respect to eternity. Psalm 90.14 amazingly informs us that humans will typically die between seventy and eighty years old of natural causes. God has given us awareness of eternity in our hearts. The combined knowledge that our life is relatively short and the comprehension of eternity in our hearts prompts us to ask ourselves a logical question regarding the relationship between our earthly life and eternity. Questioning the relationship between our earthly life and eternity prompts us to consider the consequences of living in the flesh as a selfish carnal person or living in the Holy Spirit and focusing on eternity.

A carnal person, in and of the world, loves the world and worldly things, especially themselves. I John 2.15-17 tells us to not love the world or things in the world. A carnal person exposes their self-centeredness by their cravings for earthly things, the insatiable lust for all they see and the boasting of their job and their possessions. Carnal people may boast of what they have and what they do; the carnal man may take wicked enjoyment by possessing what others do not have. When my wife and I were first married, I had finished my degree in engineering and my wife did not have her bachelor's degree in Occupational Therapy. Some college-educated women, creatures of instinct, seem to have a desire to humiliate other women who do not have a degree. At my employer sponsored picnics, numerous women there would first ask the other women their name, then, asked what their college degree was and what college they attended. My wife had no degree yet and felt the women were not being friendly in their conversation; the women were covertly boasting of their degree and establishing they were educated and of higher rank as a pack leader. People who have not been born again with the Holy Spirit often seem to fixate on earthly life and place all value on earthly achievements.

Jesus' parable, in Luke 12.16-21, regarding life in the flesh and eternity, provides supernatural clarity on the subject. A rich man, living as a carnal man in the flesh, had a very productive harvest in his fields. His crop yield was so large, it exceeded the storage capacity of his barns. The man evidently did not plan to share his crops with others, but he planned to tear down his barns and build larger barns to store the crops for himself for the future. Ironically, God informed the rich man he would die that night. Others left behind on earth will enjoy the crops he stored for himself.

The preacher king, writer of Ecclesiastes had many profound thoughts to share regarding life being temporary and things unseen being eternal. The king had accumulated much earthly treasures. The king labored extensively and rewarded himself with any pleasurable activity his eyes desired. However, all his pleasurable activities and accumulation of treasures did not bring him true joy and peace. He declared all his labor, activities, and possessions vanity and meaningless. The wise king understood that all possessions are temporary. The pleasurable activity vanishes the moment it is completed. The treasures he collected, including gold and silver, will remain behind when he dies. Other treasures of the king may rust or be stolen before he dies. In chapter 3 of Ecclesiastes, the preacher king indicates that God set eternity in the hearts of men. Regardless of what our carnal instincts drive us to do, humans have the understanding of our future death and eternity.

The understanding of eternity prompted the writer of Ecclesiastes to determine all possessions and activities in life to be vanity, that is, meaningless, with respect to eternity. The preacher deduced that since the treasures and activities in life are meaningless, we are to fear God and keep His commandments. Perhaps Ecclesiastes' most profound conclusion was that life is meaningless by itself, but God will judge the deeds in our earthly life to determine where we spend eternity. The preacher acknowledges that God will judge all our deeds, including those done in secret, to be good or evil.

I have witnessed what Ecclesiastes preached about. Most of us work for many years, buy a home, cars, clothes, and appliances. Eventually people get old. The new cars people purchase age, rust, and end up in a junkyard. Clothes and appliances also age and are eventually discarded. Ultimately, people die and their homes are sold to someone else. Life could be deemed vanity, meaningless. However, life is not truly meaningless; life is an opportunity to love God, obey His commandments, and love your neighbor as yourself. The unseen is eternal.

The knowledge of eternity that God places in our hearts is a true notification for us to investigate what is unseen. Scripture tells us that we do not have an excuse to deny the existence of God or eternity. The wonder of creation tells us God exists. Jesus explained that those who have not seen Him in person, but still believe in Him, are blessed. People have the choice to ignore God, deny eternity, and ignore God's laws. However, those who deny God and focus on oneself are not rich toward God. God will call each of us to leave this earthly life and we will each die.

A very brief and amazingly profound declaration by Jesus Himself is found in Matthew 10.28. Jesus specifically warns us to fear God because He has the absolute power to send our eternal soul to hell when our bodies die! That statement by Jesus, the Son of God, raises the hairs on my arms if I ponder the implications of what He said. As humans, we have the ability to choose to embrace evil and live fully for what is seen. We can partake of the cravings of sinful man. We are able to break some or all of God's commandments. However, Jesus, who tells the truth, clearly stated we HAVE a soul that is eternal and the soul is not of the body; the soul is of the spirit. Furthermore, Jesus said His Father, God, has the ability to destroy our body and send our eternal soul to HELL! The concept of spending eternity in Hell as a consequence of spending seventy to eighty years in the body succumbing to lusts and evil activities seems very unwise to me. Since I enjoy pleasing my heavenly Father and try my best to be holy, I truly have no desire to be evil and spend eternity in Hell. The more one lives a holy life, the more at peace one becomes. Ultimately, being Godly and spending eternity in paradise seems like a win-win scenario to me.

The choice before us is clear. Do we live our life according to God's laws, earn an honest income, and prepare for eternity in Heaven? Or do we live as creatures of instinct, absorbed in our selfish desires, disobey God's laws, and live only for the things seen in the present? The consequences of our decision will last for eternity.

Let us pray. Heavenly Father, thank you for placing eternity in our hearts to remind us you are God and we are not. Let us remain humble and focused on pleasing you God, rather than trying to impress or intimidate others by boasting of what we have or what we do. Amen.

# CHAPTER 21

# Children of the Devil or Children of God

And there was war in heaven, Michael and his angels waging war with the dragon. The dragon and his angels waged war, and they were not strong enough, and there was no longer a place found for them in heaven. And the great dragon was thrown down, the serpent of old who is called the devil and Satan, who deceives the whole world; he was thrown down to the earth, and his angels were thrown down with him. Revelations 12.7-9 NASB

The LORD said to Satan, "From where do you come?" Then Satan answered the LORD and said, " From roaming about on the earth and walking around on it." Job 1.7 NASB

For our struggle is not against flesh and blood, but against the rulers, against the powers, against the world forces of this darkness, against the spiritual forces of wickedness in the heavenly places. Ephesians 6.12 NASB

The LORD smelled the pleasing aroma and said in his heart: "Never again will I curse the ground because of man, even though every inclination of his heart is evil from childhood. And never again will I destroy all living creatures, as I have done. Genesis 8.21 NIV

He came to His own, and those who were his own did not receive Him. But as many as received Him, to them He gave the right to become children of God, even to those who believe in His name, who were born, not of blood, nor of the will of the flesh nor the will of man, but of God. John 1.11-13 NASB

Now there was a man of the Pharisees named Nicodemus, a member of the Jewish ruling council. He came to Jesus at night and said, "Rabbi, we know you are a teacher who has come from God. For no one could perform the miraculous signs you are doing if God were not with him." In reply Jesus declared, "I tell you the truth, no one can see the kingdom of God unless he is born again. John 3.1-3 NIV

He went on: "What comes out of a man is what makes him 'unclean.' For from within, out of men's hearts, come evil thoughts, sexual immorality, theft, murder, adultery, greed, malice, deceit, lewdness, envy, slander, arrogance and folly. All these evils come from inside and make a man 'unclean.'" Mark 7.20-23 NIV

Jesus replied and said, "A man was going down from Jerusalem to Jericho, and fell among robbers, and they stripped him and beat him, and went away leaving him half dead. "And by chance a priest was going down on that road, and when he saw him, he passed by on the other side. "Likewise a Levite also, when he came to the place and saw him, passed by on the other side. "But a Samaritan, who was on a journey, came upon him; and when he saw him, he felt compassion, and came to him and bandaged up his wounds, pouring oil and wine on them; and he put him on his own beast, and brought him to an inn and took care of him. "On the next day he took out two denarii and gave them to the innkeeper and said, 'Take care of him; and whatever more you spend, when I return I will repay you.' "Which of these three do you think proved to be a neighbor to the man who fell into the robbers' hands?" And he said, "The one who showed mercy toward him." Then Jesus said to him, "Go and do the same." Luke 10.30-37 NASB

Jesus said to them, "If God were your Father, you would love me, for I came from God and now am here. I have not come on my own; but he sent me. Why is my language not clear to you? Because you are unable to hear what I say. You belong to your father, the devil, and you want to carry out your father's desire. He was a murderer from the beginning, not holding to the truth, for there is no truth in him. When he lies, he speaks his native language, for he is a liar and the father of lies. Yet because I tell the truth, you do not believe me! Can any of you prove me guilty of sin? If I am telling the truth, why don't you believe me? He who belongs to God hears what God says. The reason you do not hear is that you do not belong to God. John 8.42-47 NIV

But these men blaspheme in matters they do not understand. They are like brute beasts, creatures of instinct, born only to be caught and destroyed, and like beasts they too will perish. 2 Peter 2.12 NIV

The children of God and the children of the devil are revealed in this way: all who do not do what is right are not from God, nor are those who do not love their brothers and sisters. I John 3.10

Sin is lurking at the door; its desire is for you, but you must master it." Genesis 4.7B

For we know that the law is spiritual; but I am of the flesh, sold into slavery under sin. I do not understand my own actions. For I do not do what I want, but I do the very thing I hate. Romans 7.14-15

God sent forth his Son, born of woman, born under the law, to redeem those who were under the law, so that we might receive adoption as children. And because you are children, God has sent the Spirit of his Son into our hearts, crying, "Abba! Father!" So through God you are no longer a slave but a child, and if a child then an heir, through God. Formerly, when you did not know God, you were enslaved to beings that by nature are not gods. Galatians 4.4b-8

But when Jesus heard this, He said, "It is not those who are healthy who need a physician, but those who are sick. "But go and learn what this means: 'I DESIRE COMPASSION, AND NOT SACRIFICE,' for I did not come to call the righteous, but sinners." Matthew 9.12-13 NASB

What man among you, if he has a hundred sheep and has lost one of them, does not leave the ninety-nine in the open pasture and go after the one which is lost until he finds it? "When he has found it, he lays it on his shoulders, rejoicing. "And when he comes home, he calls together his friends and his neighbors, saying to them, 'Rejoice with me, for I have found my sheep which was lost!' "I tell you that in the same way, there will be more joy in heaven over one sinner who repents than over ninety-nine righteous persons who need no repentance. Luke 15.4-7 NASB

I initially thought this topic of being children of God or children of the devil would be a clear choice between good and evil. However, as I researched more, I was surprised to learn that children belong to heaven, but after we humans mature past childhood, we are creatures of instinct in our natural carnal state; **our hearts are filled with evil from within**. Ouch! Jesus indicating we must be born again to see the Kingdom of God surprised me. Knowing that we are pre-condemned and we have a predisposition to evil was upsetting to me; I thought I was always a good guy. The Holy Bible has a reoccurring message that we are dead in sin and we must be born from above to enter the kingdom of God.

I humbly admit that I never understood why we humans must be born again or where evil originated until the evening I am typing this paragraph. God is teaching me details I miss as I type the chapters and He does not want to overexert my brain by giving me too much information at once. God is coaching me gently as I type this book. Now that my pastor and my wife each referred me to Revelations 12.7-10, and I found Job 1.7, I can move into the topic of where the devil came from. I am not necessarily a fast researcher, just a persistent one.

Revelations 12 explains the devil and his angels were spiritual beings living in Heaven; they were not flesh and blood like humans. Angel Michael and his fellow angels threw the devil and his evil angels out of Heaven to EARTH! Job 1.7 confirms and clarifies that Satan is roaming on the earth and is walking on it. We humans are living and walking on the earth also. Therefore, we coexist with Satan and his evil angels on earth. We humans exist as flesh and blood with a spiritual soul; Satan and his fallen angels exist as the spiritual forces of wickedness! The war between the devil, with his fallen angels, and the good angels in Heaven has been transferred to EARTH. We humans are now in a spiritual war against the spiritual forces of wickedness on earth. We humans, being both of the flesh and of the spirit, are in a war involving good and evil, God and Satan. Neutrality is not an option in this war. We are either for Jesus and oppose evil or embrace evil and are against Jesus. The sin of Adam and Eve against God established the sinful nature of humanity. Humans are born of man, born of the earth, influenced by Satan, and inclined toward evil.

Genesis 8.21 and John 1.11-13 are very powerful statements in scripture. Genesis 8.21 occurred after God caused the great flood and drowned the people of the earth except those in the ark. Noah then exited the ark, and made a burnt offering to God. God declared that the inclinations of our hearts are evil from childhood. This concept of being evil from childhood was foreign to me. Perhaps self-centered behavior is the same as carnal behavior or living in the flesh. John 1.11-13 indicates that Jesus was rejected by His own Jewish people, but was received by many others. God bestowed the right to be called children of God to those who believe in Him by being born again of God Himself. It is humbling that we can be born again, not of earthly parents, but born again as a child of the Creator of all, God.

Jesus describes what comes out of a human: evil thoughts, sexual immorality, theft, murder, adultery, greed, malice, deceit, lewdness, envy, slander, arrogance and folly. After reading Jesus' list of what comes out of a carnal human, those living in the flesh, also known as a creature of instinct, we can understand what is a child of the devil. **Shocking to me, without believing in God, we default to being children of the devil!** John declared the whole world lies under the power of the evil one.

Now I understand why many people are selfish in business, driving, and many aspects of everyday life; that is frightening. Understanding the whole world lies under the power of evil brings clarity and simultaneously a watchful recognition of the evil around us. Jesus listed evil thoughts first in the list of things coming out of the heart of man. Our brain must first conceive an evil thought to direct our bodies, including our tongue, to perform an evil deed. Evil thoughts are indeed the predecessor of evil deeds. It is prudent to resist our evil thoughts; this can prevent the escalation of an evil thought into evil deeds. By our sinful nature, we have the instinct to do evil. My two children did not share instinctively when they were infants. My wife and I taught our children to share. My children were not patient, they cried when they wanted their bottle or their diaper changed. My wife and I taught our child to wait.

As children become young adults an inborn sense of fairness evolves. Fairness involving selfish interests develops in both the evil and the good. A self-centered person is acutely aware of fairness. Thinking of fairness not only for oneself, but fairness toward others indicates the development of spiritual maturity. God instilled a conscience in humans and the ability to choose good or evil.

Jesus spoke with Nicodemus one night and provided insight regarding how to be a child of God. Jesus said we must be born again. Being born again involves believing in Jesus as our Savior and filling our hearts with the Holy Spirit of God, rather than our carnal instincts to sin. Although we choose Christ as our Savior, the temptation to sin remains. Being born again is the start of our journey toward holiness; being born again is not the completion of our spiritual journey.

In Matthew 4.1-10, the devil tempted Jesus three times after He spent forty days in the wilderness. The devil first tempted Jesus with the carnal instinct to eat bread. Next, the devil wanted Jesus to test God by throwing Himself off the pinnacle of the Temple. Thirdly, the Devil tempted Jesus to worship the devil in exchange for earthly power. Jesus never sinned.

The temptation of Jesus illuminates what Satan used to tempt Jesus. In addition, the temptation of Jesus revealed that the devil exists and the devil knows Jesus exists. Human beings acquired the knowledge of good and evil in the Garden of Eden, as documented in Genesis Chapter 3. Acknowledging Jesus exists does not imply salvation and eternal life; Satan himself knows Jesus and talked with Jesus! Hebrew 10.16 indicates being born again involves listening to the laws God put in our hearts and wrote on our minds. Being born again to be children of God involves loving and believing in Jesus and obeying his teaching.

When we are born again, we choose to minimize our sinful, carnal, and instinctive nature and begin to live in the spirit. Galatians Chapter 4 indicates we become adopted sons and daughters of God, children of God, when Jesus redeems us. John 1.11-13 provides another clear explanation of being born again; those that are born again become children of God, born not of flesh, but born of God! Jesus died on the cross as a perfect sacrifice for our sins.

Jesus explained the distinction of being born again as a child of God or being a child of the devil in John 3 and John 8, respectively. We each have the ultimate choice of being a child of the devil or living and believing in Jesus of Nazareth. Our choice in life is reviewed before the judgment seat of Christ and has eternal ramifications. Some people choose to be evil and follow the devil. Some people commit to be righteous and follow Jesus throughout their lives.

Jesus also spoke of coming for sick people and for lost people; these people are not totally committed to evil or righteousness. Let us first ponder the sick or broken people who need healing from the chief physician, Jesus.

Broken people may have lost their faith through pain. We all have basic requirements in life, including love, food, clothing, shelter, and work. When we lose something in life, it is natural to grieve. A person may become broken when events in their life shatter their self-confidence or their self-esteem. Bitterness and anger may fill the lives of the broken. The broken are similar to those in the Parable of the Sower, from Matthew 13. The broken are like seed that falls among rocky places. When affliction or persecution occurs, the broken fall away from faith.

Jesus also came to save the lost. The lost people may have never known God or may have known God and wandered away. Jesus seeks to find the lost and invite them back into His presence. The lost may not even understand that they need a savior. The lost are similar to those in the Parable of the Sower, from Matthew 13, whose seed was sown beside the road. The evil one snatched the seed of the kingdom that the lost did not understand. The lost must repent of their sins or face the consequences when they die. The lost seem to be more common in society. With the amount of stimulus in media and communication increasing, it is easier to not think about God. Unfortunately, I know many lost people personally. Many of the lost I know are college educated and kind people. Other lost people I know are less educated. I am trying to guide the lost to God, but they must make the choice themselves. However, the Holy Bible clearly states we do not gain salvation and enter Heaven by our deeds. Romans chapter 3 indicates we are forgiven by grace through faith in the redemption that is in Christ Jesus, by His sacrifice of atonement by his blood.

There may be a large number of lost, but ethical people. Outwardly, these lost people may appear to obey some of the commandments, such as not murdering, not stealing, and not committing adultery, however the motive is not to obey God, but to worship themselves. Lost ethical people may understand that:

- Murdering others is a crime punishable by life imprisonment or execution
- Stealing is a crime punishable by imprisonment
- Making false statements is perjury and may be a crime
- Vandalism is a crime
- Abusing one's neighbor physically is a crime
- Committing adultery will destroy one's marriage
- Harassing a coworker is a crime and may result in termination of employment
- Cheating customers is a crime and reduces repeat customers
- Being kind and friendly to people increases sales and profits
- Speaking to people in an assertive manner, without insulting them, is ultimately beneficial in attaining one's goal.

Some may act politely and not abuse their neighbor, but deny God. Those that deny God are not born again and are not children of God. Jesus plainly declares that no one can see the kingdom of God unless he is born again in John 3.1-3. We are justified by faith, not by works! Those who act in an ethical manner that conforms to social norms, but reject God, do not conform to the likeness of Jesus. The first four of the Ten Commandments indicate:

- We are not to have other gods before God
- We are not to make an idol, or worship an idol
- We are not to make wrongful use of the name of the Lord your God
- We are to remember the Sabbath and keep it holy.

Those who reject the Lord God may have placed themselves as a god before the Lord God. Those who reject God may worship the idol of earthly power, money, or themselves. Those who reject God may use the Lord's name inappropriately; they may blame Him, but give Him no praise. Those who reject God have no intention of keeping the Sabbath holy. No matter how polite and kind people may act, all have sinned and fall short of the glory of God. Those who reject God are sinners who may be guilty of breaking at least three commandments of God and not repenting. Those who reject God choose this world and reject eternal life in Heaven!

Jesus came to earth to save the broken and the lost. When Jesus returns, the division will be between the children of the devil and the children of God. The lost and the broken will be judged to be the wheat or the chaff.

"He who is not with Me is against Me; and he who does not gather with Me scatters." Matthew 12.30 NASB

To be a Child of God, Jesus commands us to show mercy on our neighbors. The parable by Jesus recorded in Luke 10 explains worthless honoring with lips versus loving one's neighbor. Jesus tells of a man traveling to Jericho who was robbed, beaten, and left half dead. A priest saw the injured man and crossed to the other side of the road to avoid becoming involved. A Levite, a person from a religious Jewish tribe, did not attend to the injured man, but rather crossed to the other side. A Samaritan, considered not part of the chosen people, cared for the injured man. The Samaritan bandaged the injured man and took care of him. Jesus asked who was a neighbor to the injured man. The expert of the law replied to Jesus the one who showed mercy. Children of God build up, help, and love their neighbors.

Let us pray. Heavenly Father, thank you for inviting us to be your adopted children, children of God! Through our carnal and sinful nature, we are children of the devil and creatures of instinct. Only by being born again and becoming your adopted child do we begin to understand love, peace, contentment, righteousness, and are invited into eternal life in Heaven. It is from Jesus' love and sacrifice that we are saved from eternal death, not our works. Amen

# CHAPTER 22

# Peace in Heaven; Struggles on Earth

Then to Adam He said, "Because you have listened to the voice of your wife, and have eaten from the tree about which I commanded you, saying, 'You shall not eat from it'; cursed is the ground because of you; in toil you will eat of it all the days of your life. Both thorns and thistles it shall grow for you; and you will eat the plants of the field; by the sweat of your face you will eat bread, till you return to the ground, because from it you were taken; for you are dust, and to dust you shall return." Genesis 3.17-19 NASB

Be of sober spirit, be on the alert your adversary, the devil, prowls around like a roaring lion, seeking someone to devour. I Peter 5.8 NASB

BLESSED IS THE KING WHO COMES IN THE NAME OF THE LORD; Peace in heaven and glory in the highest!" Luke 19.38b NASB

Do not think that I came to bring peace on the earth; I did not come to bring peace, but a sword. He who has found his life will lose it, and he who has lost his life for My sake will find it. Matthew 10.34, 39 NASB

Jesus said to them, "Truly, truly, I say to you, before Abraham was born, I am." Therefore they picked up stones to throw at Him, but Jesus hid Himself and went out of the temple. John 8.58-59 NASB

Beloved, I urge you as aliens and strangers to abstain from fleshly lusts which wage war against the soul. I Peter 2.11 NASB

"You will be hearing of wars and rumors of wars. See that you are not frightened, for those things must take place, but that is not yet the end." Matthew 24.6 NASB

But you have dishonored the poor man. Is it not the rich who oppress you and personally drag you into court? James 2.6 NASB

The Light has come into the world, and men loved the darkness rather than the Light, for their deeds were evil. John 3.19b NASB

If you were of the world, the world would love its own; but because you are not of the world, but I chose you out of the world, because of this the world hates you. John 15.19 NASB

"Blessed are you when people insult you, persecute you and falsely say all kinds of evil against you because of me. Rejoice and be glad, because great is your reward in heaven, for in the same way they persecuted the prophets who were before you. Matthew 5.11-12 NIV

So Jesus then said to them plainly, "Lazarus is dead." When Jesus therefore saw her weeping, and the Jews who came with her also weeping, He was deeply moved in spirit and was troubled. Jesus wept. John 11.14, 33, 35 NASB

Then Pilate said to the chief priests and the crowds, "I find no guilt in this man." Luke 23.4 NASB

And Herod with his soldiers, after treating Him with contempt and mocking Him, dressed Him in a gorgeous robe and sent Him back to Pilate. Luke 23.11 NASB

So Pilate said to Him, "You do not speak to me? Do You not know that I have authority to release You, and I have authority to crucify You?" As a result of this Pilate made efforts to release Him, but the Jews cried out saying, " If you release this Man, you are no friend of Caesar; everyone who makes himself out to be a king opposes Caesar." So he then handed Him over to them to be crucified. John 19.10, 12, 16 NASB

Peace I leave with you; my peace I give you. I do not give to you as the world gives. Do not let your hearts be troubled and do not be afraid. John 14.27 NIV

"I have told you these things, so that in me you may have peace. In this world you will have trouble. But take heart! I have overcome the world." John 16.33 NIV

When the Canaanite king of Arad, who lived in the Negev, heard that Israel was coming along the road to Atharim, he attacked the Israelites and captured some of them. Then Israel made this vow to the LORD: "If you will deliver these people into our hands, we will totally destroy their cities." The LORD listened to Israel's plea and gave the Canaanites over to them. They completely destroyed them and their towns; so the place was named Hormah. Numbers 21.1-3

Finally, be strong in the Lord and in the strength of His might. Put on the full armor of God, so that you will be able to stand firm against the schemes of the devil. For our struggle is not against flesh and blood, but against the rulers, against the powers, against the world forces of this darkness, against the spiritual forces of wickedness in the heavenly places. Ephesians 6.10-12 NASB

"While I was with you daily in the temple, you did not lay hands on Me; but this hour and the power of darkness are yours." Luke 22.53 NASB

Come to Me, all who are weary and heavy-laden, and I will give you rest. Take My yoke upon you and learn from Me, for I am gentle and humble in heart, and YOU WILL FIND REST FOR YOUR SOULS. Matthew 11.28-29 NASB

To keep me from becoming conceited because of these surpassingly great revelations, there was given me a thorn in my flesh, a messenger of Satan, to torment me. Three times I pleaded with the Lord to take it away from me. But he said to me, "My grace is sufficient for you, for my power is made perfect in weakness." 2 Corinthians 12.7-9a NIV

❖ ❖ ❖

Human beings, although made in God's image, are very different than God. We humans make mistakes, are carnal creatures of instinct, and learn to love others by training or by the grace of God. Each of us has the choice to be slaves of sin or choose to obey God and walk in righteousness. Genesis 3.17-19 explains that life on earth will be a struggle for human beings. God explained that the ground of the earth is cursed because of Adam and Eve's sin of disobeying God and eating of the tree of the knowledge of good and evil. Mankind must toil amongst the thorns and thistles to grow food. My wife suggested that poison ivy might be one of the thistles in life. We humans will only eat, and stay alive, by the sweat of our face. Ultimately we will die, return to the ground and return to dust! Genesis explains in meticulous detail that we will struggle against the world and work to stay alive. In addition to struggling by working, humans will struggle against illness and the wearing out of our bodies. Regardless if we work diligently and struggle against illness and the aging process, we will each die. The book of Genesis makes it very clear God is in charge and we are not.

If we survive the struggle with shelter, starvation, and illness, we will struggle against our fellow man. Thousands of years ago, King David prayed to God to deliver him from his enemies:

O God, hasten to deliver me; O LORD, hasten to my help! Let those be ashamed and humiliated Who seek my life; Let those be turned back and dishonored Who delight in my hurt. Psalm 70.1-2 NASB

A scripture verse on needing God when in trouble:

He restoreth my soul: he leadeth me in the paths of righteousness for his name's sake. Yea, though I walk through the valley of the shadow of death, I will fear no evil: for thou art with me; thy rod and thy staff they comfort me. Psalm 23.3-4 KJV

## Alpha Leaders

My wife and I have owned two or three dogs simultaneously for many years. I have a clear understanding that pack animals have an alpha leader, called the alpha dog. The instinctive social structure of dogs is carnal and appropriate for survival in the wild. If two or more dogs are together, the dogs will compete amongst themselves for power and one will emerge as the alpha dog. The alpha dog will actually dominate the other dogs. If one owns dogs as house pets, the human owner must take the role as the alpha leader of the pack. Similar to other pack animals, humans are carnal beings that will fight one another to establish themselves as the alpha leader. Dogs are typically honorable to one another when establishing the alpha leader. When the strongest dog approaches a weaker dog, the weaker dog may indicate it surrenders; dogs indicate surrender by lying on its back with its chest exposed. The stronger dog typically graciously accepts the surrender of the weaker dog. I have seen puppies instinctively surrender to any visiting adult dog to clearly communicate it is not a threat.

The human desire to be the alpha leader was demonstrated through the first sin of Adam and Eve. Adam and Eve wanted to have control equal to or exceeding God. Adam and Eve competed with God for control and power. Perhaps the craving in humans to have control and power over others is the primary source of struggles between all humans. If we all followed Jesus' command to love our neighbor as our self, struggles between people would be greatly reduced.

Humans may exhibit a wicked and vicious behavior when competing for the alpha leader position that surpasses that of animals. In the human competition for alpha leader, surrender may not even be requested. Cain murdered his brother Abel because God found favor with Abel's offering. There was no mention that Abel was competing with Cain. Rather than Cain make a suitable offering to God and achieve God's favor, Cain opted to murder his competition. The apostle John wrote in 1 John 3.11-12 that Cain killed Abel because Cain's deeds were evil and Abel's deeds were righteous. A righteous person may be murdered simply for being righteous and not evil!

Peace on earth is very difficult to achieve. Humans are born carnal creatures of instinct with a heart inclined toward evil.

For from within, out of the heart of men, proceed evil thoughts, adulteries, fornications, murders, thefts, covetousness, wickedness, deceit, lasciviousness, an evil eye, blasphemy, pride, foolishness: All these evil things come from within, and defile the man. Mark 7.21-23 KJV

By contrast, humans also have an understanding of righteousness, rightful ownership, protection of their loved ones, holy marriage, freedom, joy, contentment, and kindness. Humans having diametrically opposing inclinations:

- Evil versus righteousness
- Theft versus hard work and rightful ownership

- Murder versus protection of loved ones
- Adultery versus holy marriage
- Deeds of wickedness versus freedom to pursue joy
- Coveting versus contentment
- Deeds of deceit and slander versus kindness.

As I previously declared, **reciprocity is the test of fairness.** Any human being that treats someone in a wicked or unkind manner or steals from another will complain, protest, and be outraged if he or she is treated in a reciprocal manner. Humans know right from wrong. God Himself wrote His commandments on our minds. Carnal people may enjoy abusing others, but will whine if they are treated unkindly. Conflict and tension on an interpersonal level seem to be a natural part of mankind's fallen nature.

Many years ago, when my physician son was in grade school, he was a miniature doctor in training. My son enjoyed baseball, music, travel, the arts, and museums. To balance our son's artistic and cerebral behavior with athletic ability and physical coordination, my wife and I enrolled our son, along with our daughter, in martial arts school. I joined the martial arts program with my children to assist in training them. After numerous years of training three times weekly, my daughter earned a red belt and my son and I attained red black belts in Tae Kwon Do. My son grew into a polite young intellectual and martial artist long before high school. My son's classmates had known he was a martial artist and he lived a peaceful childhood free of harassment. One summer, my wife and I sold our home in the country and moved to an upscale suburb with an excellent school system. My wife and I purchased a larger home in a good suburb to raise and educate our family.

When fall came, our son and daughter began attending the new school. At first all seemed well. After a few weeks at the new school, my previously tranquil son seemed stressed. When asked, my son indicated he was not troubled. Within a month of attending the new school, he was feeling sick to his stomach before and after classes. After our son's stressed state and upset stomach could no longer be ignored, he finally responded to our repeated questions concerning his emotional state. Our son indicated a bully was tormenting him at school. As a fellow male, and one who understands carnal man's inclination to dominate in an abusive and brutal manner, I sadly acknowledged that every inclination of a human's heart is evil from childbirth. If a person does not choose to live according to the Spirit, he lives according to the flesh. I told my son that he must tell the bully to stop tormenting him immediately; if the bully continued, my son must defend himself. My son looked at me as if I said something crazy. My son asked, "Dad, do you want me to fight?" I replied, "Son, I love you and you must defend yourself or the tormenting will not stop." I reviewed several martial arts sparing techniques with my son and told him to fight the bully the next time the bully bothered him. The next day the bully punched my son in the back. My son, wise beyond his physical age, understood he must neutralize the abuse, but not escalate the situation to a higher level of hostility. My son responded by punching the bully in the face with one properly placed tight horizontal fist with sufficient acceleration and momentum. My son paused after his single punch to the bully's face, entered into a martial arts fighting stance, and looked at the bully.

My son had years of training in the martial arts to punch an attacker in the face with his right hand, punch the attacker's throat with his left hand, then do an elbow strike to the left temple of the attacker to disorient him. Once the attacker was dazed, my son could have delivered various kicks and punches to cause severe or permanent physical damage to the bully. However, my son was a child of God and knew his life was not in danger at that time. Being a child of God, and not a child of the devil is always a split second choice we each must make repeatedly in life. My son chose to place a single punch, stop, and wait. After a few moments, the bully ran past my son crying in retreat and never bothered my son again. The bully respected my son for being honorable. The bully had to know that my son chose to land one punch and wait to see his reaction; my son had sufficient training and stamina to have easily retaliated with revenge involving dozens of punches and kicks. My son inspired me with the clarity of the choice between being a child of God or a child of the devil. My son wisely spoke that we must respond when we are attacked, but with the least amount of force needed to neutralize, but not escalate the situation. As a physician, my son has much better verbal skills than me. When a patient or colleague speaks to my son with malice, he is able to verbally deflect the hostility with humor and neutralize the attack. I am not able to think quickly enough to diffuse a verbally hostile attack with humor. As one who thinks as slow as a turtle, I tend to respond to verbal wickedness with a wicked tongue myself or at best, a blunt rebuke.

## Local Struggles

Remembering the story of the bully and my son generates an emotion of sadness in my heart. My wife and I sold our home and moved to a better school system to give our children more educational opportunities. Rather than finding peace and more opportunities for education in an affluent community, we found that all humans, even children, either choose to treat others as they would like to be treated or choose evil. The tormenting of my son by a bully in school provided clarity that mankind's carnal instincts to control, over-power, abuse, dominate, covet, steal, and murder will prevent peace from occurring on earth without installing systems to promote peace. I became a police volunteer after the 9/11/2001 terrorist attack of the Twin Towers in New York City. A police officer is also called a peace officer. People have known, since Cain murdered his brother Abel, that humans have the choice to love God and love their neighbor or ignore the laws of God placed in their hearts and harm their neighbor. Peace officers and police forces were created by civilized societies to keep the peace. Police officers are not soldiers to fight invading enemies; peace officers limit the acts of evil done by people within the society to one another at times of "peace."

Mankind's self-centeredness and desire to treat others with malice can be somewhat controlled by the threat of pain and dominance by another. Evil behavior is punished by the coordinated efforts of police officers and the judicial system. Wrong doers may incur any of the following repercussions: hand cuffed during the arrest process, required to pay a financial punishment, seizure of their property, jail time, or ultimately execution. A civilized society attempts to minimize evil acts by the threat of punishment and actually dispensing punishment as necessary.

Unrighteous people with authority may gravitate to abuse others. Luke chapter 23 records that Pontius Pilot knew that Jesus was an innocent man that was guilty of no crimes. John chapter 19 indicates that Pilate told Jesus that he has the authority to release or crucify Jesus. Pilate then knowingly and willfully had a guiltless Jesus crucified! John 19.12 details that perhaps Pilate decided to authorize the murder of Jesus for a political advantage with Caesar and the outspoken Pharisees!

I have pondered for many years what is the primary root cause of emotional stress between humans. Jesus clearly explained the primary root cause of emotion stress between humans in three words in Luke 22.53: "power of darkness." I swiftly passed across these words on my numerous times listening to or reading the Gospels. It was only when I pondered these three words, with the help of the Holy Spirit, did the powerful meaning become unveiled. Humans are either acting for God or against God, there is no middle ground. The power of the Holy Spirit is used in positive creativity and to act in righteousness. Teaching and mentoring others demonstrates Godly goodness.

When someone is using their power to treat others in a manner he or she would not want to be treated, the power is from darkness. Directing or controlling others to demonstrate authority, coerce others, or dishonor one's neighbor is rooted in the power of darkness. Jesus identified his pending torture and murder as examples of the power of darkness. The power of darkness is present when people dominate or control others to dishonor or physically harm another. The power of darkness may be demonstrated when someone hurtfully excludes another. The power of darkness is present when someone abuses his or her authority to unfairly treat another to flaunt his or her authority. The power of darkness was demonstrated when Jesus was murdered to try to silence his teachings and to try to stop others from following Jesus. Jesus permitted the power of darkness to reign momentarily, but his resurrection from the dead won the battle with sin and death. We must each be aware when the power of darkness is being waged against God, the children of God, and righteousness. We must take our stand against the devil's schemes.

John 3.19 indicates the children of darkness hate the light; when the light shines on them, the light exposes their evil deeds. The power of darkness also includes deeds done by cowards, who hide their deeds in the cover of darkness and anonymity. The people of the light are aware that God knew us before we were born. The people of the light know there is nowhere to hide from God. Only the cowardly children of darkness think they can cloak their evil deeds in darkness and anonymity. Slanderous or hurtful words written or spoken in cowardly anonymity are from the power of darkness. On the Day of Judgment we will be justified or condemned by our words, words conveyed in darkness and anonymity or in the light.

Struggles Related to Work

Genesis 3.19, Matthew 25. 14-30, and 2 Thessalonians 3.7-11 teach that humans must work to eat; those too lazy to work are not to eat. A properly operated business may actually promote peace and cooperation among workers. Workers in a functioning business must cooperate to produce a quality product and achieve sales. Workers that quarrel with coworkers or are unproductive are terminated. Workers attending a board meeting to solve problems and achieve results must work in peaceful cooperation to maintain their employment, maintain productivity and earn profits. The agricultural systems mentioned in the Bible are very applicable to our lives. Workers who do not plant or harvest are worthless. In my job as an engineering manager, I frequently have conference calls with my colleagues in Italy, Ireland, Germany, and numerous cities in the United States. We carefully plan our efforts to manufacture products that our customers will purchase. The system of making and selling goods promotes teamwork and harmony. I wake up every weekday at 6:30 AM and drive in my automobile to my office. I work often until 6 PM. Why do my colleagues and I wake up every day, rain, snow, or sunshine to work? We work to be paid money as appreciation for a job well done. Suppliers of raw materials provide quality products with mutual respect to maintain our business relationship. Buying and selling items promotes a behavior that is good for society. Competition and a free economy promote good products and good service. Those that provide poor quality products or poor service will cease to exist because customers will migrate to better suppliers.

As the professions of humans have diversified from farming to manufacturing and business, perhaps the thorns and thistles may have diversified into hostile coworkers and unpleasant work environments. Following this command from Jesus Christ will help keep workers engaged in their work, productive, and content:

Treat others the same way you want them to treat you. Luke 6.31 NASB

Giving workers clear and attainable goals, and treating them with kindness and fairness enables workers to focus on accomplishing their job. When workers are treated unfairly, they will not focus on the work, but rather the work environment.

President Teddy Roosevelt made a profound statement regarding leadership:

The best executive is one who has sense enough to pick good people to do what he wants done, and self-restraint enough to keep from meddling with them while they do it.[14]

There is an inherent struggle with work itself. God told us in Genesis that we will eat by the sweat of our face. As society and technology changes, professions and entire industries may be eliminated or require adaptation. The demand for professions related to the widespread use of horses for personal transportation diminished as trains replaced horse travel. As automobiles and airplanes became more popular for travel than trains, employment shifted again. As much manufacturing shifted from the United States to China, the demand for manufacturing personnel and engineers decreased in the United States and increased in China. Acknowledging that we must adapt our occupations as society and technology changes may reduce our stress. The Holy Bible forewarns that working to eat will be a struggle.

National Struggles

The Holy Bible records that people will struggle against governments. Exodus 1-14 explains that the people of Israel migrated to Egypt. Pharaoh became concerned that the sons of Israel might fight against the government of Egypt. Pharaoh set task masters over the people and made them work as slaves. The people were forced to work as masons and farmers. Pharaoh ordered that infant male children of Israel be drowned in the river Nile at birth. The people of Israel groaned for freedom. God delivered the people of Israel from bondage in Egypt. The people of Israel formed their own government.

Kings ruled the twelve tribes of Israel. The Holy Bible documents in 1 Kings 12 that King Solomon, and then his son Rehoboam, burdened their people with heavy taxes and forced labor. The people of Israel rebelled against the government. Ten of the twelve tribes of Israel succeeded from King Rehoboam and formed Israel; the two remaining tribes, Benjamin and Judah, formed Judah.

As a society advances, the people form a civilization to protect themselves from invading societies. Civilizations may flourish when people have the ability to freely design, create and sell products. The free market promotes quality and efficiency through survival of the fittest.

If a government compromises the freedom of the people and becomes inefficient, excessive taxation seems likely to occur. The Holy Bible records that if a government continues to burden its people, the people will tend to struggle toward freedom from oppression.

International Struggles

In addition to inherent changes in technology, mankind's desire to steal, kill, and destroy may be on a international scale. The Holy Bible documents that war has been occurring for thousands of years and wars will continue. An offensive war is initiated by a society that is intent on murdering and conquering people and perhaps stealing their property. A defensive war is fought by those joined together to oppose another group of savages from stealing one's property, murdering loved ones, and assuming domination.

The book **Report From Iron Mountain on the Possibility and Desirability of Peace**[15] by Leonard C. Lewin provides interesting concepts on mankind's carnal instinct to fight and make war. Regardless if the book is a narrative from a secret government study group or a work from the private sector, the **Report From Iron Mountain** provides a unique insight into mankind's barbarian nature. The report explores the functions of war, and possible substitutions of war. War or the threat of war, in conjunction with a common enemy, politically stabilizes a nation. War or the threat of war, in conjunction with a common enemy, provides a sociological allegiance to fellow citizens and the government. By adding the alpha leader concept to the **Report From Iron Mountain,** perhaps the fear of a common enemy prompts man to accept the military leader as the alpha leader and not fight among themselves for status as the alpha leader.

Reading the **Report From Iron Mountain** inspired me to ponder war and domination relative to a carnal or born again person. The people in the United States seemed more kind to one another for the first few months immediately following the 9/11/2001 attacks. For a brief few months when people of the United States thought the country was under terrorist attack, loving your neighbor was desirable and acceptable behavior. Perhaps a carnal person feels less inclined to dominate, abuse, control, rob or murder a fellow citizen if a common enemy is trying to kill both him and his neighbor. If a carnal man robs his neighbor, his neighbor may be less inclined to join forces with the robber if legions of terrorists came marching down the street with machine guns to conquer the United States. A carnal man is less inclined to yell or fight his neighbor if he may need his neighbor to fight terrorists the next day. A born again person, filled with the Holy Spirit, will love his neighbor regardless if the nation is at war or at peace. Children of God may be kind without the real or imaginary threat a of common enemy preparing to kill us all; children of God may be kind without the expectation of kindness in return.

Police carrying deadly handguns reduces crime, but does not eliminate crime. The threat of death in war has not eliminated war. President Ronald Reagan, one of my favorite presidents, endorsed "Peace Through Strength."[16] Freedom is not free; freedom is earned and retained only through sacrifice. I am grateful to my father, who fought in World War II to oppose abuse, domination, and murder. My father was severely injured by a mortar, but survived the war. I am grateful to my late father-in-law for serving for South Korea's freedom. I am grateful to my brother for serving in Vietnam, and my late brother-in-law for serving and dying in Vietnam. I express sincere gratitude to all who serve for freedom and oppose evil.

It is prudent at this time to review the commandment listed in Exodus 20.13 "Thou shall not murder." The original King James Version translated the word as "kill." However, the New King James, the New International Version, the New American Standard Bible, and the New Revised Standard Bible all translate the word as "murder". The Holy Bible records that defending the innocent may involve killing in battle those who abuse, dominate, covet, steal, and murder. Numerous people have defended the innocent and established righteousness by fighting on the side of God and killed those who propagate the power of darkness. When the chosen people of God were about to be attacked by an invading army, David slung a stone at Goliath, hit him in the forehead, and then killed him with his own sword. The people of Israel fought many battles to survive. Numbers 21.1-3 records that the Canaanite King of Arad, heard that Israel was coming along the road to Atharim and sent his army to attack the Israelites. The LORD listened to Israel's plea and the Israelites completely destroyed them and their towns. War is horrible and complex. However, those who seek to abuse, dominate, rob, and murder others must be rebuked by force. God defended those being attacked and endorsed self-defense. God is the judge of nations.

After the fear of subsequent terrorist attacks subsided, United States citizens seemed to have less of a need for their neighbors. Years after 9/11/2001, my wife and I were at a shopping mall on a pleasant sunny day in this land of the free. I drove our automobile down an aisle, found a person exiting a spot, and waited for the vacancy. As the person backed out and pulled away, I pulled into the spot. Another driver from the opposite direction noticed the spot and attempted to race me to the spot, but I had already pulled in. I noticed the other driver sulking, waiting, and watching us exit our automobile. After we exited our vehicle and walked toward the mall, the driver sounded her car horn and sped toward us as if she wanted to run us over with her car. She adjusted the path of her sport utility vehicle to nearly miss us and chose not to murder us because I found the vacant parking spot first. Unfortunately, the **Report From Iron Mountain** seems to be accurate in the assessment that war facilitates social organization.[15] Allegiance in society appears to be predicated on a common enemy. With no fear of a common enemy, humans may fight to be the dominant alpha leader and have no need for allegiance to one another.

The fallen nature of man creates wars and struggles on multiple levels. Our human life on earth is not one of peace; Matthew 10.34-36 indicates there will be divisions among family members who are saved and unsaved and Matthew 24.6 states there will be wars and rumors of wars.

God is the Alpha and the Omega

**A mature Christian grows to understand that God is the alpha leader of all.** The mature Christian understands that God said "I am the Alpha and the Omega" in Revelations 1.8. Petty squabbles between humans might be insignificant relative to eternity. While we are living in human form, we must survive in society; however, the Christian knows God is the one Alpha leader.

Studying the actions of Jesus recorded in the Holy Bible provides much insight. For my first fifty years, I had serious misconceptions about Jesus. The more I read Jesus' words in detail, the more I actually understood Jesus is powerful, wise, articulate, proactive, and an excellent communicator. Jesus' harsh words to people behaving badly caused me to stand up and cheer when I read them for the first time. When I first taught my daughter, then a teenager, that the Holy Bible records that Jesus called numerous people hypocrites, my daughter thought I was teasing her. Matthew 23.28 records that Jesus referred to the Pharisees as hypocrites. Jesus boldly rebuked the wicked. Perhaps I inappropriately associated Jesus' dying on the cross with passivity and being a victim; those are not the characteristics of Jesus. Yes, Jesus was crucified and was murdered in a time span approximately between the third hour and the ninth hour, nine o'clock in the morning until three o'clock in the afternoon. Jesus was crucified for six horrible hours of great suffering. However, Jesus indicated, in Matthew 26.53, that he could call upon His Father to send twelve legions of angels to rescue Him. Jesus is a hero who lay down His life for us sheep.

"For this reason the Father loves Me, because I lay down My life so that I may take it again. No one has taken it away from Me, but I lay it down on My own initiative I have authority to lay it down, and I have authority to take it up again. This commandment I received from My Father." John 10.17-18 NASB

I pause here to share what I am experiencing as I type this chapter regarding Jesus' actions as a man. As the midnight hour approaches, my body grows tired from working as an engineering manager during the day and writing a book on Jesus at night. As I formulate words to explain that Jesus was a courageous, assertive, and outspoken man on earth, I begin to feel an overwhelming fear of my incompetence and unworthiness to write about God Almighty. I am not worthy to write this chapter explaining our interactions with God and man; perhaps I am not worthy to write any part of this book. A paralyzing sense of complete incompetence and complete unworthiness overcomes me and I stop typing. Gently, I begin to sense the Holiness of God in my soul and around me as I sit in still silence. A supernatural clarity comes to my mind that I am indeed unworthy to write **Jesus is Our Friend**; I am unworthy to be in God's presence and I am a dirty carnal creature of instinct myself! My eyes fill with tears as I pause, enveloped in God's Holy Spirit and I feel ashamed of all my flaws and sins. I am ashamed that Jesus died for my sins, and I feel totally unworthy to be in the spiritual presence of the purity of the Holy One. I tell God I am not worthy to write a book on His behalf. God reveals that all have sinned and fall short of the glory of God, it is only through faith that we are saved. Gently, I feel a supernatural peace fill my soul. I gain a clear understanding that I am indeed a foolish mortal sinful man and a creature of instinct; however, I am trying to give God glory and share God's Good News. I write this book as a forgiven sinner, NOT as one who has achieved Holiness! I feel very relieved. I do not need to be perfect to write this book; I can never be perfect on my own. God loves me as I am. God guides me to keep typing my words for **Jesus is Our Friend** based on His Word recorded in the Holy Bible and I will stand in righteousness. He gently prompts me to return to the assignment He has given me. I type this paragraph and resume writing.

Jesus is strong and stands firm in opposition to the forces of darkness and the spiritual forces of wickedness. Jesus won the war against sin by His sacrificial death and resurrection to give us life after death.

As I mentioned, several years ago, my wife and I hosted a Japanese high school girl for a school year. Nana previously had never considered believing in God and no one had taught her the Gospel of Jesus. My wife and I had the honor of teaching the gospel to Nana. The Holy Spirit and Nana are still interacting as she completes her education as a physician. My wife and I enjoyed discussing the cultures of Japan and the United States.

My wife and I subsequently hosted an exchange student from a communist Asian country a few years later. Our second exchange student had no doubts regarding the existence of God; she was positive there was no God. Her rulers placed their laws in her mind and she had no interest for the laws of God. My wife and I did indeed learn about an atheist culture, but we did not enjoy the experience. Interacting with a true athiest for nine months was a painful educational experience. Like the good Samaritian, my wife and I gave her a home to live in, fed her, and provided transportation to school activities. Observing the behavior of my atheist guest provided me with a clearer understanding of being a Christian. An atheist thinks a human being is a body in the flesh; there is no spiritual and eternal soul.

With no God, day to day life for an atheist centers on one's self-interest and perhaps the government as a law giver and ruler. From personal experience, I say loving someone who does not value me as a living entity created in God's image, with an eternal soul, is difficult. We loved our athiest guest as a human being, but living with her behavior was challenging. I can not generalize that all athiests do not value human life. However, her training was apparent in her behavior. One day my wife and I arrived to pick her up from a school play reheral and saw an ambulance drive away. When we inquired if someone was injured, she replied, "A boy fell and hurt his leg, but he was no one important. Someone else can take his place and the play will go on." My wife and I were stunned with her indifference to the value of human life.

The foundation of valuing human beings is God. Knowing God created human beings in His image and we have an eternal soul is the origin of loving our neighbor. Without God, a false god is necessary to fill the void in the human soul, such as education, wealth, power, or position in society. In an atheistic view, perhaps a human being, an automobile, and a piano are perceived as having equal value. Perhaps our guest would have been more disturbed if the piano had broken, requiring the reheral to be cancelled.

Living with an atheist in our home for nine months taught me much about my values regarding loving God and loving our neighbor. It is difficult to explain, but I truly perceived our atheist guest did not value my human life. There was no concern of me as a person with a soul; my only value to her pertained to providing food, transportation, and housing. I prayed for weeks to understand what lesson I learned from our atheist guest and found the answer in scripture:

For those who are according to the flesh set their minds on the things of the flesh, but those who are according to the Spirit, the things of the Spirit. Romans 8.5 NASB

An atheist lives according to the flesh and assigns worth according to the flesh. In dramatic contrast, Christians live according to the Spirit and are to focus on two commands, loving God and loving your neighbor.

It is prudent we understand that until carnal life on earth ends, the battle between good and evil, interpersonal disputes, and war will continue. Jesus said in Matthew 24.6 that there will be wars and rumors of war, but this is not the end. The need for law, police officers, and armies will continue.

Spiritual Struggles

Christians are to be the light in a dark fallen world. Jesus went into the world and ate with sinners and tax collectors to be a beacon of light, to teach and to share the good news. We walk amongst the people of the earth as aliens in the war against the soul. We are commanded to love our neighbor. In addition to loving our neighbors, we are to serve and do good works to give glory to God our Father. When a parent loves a child, the parent wants to teach the child to act appropriately. If a child tells a lie, the loving parent will rebuke the child and tell the child not to lie. If a child acts in a selfish manner to others, a loving parent will rebuke the child and tell the child to share. Rebuking those who mistreat us is a sign of love.

Jesus indicated in John 15.19 that the world loves it own, but the world hates those chosen by Jesus. If we understand that Christians may be hated because we are Christians, we acknowledge reality. Jesus called numerous teachers of the law and Pharisees hypocrites and informed them of their evil ways. We are not to be timid in the world. We are to rebuke those who sin against us. Love involves a balance between rebuking and forgiving. We are to turn the other cheek if we are slapped, but we only have two cheeks. Be patient with others, but do not have the delusion that all people are kind. Jesus walked away when workers at the temple were about to stone Him; Jesus had more to accomplish. If another sins repeatedly against us and does not repent, have nothing to do with them.

Warn a divisive person once, and then warn him a second time. After that, have nothing to do with him. Titus 3.10 NIV

In addition to earthly wars for material possessions and earthly domination, we are also in a spiritual war. Ephesians 6.10-12 explains that we are in a struggle against the world forces of this darkness and the spiritual forces of wickedness.

Scripture uses words in very powerful ways. People of God are indeed in a struggle against the spiritual forces of wickedness. If a person describes herself as spiritual, but not affiliated with God, she could endorse the spiritual forces of wickedness. Regardless if people accept the existence of good and evil, we are in a spiritual war. A follower of God follows the Spirit of God. Pagans and children of the devil are opposed to the spirit of God and are worshipping a false god.

As I continue to write this book, and slowly approach a likeness of Jesus, the more the children of darkness openly hated me. I find it very difficult to love my enemies, but I am trying. It would be easier to hate my enemies than to love them. However, I am committed to staying on the narrow path to eternal life, but the road is long and difficult at times.

For our struggle is not against flesh and blood, but against the rulers, against the powers, against the world forces of this darkness, against the spiritual forces of wickedness in the heavenly places. Ephesians 6.12 NASB

The devil and his many followers want to tell lies, and steal, kill, and destroy all that is good. The apostle Paul was precisely correct in declaring that we are in a struggle with the world forces of darkness. It seems to me that too many people are self-absorbed in the desire for earthly treasures and earthly powers, and they are unaware there is an ongoing war between righteousness and the spiritual forces of wickedness. We must put on the full armor of God, the helmet of salvation, and grasp the sword of the Spirit, which is the word of God, to stand firm against the schemes of the devil.

Struggles with Possessions
"Do not store up for yourselves treasures on earth, where moth and rust destroy, and where thieves break in and steal. But store up for yourselves treasures in heaven, where neither moth nor rust destroys, and where thieves do not break in or steal; for where your treasure is, there your heart will be also." Matthew 6.19-21 NASB

I understand what Jesus said on multiple levels as an older person now. My wife and I saved our money for several years, bought and sold our starter homes, then ultimately moved to a suburban home. We made house payments for fifteen years and all was well. For the first time in over thirty years of marriage, we started to accumulate a little surplus money in our savings account! A strong wind came one day and tore off a ten foot section of roofing from our home. After requesting several quotes, it was obvious our roof aged and it needed to be replaced. We replaced our roof at a cost of two months pay. Within a year of our roof being replaced, the "new" "durable" clothes dryer we purchased eight years ago broke for the second time and we replaced it. Within a month of the clothes dryer breaking, the clothes washer machine started leaking from the main seal; we replaced the clothes washing machine. We then learned hot water heaters often last thirteen years as our water heater started leaking; that too was replaced. After buying a new roof and three major appliances, our surplus saving was nearly depleted. These are concrete examples of Jesus' warning: do not store up treasures on earth where moth or rust destroy. The longer we live, the more we see our possessions become destroyed over time.

Nature reveals all of life is in tension. The moon remains in orbit around the earth because the gravity of the earth is equal to the centrifugal acceleration of the moon. A suspension bridge does not collapse because the tension on the cables oppose gravity. Those who love God and those who do not love God are in tension.

In the book, **Awareness** by Anthony de Mello, Mr. de Mello indicated that happiness might be more readily attained if one rejects society's conditions for happiness.[17] I thoroughly agree that life is more peaceful when one embraces the principles found in the Holy Bible. Mr. de Mello proposed that problems in the life of humans are caused by improper expectations in one's mind and that people create some their own problems; people suffer when their expectations do not agree with reality. Mr. de Mello profoundly indicated that we humans may increase our joy by limiting the biases created by society that serve as prerequisites to our happiness. Making our success and happiness conditional on achieving a certain rank in the workplace or owning a certain type of automobile will delay and impede happiness. Ironically, achieving the job rank or buying the certain type of automobile may not make us happy either! Things will not make us happy.

God created us humans with emotions that cannot be eliminated, no matter how hard we try. Followers of Jesus love people and feel sadness when a loved one dies. Although I acknowledge death is inevitable, I feel emotional pain when a loved one dies. Jesus Himself was troubled when He saw Mary and others weeping because Lazarus died; Jesus Himself wept. Although I fully acknowledge and accept I have a chronic breathing disease, I physically and emotionally suffer when I am suffocating. We each have both a body and soul while we live. Our body will cause us to suffer when we cannot breathe in sufficient air. Our bodies will feel stress without water, sleep, or food. Our souls will ache when a loved one is ill or dies.

Jesus clearly declared that we will experience trouble in this world. However, Jesus told us how to find rest for our souls. Jesus invites us to come to Him when we are weary and heavy-laden. Jesus offers to teach us how to have peace in our souls. The apostle Paul had a troubling thorn in the flesh. Paul was tormented by a thorn in his flesh and prayed to God to heal him. God did not heal Paul the first time he prayed. Paul pleaded with God a second and third time to remove his thorn in the flesh.

God did not heal Paul's body; God told Paul:

"My grace is sufficient for you, for my power is made perfect in weakness."
2 Corinthians 12.9a

Jesus did not preach that His followers will be healthy, wealthy, and wise! Please do not be shocked and angry with God if one encounters troubles and struggles in life after giving one's life to Jesus. Jesus provides the gift of grace to help us endure challenges in life. God also has other Godly people available to help us. God provides healing through clergy, physicians, therapists, dentists, other professionals, and common children of God to work in concert with His grace.

Therefore put on the full armor of God, so that when the day of evil comes, you may be able to stand your ground, and after you have done everything, to stand. Stand firm then, with the belt of truth buckled around your waist, with the breastplate of righteousness in place, and with your feet fitted with the readiness that comes from the gospel of peace. In addition to all this, take up the shield of faith, with which you can extinguish all the flaming arrows of the evil one. Take the helmet of salvation and the sword of the Spirit, which is the word of God. Ephesians 6.13-17 NIV

If God is for us, who can be against us? Romans 8.31b NIV

Let us end in prayer. Dear Heavenly Father, we come before you as humble servants. It is only by the sweat of our face that we eat bread, until we return to the ground. We acknowledge our struggle is against the rulers of this world, the forces of darkness and the spiritual forces of wickedness. Please give us the strength and courage to flourish and be an advocate for good on earth. Heavenly Father, you know our enemies, please disrupt their evil schemes against your people. Please give us your grace to yield the sword of the Spirit, which is the word of God, to rebuke the enemies of righteousness. LORD, please give us the wisdom to never forget that You, God, are the all-powerful alpha leader. A sparrow does not fall to the ground apart from the Father. The Lord God is the Almighty Alpha and the Omega. Your grace keeps us strong God when we are weak.

For I am convinced that neither death, nor life, nor angels, nor principalities, nor things present, nor things to come, nor powers, nor height, nor depth, nor any other created thing, will be able to separate us from the love of God, which is in Christ Jesus our Lord. Romans 8.38-39 NASB

# CHAPTER 23

# Discerning Good and Evil

Then the LORD God said to the woman, "What is this you have done?" And the woman said, "The serpent deceived me, and I ate." Genesis 3.13 NASB

The thief comes only to steal and kill and destroy; I came that they may have life, and have it abundantly. John 10.10 NASB

When the devil had finished every temptation, he left Him until an opportune time. Luke 4.13 NASB (Him is referring to Jesus.)

Discipline yourselves, keep alert. Like a roaring lion your adversary the devil prowls around, looking for someone to devour. I Peter 5.8

As a result, we are no longer to be children, tossed here and there by waves and carried about by every wind of doctrine, by the trickery of men, by craftiness in deceitful scheming; Ephesians 4.14 NASB

You are of your father the devil, and you want to do the desires of your father He was a murderer from the beginning, and does not stand in the truth because there is no truth in him Whenever he speaks a lie, he speaks from his own nature, for he is a liar and the father of lies. John 8.44 NASB

For everyone who does evil hates the Light, and does not come to the Light for fear that his deeds will be exposed. John 3.20 NASB

For everyone who partakes only of milk is not accustomed to the word of righteousness, for he is an infant. But solid food is for the mature, who because of practice have their senses trained to discern good and evil. Hebrews 5.13-14 NASB

"But while his men were sleeping, his enemy came and sowed tares among the wheat, and went away. But when the wheat sprouted and bore grain, then the tares became evident also. 'Allow both to grow together until the harvest; and in the time of the harvest I will say to the reapers, First gather up the tares and bind them in bundles to burn them up; but gather the wheat into my barn.' The field is the world; and as for the good seed, these are the sons of the kingdom; and the tares are the sons of the evil one." Matthew 13.25, 26, 30, 38 NASB

You let your mouth loose in evil And your tongue frames deceit. Psalm 50.19 NASB

For out of the heart come evil thoughts, murders, adulteries, fornications, thefts, false witness, slanders. Matthew 15.19 NASB

The good man out of the good treasure of his heart brings forth what is good; and the evil man out of the evil treasure brings forth what is evil; for his mouth speaks from that which fills his heart. Luke 6.45 NASB

But Jesus asked him, "Judas, are you betraying the Son of Man with a kiss?" Luke 22.48 NIV

People will be lovers of themselves, lovers of money, boastful, proud, abusive, disobedient to their parents, ungrateful, unholy, without love, unforgiving, slanderous, without self-control, brutal, not lovers of the good, treacherous, rash, conceited, lovers of pleasure rather than lovers of God— having a form of godliness but denying its power. Have nothing to do with them. 2 Timothy 3.2-5 NIV

Behold, I send you out as sheep in the midst of wolves; so be shrewd as serpents and innocent as doves. Matthew 10.16 NASB

But those who want to get rich fall into temptation and a snare and many foolish and harmful desires which plunge men into ruin and destruction. 1 Timothy 6.9 NASB

Do not let any unwholesome talk come out of your mouths, but only what is helpful for building others up according to their needs, that it may benefit those who listen.

Ephesians 4.29 NIV

He said to His disciples, "It is inevitable that stumbling blocks come, but woe to him through whom they come! "It would be better for him if a millstone were hung around his neck and he were thrown into the sea, than that he would cause one of these little ones to stumble." Luke 17.1-2 NASB

There are six things the LORD hates, seven that are detestable to him:
haughty eyes,
a lying tongue,
hands that shed innocent blood,
a heart that devises wicked schemes,
feet that are quick to rush into evil,
a false witness who pours out lies
and a man who stirs up dissension among brothers. Proverbs 6.16-19 NIV

"For God did not give us a spirit of timidity, but a spirit of power, of love and of self-discipline." 2 Timothy 1.7 NIV

Most of our daily activities are tangible, such as praising God, serving others, family fellowship, earning an income, maintaining a home, recreation, commuting, and sleeping. If we do not schedule time to read the Holy Bible and talk with God, we can condition ourselves to not listen for God's guidance. Thinking about and talking with God one hour weekly is insufficient.

For those who are according to the flesh set their minds on the things of the flesh, but those who are according to the Spirit, the things of the Spirit. Romans 8.5 NASB

Living and thinking primarily in the world will likely cause us to minimize our thoughts regarding things of the spirit. God created us humans with a longing for Him, like a deer pants for water. However, we have the ability to harden our hearts and close out God's words. Living according to the flesh will cause one to set their minds on things of the flesh.

Setting our minds on the Spirit of God will nudge us to live according to the Spirit. When we first commit our lives to Jesus, we are infants in

Christ. Believers in Christ often start their spiritual journey obeying the Ten Commandments. Christians who follow the teachings of Jesus and study scripture are on a spiritual journey to become mature in their faith. Mature Christians gain a spiritual understanding of more abstract concepts regarding good and evil. Mature Christians, who live in the physical world, but also embrace the spiritual world of Christianity, perceive good and evil in their daily lives. Jesus clearly told people to live in righteousness.

Jesus commanded that we are to be as shrewd as serpents and innocent as doves, as we live amongst the wolves in life on earth. The evil one or his followers have also been compared to a roaring lion, chaff, or tare, also known as weeds. Jesus told a parable that the world is a field; wheat represents the sons of the kingdom, and the tare, or weeds, are the sons of the evil one. The wheat and the tare are allowed to grow together until the harvest, which is death. In this brief, but profound metaphor, Jesus explained that the sons of the kingdom and the sons of the evil one live together in the field of life. To live shrewdly as wheat among the tare, it is best to understand the goals and activities of our evil enemies.

Jesus summed up the law and the prophets with two commandments found in Matthew 22.37-40 and explained how to love your neighbor in Luke 6.31 NASB:

- Love God with all your heart, soul, and mind
- Love your neighbor as yourself
- Treat others the same way you want them to treat you.

Perhaps the goals and activities of the forces of evil can be summed up as follows:
- Disobey and hate God with all one's heart, soul, and mind
- Hate one's neighbor
- Treat others the way one would not want to be treated.

Evil can be described as spiritual forces of wickedness that are in opposition to the Way, the Truth, and the Light of God.

The actions of evil seem to have not changed much from the beginning. The foundation of the ability to decipher good and evil should include knowledge of the methodology of evil. Scripture teaches that the forces of evil come to:

| | |
|---|---|
| Control | Exert Power of Darkness |
| Tempt | Oppose (adversary) |

| | |
|---|---|
| Hate | Envy |
| Steal | Dishonor |
| Lie | Devour |
| Destroy | Kill |
| Hide | Scheme |
| Cause dissention | Be arrogant |
| Accuse | Abuse |
| Deceive | |

God told Adam and Eve they may eat freely from any tree in the garden, but not to eat of the tree of the knowledge of good and evil. Eating of that tree would cause their death. Adam and Eve initially had no fear or shame, and would not die; Adam and Eve had a very pleasant life. The devil told Eve disobeying God would make her wise like God and she would not die. Adam and Eve believed the devil and ate of the tree of the knowledge of good and evil. Why did Adam and Eve risk God's wrath through disobedience? Adam and Eve ate of the one forbidden tree because of their desire for **control** and **power**. Adam and Eve did not want to be controlled by God or obey God; Adam and Eve wanted to specifically disobey God. The second motivation was power. Jesus refers to power in opposition to God as the **power of darkness**. Adam and Eve attempted to compete with God Himself for knowledge. Adam and Eve were displeased God possessed the knowledge of good and evil and they wanted to be as great as God. Perhaps the choice to yield to the carnal instincts for control and power prompted mankind's first sin and downfall. Mankind's craving for control and power over others has not diminished. We each feel the pain caused by others attempting to control us and exert power over us in our daily life, in our jobs, in our government, and in national conflicts.

Adam and Eve's sin had major consequences. Humans became mortal and disease entered our lives. The need for clothing, shelter, and the struggle to survive began when Eve and Adam disobeyed God and followed the devil. The devil's message of deception seems to have remained the same for thousands of years:

- Disobey God
- God's commands are not for mankind's benefit
- The consequences of disobeying God's commands are not real
- Mankind can elevate himself to be equal to God.

The devil's message of deception can be identified whenever there is a challenge to God's authority, truth, or sovereignty.

Telling lies is an integral part of the deceiving others. Jesus referred to the devil as the father of lies. The evil one and his children tell lies to manipulate the behavior of others to advance the forces of wickedness. Whenever a lie is being told in person or in the media, evil is involved.

Jesus indicated, in Luke 17.1-2, that it is inevitable that stumbling blocks, also known as temptation, will come into our lives! Temptation is the suggestion to commit sin; temptation may come from our own thoughts, by other humans, by the devil, or by something that triggers our minds to be tempted. Per Luke 17.1-2, Jesus sternly warns that it is better to be drowned at sea with a millstone around one's neck than to tempt children to sin! Temptation does not necessarily involve a lie or deception, but lies often accompany temptation. As recorded in Matthew 4, the evil one tempted Jesus to:

- Change stones into bread to eat; bread may be a metaphor for earthly goods
- Test God by throwing Himself off the pinnacle of the temple
- Worship the devil to have power over kingdoms in the world.

In addition to his lies, the temptations of the devil have been fairly consistent for thousands of years. Satan tempts us to live according to the flesh and set our minds on the things of the flesh. The devil also tempts us to test God's love for us. Life is often difficult. We are tempted to blame God for earthly struggles and perhaps reject God's love and all things holy. I have personally interacted with quite a few people who seemed to have joined with the forces of darkness for earthly power and treasures.

Evil is opposition to God and opposition to the children of God. The fruits of the Spirit are love, joy, peace, patience, kindness, gentleness, and self-control. The products of evil are hate, despair, discontentment, impatience, abusiveness, brutality, and carnal instinctive reactions. While I was writing the last few chapters of **Jesus is Our Friend**, I was afflicted with shingles, a painful adult reoccurrence of the chicken pox virus. Shingles causes pain to the nerves of the skin, muscle aches, and fatigue. Perhaps the devil was opposing and tormenting me to tempt me to lose faith in God and give up writing this book. I visited my physician and received a steroid injection and anti-viral medicine for seven days. I kept on writing this book throughout the duration of the inflammation. I was healed in only eight days. The devil may overtly oppose those trying to share the good news of God, but we must fight the good fight.

As a young man, I reacted to being mistreated with confusion. My confusion involved questioning if I was truly being mistreated and why. As I matured and trained myself to decipher good and evil, mistreatment is clearly identifiable without confusion. Jesus teaches us that the thief, perhaps a metaphor for evil in general, comes only to steal, kill, and destroy. The goal of evil is to simply steal, kill, and destroy. There is no complex and logical secret to understand. Despair, death of goodness, and destruction are the goals of evil.

When my daughter was in grade school, she joined a neighborhood swim team. One day after a swim race, she returned to her chair and discovered her eyeglasses were bent out of shape and deformed beyond repair. Whoever deformed my daughter's glasses did so to temporarily steal my daughter's vision and destroy her eyewear. As her dad, I spent two to three days' wages to purchase a new pair of eyeglasses for my daughter. Evil deeds are simply done to commit evil. Envy, abuse, and dishonor involve the devil's deception that hurting or destroying one's neighbor elevates the evildoer. The person who destroyed my daughter's eyeglasses did not elevate herself. An extreme example of envy, abuse, kill, and destroy is Cain murdering Abel. God was pleased with Abel's heartfelt offering. Cain envied Abel's relationship with God. Cain killing Abel did not benefit Cain, nor make God love Cain. There is nothing complex to understand when encountering evil behavior; there is nothing to be confused about. Evil comes to steal, kill, and destroy.

Scripture tells us evil can be manifested in the following:

1. The evil one himself, the devil. The devil is the father of lies. The devil comes to steal, kill and destroy.
2. Evil mouth. An evil mouth is also used to steal, kill, and destroy. An evil mouth seeks to steal treasures or happiness from others. An evil mouth lies, brutally insults others, slanders the innocent, is ungrateful, is conceited, degrades others, elevates the wicked, is boastful, is greedy, and stirs up dissension. An evil mouth conceals the truth to avoid helping others, tempts others, manipulates others, and causes confusion.
3. Evil thoughts. Evil thoughts are suggestions by our own heart; our hearts are inclined to evil since childhood. Evil thoughts are also temptations from the devil. Evil thoughts include conceit, discrimination, favoritism, jealousy, greed, and lust.
4. The tares in the field of wheat; the sons and daughters of the evil one, they are evil men and women.

5. Evil treasures. Evil treasures of evil people may include evil power gained by destroying righteous people and theft.

6. Evil schemes. Evil schemes are premeditated plans to do evil deeds. The devil deceived Eve and prompted the fall of mankind.

7. Evil gestures. God Himself hates evil gestures. A pompous expression with haughty eyes to insult those of lesser status is displeasing to God.

8. Evil deeds. Evil deeds may be involve overt physical actions, such as murder, adultery, fornication, theft, lies, persecution, brutality, deception, stirring up dissention, or worship of false gods.

   Evil deeds may be more abstract, such as treating others differently than that person would treat himself, abusing others, being ungrateful, being conceited, and being selfish.

The aforementioned manifestations of evil are illustrated many times in the Holy Bible. Luke 4.13 is a powerful statement: after the devil tempted Jesus numerous times, the devil left Jesus until an opportune time to return. Scripture teaches the devil is relentless in his pursuit to steal, kill, and destroy us. Passing through the narrow gate and ultimately enduring to the end in goodness is a struggle. Whatever our temptations may be, earthly idols of money or power, adultery, or any sin, the devil returns again and again in an attempt to separate us from God. If Jesus, with His supreme holiness, was repeatedly tested by the devil, we will be repeatedly tempted by the devil. When tempted, let us imitate Jesus and tell the devil:

Jesus said to him, "Away from me, Satan! For it is written: 'Worship the Lord your God, and serve him only.'" Matthew 4.10 NIV

It seems also that God's name is seldom mentioned in the mainstream media. However the word "god" is dramatically mentioned in the media when a murder kills someone and declared "god" told him to murder. Let me reiterate, there are false gods. God's first commandment is to have no other gods before Him, the second commandment is not worship an idol. If someone does not live and believe in God, repent, and be born again, the person will worship something, perhaps himself, money, education, hate, a pagan god, or the devil. The forces of darkness may suggest a person murder someone, but not God, the Creator of the universe, who brought His people out of Egypt. The next time the media declares that someone said "god" told him to murder innocent people, remember the murderer was listening to the father of lies or his own wicked thoughts.

In John 10.1-5, Jesus explained He is the good shepherd, His sheep know His voice, and follow Him. It is crucial for the Christian to recognize the voice of God as He calls us by name and we perceive His love. Let me disclose my personal experience with deciphering God's voice and the temptation of the devil. When God spoke to me when I prayed for months to stop stuttering, God called me by my name and made a statement: "Carl, I love you as you are." When I prayed and again asked Him to cure me of my stuttering, God repeated the exact phase He said previously. Jesus indicated He comes to bring life. My stuttering was rooted in a deep feeling of worthlessness, rooted in the abandonment I felt from my father's suicide. Jesus does not accuse us of our faults; Jesus tells us the way to life. Jesus told the woman found in adultery to sin no more, see John 8.3-11; He did not condemn her. Jesus does not dwell on our sins, we are to repent and move on with our lives. Our sins are forgiven by God's grace through His sacrifice. Jesus comes to give life. We need Jesus and He is our Friend.

Negative thoughts, attacks on our personal value or attacks on our shortcomings in life are from the evil one. Revelations 12.10 teaches that the devil is the accuser of brethren, that is, fellow Christians. The devil accuses us of being worthless and inadequate human beings. The devil seeks to fill humans with thoughts of helplessness and sadness. The devil's quest to steal, kill and destroy are opposite of God's goal. The devil attempts to disrupt our walk with Jesus. As humans, we have a sinful nature and we are imperfect. Thoughts to steal, murder, or destroy are from the forces of darkness.

Caiaphas, the high priest, used his evil mouth to falsely accuse Jesus of blasphemy in Matthew 26.65. Caiaphas told more lies in saying to Pilate that Jesus opposed Caesar in John 19.12. Similar to Cain's motive in killing Abel, Caiaphas, the chief priest, arranged the death of Jesus because God found favor with Jesus. The forces of evil accuse us of our faults, not God.

The tares in the field, the children of the devil, choose to follow the devil and not God. Judas Iscariot chose to sell information concerning the location of Jesus for thirty pieces of silver. Perhaps Judas loved money more than Jesus, or perhaps he wanted to test Jesus to fight the Romans and become an earthly king.

Vast manifestations of evil were involved in the murder of Jesus. Remembering the commandments and remembering what God hates helps train us to decipher good and evil.

Evil may also be done by omission. Jesus' parable of the merciful Samaritan in Luke 10 teaches that love requires action to be effective. Jesus told us he requires mercy, not sacrifice. In the parable, a man is beaten and left to die in a road. A priest passed by the beaten man, and did not assist him in his pain. A Levite, a member of the tribe that carried the Ark of the Covenant, passed by the injured man. A Samaritan, a non-Jew, aided the injured man and took him into town. The Samaritan paid the innkeeper to care for the injured man. Jesus tells us to do likewise and care for our neighbors. Jesus commands us to do good works by caring for others. Declaring oneself a Christian, but doing nothing to help others, is contrary to Jesus Christ's command.

Deciphering good and evil is beneficial for our daily lives, with applications including:

- Be aware when someone is jealous and pleased with our pain, or has come to steal, kill and destroy us
- Be aware when we are tempted to act in a manner displeasing to God
- Be aware when we have sinned, as all have sinned, and repent.

We are to note when someone is speaking to us in an abusive or destructive manner, rather than instructing us or building us up. The forces of evil seek to steal our joy, kill our heart, soul, and mind, and destroy our holy endeavors. The Holy Spirit has given us the boldness to rebuke those who attempt to abuse us. Jesus commanded we are not to fear those who can only kill the body, only fear God who can destroy both soul and body in hell. If someone speaks unkindly to us, we can kindly rebuke him and tell him not to talk to us in that manner. We can question our attacker and ask "why?" Jesus was an excellent communicator. We can imitate Jesus and speak for righteousness.

Being aware of evil and responding accordingly is important. A favorite example of someone avoiding temptation is Joseph. Refer to Genesis 39.7-13. Potiphar placed Joseph in charge of his home and all his property. One day Potiphar's wife asked Joseph to engage in an adulterous relationship with her. Joseph fled from her presence and went outside. If we sense someone may lead us down a path of sin, flee.

The ability to decipher good and evil lets us look at ourselves and acknowledge when we have sinned. Our human carnal nature prompts us to sin. Jesus told us that it is inevitable that stumbling blocks, also known as temptation, will come to us. Only Jesus is perfect and sinless, we are imperfect and sinful. Jesus indicated in Luke 15.10, we are to repent of our sins.

Let us end this chapter in prayer. We walk as sheep amongst wolves. Heavenly Father, as we mature in our faith in Jesus, please teach us to decipher good and evil. Let us rebuke those who do evil and forgive those who repent. Please forgive us for our trespasses, for all have sinned and we are not perfect. The forgiveness of our sin comes from the gift of Jesus' sacrifice for us on the cross. Thank you Jesus for your mercy. You desire us to be merciful, please guide us to be merciful. Amen.

# CHAPTER 24

# Jesus is Our Friend

When the Sabbath came, He began to teach in the synagogue; and the many listeners were astonished, saying, "Where did this man get these things, and what is this wisdom given to Him, and such miracles as these performed by His hands? "Is not this the carpenter, the son of Mary, and brother of James and Joses and Judas and Simon? Are not His sisters here with us?" And they took offense at Him. Jesus said to them, "A prophet is not without honor except in his hometown and among his own relatives and in his own household." Mark 6.2-4 NASB

But God proves his love for us in that while we still were sinners Christ died for us. Much more surely then, now that we have been justified by his blood, will we be saved through him from the wrath of God. Romans 5.8-9

Jesus replied, "If anyone loves me, he will obey my teaching. My Father will love him, and we will come to him and make our home with him." John 14.23 NIV

"I am the good shepherd. The good shepherd lays down his life for the sheep. The hired hand is not the shepherd who owns the sheep. So when he sees the wolf coming, he abandons the sheep and runs away. Then the wolf attacks the flock and scatters it." John 10.11-12 NIV

"And I say to you, everyone who confesses Me before men, the Son of Man will confess him also before the angels of God. When they bring you before the synagogues and the rulers and the authorities, do not worry about how or what you are to speak in your defense, or what you are to say; for the Holy Spirit will teach you in that very hour what you ought to say." Luke 12.8, 11-12 NASB

Love is patient, love is kind and is not jealous; love does not brag and is not arrogant. 1 Corinthians 13.4 NASB

For we do not have a high priest who cannot sympathize with our weaknesses, but One who has been tempted in all things as we are, yet without sin. Hebrews 4.15 NASB

"This is my commandment, that you love one another as I have loved you. No one has greater love than this, to lay down one's life for one's friends. You are my friends if you do what I command you. I do not call you servants any longer, because the servant does not know what the master is doing; but I have called you friends, because I have made known to you everything that I have heard from my Father. You did not choose me but I chose you. And I appointed you to go and bear fruit, fruit that will last, so that the Father will give you whatever you ask him in my name. I am giving you these commands so that you may love one another. John 15.12-17

And he came to Nazareth, where he had been brought up: and, as his custom was, he went into the synagogue on the Sabbath day, and stood up for to read. Luke 4.16 KJV  Referring to Jesus Christ.

But the LORD said to Samuel, "Do not look at his appearance or at the height of his stature, because I have rejected him; for God sees not as man sees, for man looks at the outward appearance, but the LORD looks at the heart." I Samuel 16.7 NASB

Do not judge by appearances, but judge with right judgment. John 7.24

This is My blood of the covenant, which is poured out for many for forgiveness of sins. Matthew 26.28b NASB

Then Jesus gave a loud cry and breathed his last. And the curtain of the temple was torn in two, from top to bottom. Now when the centurion, who stood facing him, saw that in this way he breathed his last, he said, "Truly this man was God's Son!" Mark 15. 37-39

Straightening up, Jesus said to her, "Woman, where are they?  Did no one condemn you?" She said, "No one, Lord." And Jesus said, "I do not condemn you, either Go From now on sin no more." John 8.10-11 NASB

Who will bring a charge against God's elect? God is the one who justifies; who is the one who condemns?  Christ Jesus is He who died, yes, rather who was raised, who is at the right hand of God, who also intercedes for us. Who will separate us from the love of Christ? Will tribulation, or distress, or persecution, or famine, or nakedness, or peril, or sword? Romans 8.33-35 NASB

"So I say to you, Ask, and it will be given you; search, and you will find; knock, and the door will be opened for you. For everyone who asks receives, and everyone who searches finds, and for everyone who knocks, the door will be opened. Is there anyone among you who, if your child asks for a fish, will give a snake instead of a fish? Or if the child asks for an egg, will give a scorpion? If you then, who are evil, know how to give good gifts to your children, how much more will the heavenly Father give the Holy Spirit to those who ask him!" Luke 11.9-13

Because of the increase in wickedness, the love of most will grow cold, but he who stands firm to the end will be saved. Matthew 24.12-13 NIV

The Holy Bible is a detailed history book. However, history is only a portion of the value of the Holy Bible.

The Holy Bible is a love letter from God. God's love letter to humans teaches:

- God is Almighty
- God is a jealous God
- God loves us
- Faith and life in Jesus is the path to eternal life
- Jesus loved us enough to die for our sins and be our redeemer
- Jesus prepared mansions for the righteous in heaven.

God told us in the book of Genesis that creation is good. Life is indeed good. False expectations in life and intermittent struggles may cause us to stumble, but life is good. Jesus clearly teaches that we are to endure and keep our faith to the end to be saved and have eternal life in Heaven. God is gracious and loving. God wants us to be filled with joy and peace. Jesus, the Son of the Living God, came to earth to demonstrate his extreme love for us.

The gospel books of Matthew, Mark, Luke, and John, provide insight into the actions, emotions, and personality of Jesus. Jesus, in addition to being

God, was born of a woman and lived on earth as a human being. Jesus spent much of His time in the community of common people. As a child, Jesus was protected by Joseph, the husband of Mary; Joseph, worked as a carpenter.

Mark 6 records that Jesus had four earthly half brothers and some half sisters. Jesus' brothers were James, Joses, Judas, and Simon. The names of Jesus' sisters are not mentioned in the Bible. Jesus became friends with his apostles, and others including, Lazarus, Mary, and Martha. Jesus felt the emotional pain of being betrayed by Judas Iscariot. Jesus was disappointed when His apostles fell asleep when he asked them to stay awake on the night when the Jewish guards took Him away.

The human qualities of Jesus revealed in the Holy Bible are different from what I had conceived. Prior to starting his ministry, Jesus, like Joseph, worked as a carpenter. The activities of a carpenter would include discussing the scope of the job with a potential customer, designing the project, measuring, creating a list of necessary materials, and producing a cost estimate for the project. If the customer would award the carpenter the job, the carpenter would serve as project engineer, purchase the necessary wood and hardware, travel to the worksite, and utilize his talents to skillfully build the structure. When the job was completed, the carpenter would be paid. A carpenter would be familiar with business, engineering, mathematics, skilled trades, and working until one is tired and needs rest. Jesus had the income of a common carpenter; He did not live in self-indulgent luxury. Jesus lived as a common man. Jesus did not live as a political king or earthly ruler.

Jesus was familiar with boating and fishing. Luke 5 records that Jesus called Simon Peter, James, and John while they were fishing. Jesus' numerous parables about planting seeds and harvesting indicate He had a detailed knowledge of farming. Jesus referred to Himself as the good shepherd. The good shepherd lays down His life for his sheep. Jesus was familiar with sheep herding.

Jesus frequently visited the temple to worship God the Father. Luke 4 documents that Jesus read the Holy Bible, including the book of the prophet Isaiah. Jesus conversed with the teachers in the synagogue regarding the law and the prophets.

Understanding that Jesus Christ, the Son of the Living God, was in business as a carpenter, was familiar with fishing and farming, and read the Holy Bible enables us to relate to Jesus as a human being. It is comforting that Jesus experienced the life of a common man. Many of us have done activities similar to Jesus: sales, marketing, engineering, carpentry, fishing, farming, attending church, and reading the Holy Bible! We each have much in common with Jesus. I truly now feel a connection with Jesus that I never experienced prior to reading the details of Jesus' life in the gospels.

Jesus ate with common people, including those outside the church and tax collectors. The self-declared religious authorities judged Jesus and His followers by appearances. I Samuel 16.7 declares the LORD looks at the heart of a man, but people look at the outward appearance. Jesus affirmed that we are not to judge by appearances in John 7.24. Jesus' personal experiences as a human being exposed Him to our struggles and weaknesses. Jesus is able to sympathize with the challenges that exist in our daily life. Jesus calls the common person His friend.

To be accepted as a friend to the world, we may need to meet criteria outside our control. The world creates barriers to keep common people on the outside and excluded. The arrogant, the rulers, and the authorities of this world may establish barriers to join their clique; barriers may include: a particular family birthright, age requirements, prestigious education, wealth, social status, or membership in a specific organization. Social barriers are created in an attempt to promote the selfish status of those creating the barriers and degrade the uninvited. In Luke 12.8, Jesus indicated that when believers confess Jesus' name before men, Jesus would confess the name of the believers before the angels. It will be the rulers and the authorities of this world that will accuse us for proclaiming the name of Jesus. The arrogant rulers and religious authorities were so blinded by their selfishness, they rejected Jesus as the King of Kings and the Savior of the World. The absurdity of mankind's cliques and barriers to acceptance in a community is exemplified by the religious authorities' rejection of Jesus Himself.

In direct opposition to the world, Jesus loves us, rejoices when a lost sheep is found, and is not arrogant. Jesus calls us His friend when we do as He commanded us; we are to love God and love our neighbor.

Come to Me, all who are weary and heavy-laden, and I will give you rest. "Take My yoke upon you and learn from Me, for I am gentle and humble in heart, and YOU WILL FIND REST FOR YOUR SOULS. For My yoke is easy and My burden is light." Matthew 11.28-30 NASB

It is ironic that Jesus, the Son of the living God, is meek and humble, but some human beings are arrogant. Jesus teaches in Luke 18 that we must receive the Kingdom of God like a child. We do not need to have a thorough understanding of biblical history in order to live and believe in Jesus. We do not need to memorize religious terminology created by Pharisees to be saved.

I remember with clarity one Sunday years ago when my wife, my three-year-old son, and I were attending a church service. My wife and I attended a very small church where our son was the only toddler in the congregation and our son sat with us in the pew during the worship service. Our son was carefully listening to the pastor recall the words of Jesus prior to presenting communion to the congregation. The pastor said, "Then he took a loaf of bread, and when he had given thanks, he broke it and gave it to them, saying, "This is my body which is given for you. Do this in remembrance of me." And he did the same with the cup after supper, saying, "This cup that is poured out for you is the new covenant in my blood."" Our son asked my wife and I if he could partake of communion. My wife replied to our son, "You are young and may not understand communion. You can have communion when you are older." Our son replied, "OK mommy." After my wife and I received the bread and the fruit of the vine, and were about to leave the church after the service was over, our son asked, "What if Jesus does not ask me again?" We asked our son what he meant. Our son replied, "Jesus told me He loves me and invited me to have communion." My wife and I felt horrible for interrupting Jesus' invitation to our son. We told the pastor our son declared Jesus invited him to communion because He loves him. The Pastor gave our son the bread and the cup in remembrance of Jesus in his own private communion. Jesus invites each of us to be His friend, receive His love, and remember Jesus' ultimate sacrifice to grant eternal life to those who live and believe in Him. We have the choice to embrace Jesus' friendship and love or reject Him. It is amazing that Jesus, the Son of the living God, is a friend to us unworthy humans and loves us.

My three year old taught me Jesus invites all of us to enter heaven. Like the man giving a big dinner in Luke 14.16-24, Jesus invites everyone. Jesus welcomes all of us, including the poor, the crippled, the blind, the lame, the young, the old, and the repentant wayward son. Jesus clearly declared that we must be like children to enter the kingdom of heaven. I did not understand Jesus' clear message:

And they were bringing even their babies to Him so that He would touch them, but when the disciples saw it, they began rebuking them. But Jesus called for them, saying, "Permit the children to come to Me, and do not hinder them, for the kingdom of God belongs to such as these. "Truly I say to you, whoever does not receive the kingdom of God like a child will not enter it at all." Luke 18.15-17 NASB

Similar to the world, I placed a barrier around Jesus. I love my son unconditionally and initially prevented him from communing with Jesus because I thought my son was too young to understand Jesus' love. As my son's dad, I immediately accepted my mistake, and asked Jesus and my son to forgive me. I do not want to interfere with Jesus, the Son of the Living God, interacting with my son. I learned very early I do not have the authority to block God's interaction with anyone. Unfortunately, some religious rulers and authorities intentionally exert their power to attempt to control others. I was elected to serve as a church board member in a church that was controlled by a few families. At one board meeting, a meddling board member told me, I was not worthy to be a board member because I was neither a member of his church long enough, nor a member of his denomination long enough! I told him it was not his church, it was God's church. The people of the light are to rebuke those who attempt to place barriers between God and His people. Excluding people from God is the work of the devil and the children of the devil.

Whenever a person professes the name of Jesus, there will be opposition. My accuser repented and requested my forgiveness; as required by Jesus, I will forgive my accuser seven times seventy times. It is critical to note no human being has the authority to elevate oneself to be the gatekeeper to Jesus Christ. Jesus Himself declared He is the gate:

Therefore Jesus said again, "I tell you the truth, I am the gate for the sheep. All who ever came before me were thieves and robbers, but the sheep did not listen to them. I am the gate; whoever enters through me will be saved." John 10.7, 8, 9a NIV

We have the privilege of being Jesus' friend by repenting of our sins, living and believing in God, and loving our neighbor. Jesus' command is easy to understand: God loves us. We are to love God. We are to love our neighbor as ourselves. Understanding what Jesus commands is easy; a child can understand Jesus' message. Obeying Jesus' message is difficult.

It would have been enough if Jesus came to earth to die as a sacrifice for our sin, but He also came to teach us the Way, the Truth and the Life. It would have been enough if Jesus taught us the Way, the Truth, and the Life, but He made us His friend.

Jesus is indeed totally able to sympathize with our daily activities of life and our struggles. I never actually understood that Jesus lived as a common man, not royalty. I never understood that Jesus experienced all the pains in life associated with daily living and was then murdered for teaching us how to experience joy in this life and the next. Jesus sympathizes with the common man because He was one of us! Jesus came to serve and not be served. Jesus did not relate to, nor befriend pompous religious leaders with beautiful white robes who follow the religious traditions of man; Jesus said the humble would be greatest in Heaven. Jesus is a friend to the common man and woman!

Although we were still sinners, Jesus died for us for the forgiveness of our sins. Jesus does not condemn us; He tells us to sin no more. Nothing will separate us from the love of Christ; it is by the grace of God we have been saved through faith. Jesus does not judge us by outward appearances; the LORD looks at the heart of people. Jesus does not place barriers between Himself and human beings. Jesus tore the curtain in the temple from top to bottom to grant common people direct access to the LORD.

When Jesus saw their faith, he said, "Friend, your sins are forgiven." Luke 5.20b NIV

It would have been enough that Jesus forgave our sins and calls us His friend, but He also offers rest for our souls. Jesus invites the heavy-laden to come to Him for He is gentle and humble. We will find rest for our souls in Jesus. The Son of the Living God graciously invites us to ask for His help. Jesus promised to answer when we knock. Jesus' sense of humor was disclosed in Luke 11. Jesus asked if our child asked for a fish, would we give him a snake? Jesus asked if our child asked for an egg, would we give him a scorpion? Jesus then shared that if we carnal people would not give our children a scorpion, God the Father will bless us when we ask for help. Since God created us to have a sense of humor, it makes sense Jesus has a sense of humor also. Jesus is our best friend

After praying for an accurate insight of Jesus' life on earth, the Holy Spirit inspired me to compile this narrative about Jesus:

Jesus was on His throne from the beginning. With much courage, Jesus left His kingdom in Heaven and came to earth to live among the common people. Jesus came to earth to save sinners. Jesus came to free us from the prison where we were held as slaves of sin in the dominion of darkness. We slaves of sin were sentenced to death in the prison of sin. Jesus rebuked the wicked and walked amongst us to save us from certain death. Jesus calls those who follow his command his friends. Jesus tore the curtain in two, thereby granting us direct access to God. Jesus gave us the way, the truth, and the life to escape the enslavement of sin. While the courageous Jesus was freeing the imprisoned slaves, the forces of darkness and the spiritual forces of wickedness tortured and assassinated Him. The wicked wanted to tell us lies and keep us prisoners and slaves of sin. Christ died for our sins, the just for the unjust, to bring us to God. Jesus set us free and granted us eternal life in paradise, God's home. However, Jesus triumphed over evil and rose from the dead. Jesus sits at the right hand of God the Father and reigns on His throne of glory. Amen

The above narrative was inspired by the following scripture verses: Matthew 9.9-12, John 1.14, John 3.16, John 8.32, John 8.34, Colossians 1.13, John 8.42-47, John 10.30, John 11.48-50, John 14.6, Romans 6.23, Galatians 3.22, and 1 Peter 3.18.

Let us close this chapter in prayer. Dear Jesus, thank you for laying down your life for your friends, we your followers. We are honored and humbled that you, Jesus, the Son of the Living God, loves us so much, you died to give us eternal life. Like a child, let us have pure faith and unconditional love for you, Jesus. Although you now sit at the right hand of God the father in Heaven, you can sympathize with any temptation or struggle we may ever endure in life. You did not come to bring Heaven to earth; you came to justify our entry into Heaven when our life on earth is complete. Jesus, you want us to learn from your example and find rest for our souls in the journey through life. Amen.

# CHAPTER 25

# Choosing Your God

As a deer longs for flowing streams, so my soul longs for you, O God. Psalm 42.1

I am the LORD your God, who brought you out of the land of Egypt, out of the house of slavery; you shall have no other gods before me. Exodus 20.2-3

He said to him, "'You shall love the Lord your God with all your heart, and with all your soul, and with all your mind.' This is the greatest and first commandment. And a second is like it: 'You shall love your neighbor as yourself.' On these two commandments hang all the law and the prophets." Matthew 22.37-40

The woman said to the serpent, "From the fruit of the trees of the garden we may eat; but from the fruit of the tree which is in the middle of the garden, God has said, 'You shall not eat from it or touch it, or you will die.'" The serpent said to the woman, "You surely will not die! "For God knows that in the day you eat from it your eyes will be opened, and you will be like God, knowing good and evil." Genesis 3.2-5 NASB

So do not worry, saying, 'What shall we eat?' or 'What shall we drink?' or 'What shall we wear?' For the pagans run after all these things, and your heavenly Father knows that you need them. But seek first his kingdom and his righteousness, and all these things will be given to you as well. Matthew 6.31-33 NIV

If your hand or your foot causes you to sin, cut it off and throw it away. It is better for you to enter life maimed or crippled than to have two hands or two feet and be thrown into eternal fire. Matthew 18.8 NIV

Psalm 42.1 teaches that as a deer longs for flowing streams, so our souls long for God. Our souls have an inherent incompleteness that can only

be fulfilled by God. This incompleteness is similar to a missing piece of a jigsaw puzzle. My wife enjoys buying a jigsaw puzzle to be assembled during each Christmas season. Guests are invited to help assemble the puzzle. A puzzle will not be considered beautiful and complete until all the pieces are found and placed in the proper position of the puzzle. When one sees an incomplete jigsaw puzzle on a table in our home, the viewer's attention immediately focuses on the void space in the puzzle, rather than the completed parts of the puzzle. All guests and family members long to find and insert missing pieces to fill the void in the puzzle. Although hundreds of other pieces have been successfully placed into the puzzle, the puzzle workers are not satisfied and content until the void in the puzzle is filled and the puzzle is complete. Similar to a person working on a puzzle, a human is not satisfied and content until the void in one's soul is filled with the missing piece; the void in our soul is God. If our souls have a void, we will focus on filling the void to find contentment.

The way of the world does not teach us to fill the void in our soul with God. God's gift of peace in our soul was paid in full by Jesus' death on the cross and resurrection. We are justified by God's grace as a gift. Humans have the choice to fill the void in our souls with God and attain supernatural peace.

Jesus commanded us that we love the LORD our God with all our heart, and with all our soul, and with all our mind. Jesus, being God and being man, is brilliant. Throughout the gospel, Jesus articulated important teachings in brief statements. It is noteworthy that Jesus did not simply say love God. Jesus carefully commanded us to love God with all our heart, all our soul, and all our mind.

I did not comprehend the complex meaning of loving God with all our heart, soul, and mind until I wandered in the desert of life for many years and remained a committed follower of Jesus of Nazareth.

**Jesus first commanded us to love God with all our heart**. Scripture explains the involvement of our heart with respect to God:

- The LORD God led the chosen people in the wilderness to humble them and know what is in their heart. See Deuteronomy 8.2.
- God put his laws in our heart. See Hebrews 10.16
- Jesus proclaimed where our treasure is, our heart will be also. See Matthew 6.21
- Trust in the LORD with all your heart, and do not rely on your own insight. Proverbs 3.5a
- He has also set eternity in the hearts of men. Ecclesiastes 3.11b NIV

Perhaps the above scriptures indicate the heart of man encompasses the center of one's existence, character, commitment, passions, and personal values regarding good and evil. God has also placed the concept of eternity in our hearts. Perhaps our heart is the battleground between our inclination for the carnal, evil, and temporary versus the holy, righteous, and eternal.

**Jesus' second command was to love God with all our soul**. God taught the following about the soul:

- We are to fear He, that is, God, who can kill the body and send our soul to hell. See Matthew 10.28
- What good is it if we gain the world, but forfeit our soul? See Mark 8.36
- Our soul longs for God. See Psalm 42.1
- A person's soul departs from the body upon death. See Genesis 35.18.

While we are alive in the body, our soul is in the body. Our soul is affiliated with the spirit. Our souls are born with a void that can be filled only by God. When human beings lack God, there is a void in their soul and emptiness in their entire being. The human soul is the eternal consciousness that lives on after our bodies die. The body is visible and temporary, but the soul is unseen and eternal.

**Jesus' third command was to love God with all our mind**. God teaches the mind:

- God provides the gift of understanding in our minds. See Job 38.36
- The intelligent seek knowledge, but fools focus on folly. See Proverbs 15.14
- God must open our minds to understand the scripture. See Luke 24.45
- The Holy Spirit wrote the laws of God in our minds. See Hebrews 10.16
- The mind can conceive mischief and deception. See Job 15.35.

The human mind is the center of our intellect, knowledge, creativity, logic, and problem solving ability. The mind can understand the scriptures and recall the inscribed laws of God. The mind can be trained to decipher good and evil. However, the mind can conceive evil and put evil into action. The mind can be filled with knowledge or be filled with thoughts of no value.

Perhaps the mind is the battleground between logic and knowledge verses faith and trust.

Loving God with all our mind is very important in our transformation into the likeness of Jesus. Our minds may have direct contact with God, however, we must be still to know Him. We are to be still and know He is God. The Holy Spirit helps us to understand what God taught in the Holy Scriptures. I pray for you that while reading **Jesus is Our Friend,** the Holy Spirit will provide you with greater insight of the gospel of Jesus Christ and eternal life through faith. We humans must be still, pray, and read His Holy Word. The forces of this world tempt us to constantly preoccupy our minds with entertainment and transient information. Entertainment and transient information may be fine, but it is critical we allocate time to talk to God and love God with all our mind.

Our minds must not overanalyze faith in God. Proverbs 3.5 teaches that we are to trust God with all our heart and not rely on our own understanding. Our heart and our mind may be in conflict occasionally. The Holy Bible teaches that our heart is to take precedence over our mind in the arena of faith. Luke 24.12 explains that the apostle Peter wondered why Jesus' body was missing from the tomb on the third day after Jesus' crucifixion. Peter wondered with his mind why Jesus' body was gone from the tomb, rather than having faith in his heart that Jesus rose from the dead as Jesus prophesied in Luke 18.33.

Our minds must not be filled with worry. It appears the media seeks to have us live in fear of environmental catastrophe, war, or crime. Jesus taught us not to worry about needs of this world in Matthew 6. We are to seek first God's kingdom and God's righteousness and He will provide for our needs. The war between good and evil is over; Jesus triumphed over sin and death. We have nothing to fear! We battle with evil forces in our daily lives, but Jesus won the war.

It is critical that we love God with all our heart, all our soul, and all our mind throughout all of our wandering in the wilderness. We are to love God when we are in crisis, sick, poor, or in need. We are to love God when we healthy, wealthy, and wise. Those who live and believe in God rejoice in the day the LORD has made. Those who live and believe in God trust in the LORD, regardless if all is well or if they are struggling.

Jesus taught in Mathew 7 that wise people build their house on the rock. When the rain, flood, and winds came, the house did not fall. Likewise, we are to build our lives on the Truth of Jesus. Some people may reject God.

When humans are in crisis and acknowledge they cannot control their surroundings, they seem more likely to need a god. I pray and thank God when my life is good. I pray to God for healing and assistance from physicians when a loved one or I am sick. I prayed to God when I wanted to find my future wife on this big planet. I pray to God when I am troubled. I pray to God when I request to be delivered from evil. When people have a crisis in their life, many seek God for comfort. In John 14, God promised to not abandon us or leave us orphaned; the Holy Spirit dwells within those who live and believe in Jesus.

Not all people seek the Living God; some people worship false gods. Judges 2.12 records that people worshipped a false god named Baal. Matthew 6.7 records that Jesus told His followers not to pray babbling like pagans. Pagans may worship idols or creation, such as the sun, earth, fire, water, or nature, rather than the creator. The term "Mother Nature" seems to be growing in popularity in today's society. Perhaps "Mother Nature" is a present day application of paganism. "Mother Nature" implies there is a deity that created the world and controls the winds and the water, but it is not the Living God. This morning, while driving to work, I heard a radio announcer say, "Mother Nature is being good to us today. The day will be warm and sunny." I felt the Holy Spirit of God within my soul declare, "Pagan words; I am the LORD your God, You shall not have any false gods before me." I felt an uneasy acknowledgement that paganism is permeating our society. The announcer could have said "God has blessed us with a warm and sunny day; let us rejoice." The announcer chose to refer to an impersonal pagan god.

Why does paganism exist? Paganism allows people to acknowledge the world exists and there is order in the universe. Those that embrace paganism fashion an impersonal god in their own mind. This god is not all-powerful. Since the pagan fashions his own god, he is not accountable to anyone but himself. The pagan does not follow the laws of God, but rather follows the traditions of man. In opposition to paganism, acknowledging that the Living God exists would validate that the laws written in our minds are from God and are to be obeyed.

Acts 19 records that people have worshipped other false gods, such the goddess Artemis. Paul's teaching about Jesus Christ reduced the profits of a silversmith named Demetrius. Demetrius' sales of silver idols to worshippers of the goddess Artemis decreased when people began to worship the true God. Please note here a very important fact, businessmen may create idols and false gods to make money. The love of money is the root of much evil, including creating false gods or goddesses for profit.

"What profit is the idol when its maker has carved it, Or an image, a teacher of falsehood? For its maker trusts in his own handiwork When he fashions speechless idols." Habakkuk 2:18 NASB

Another false god is superstition. Jesus taught that God knows the number of hairs on our heads. In Matthew 10, Jesus tells us that even a sparrow does not die and fall to the ground apart from God's authority. Superstition entrusts the control of our lives in magic or the occult; superstition places a false god before God. We must remember scripture tells us that God is sovereign over all creation.

People may invent their own version of god. I made my god the god of the healthy, wealthy, and wise. My false belief prompted me to think God did not care about me and He was not involved in my daily life. By being ignorant of the Bible, I mistakenly thought believers in god would be guaranteed a life of health, wealth, and wisdom. God blesses us as believers, but the rain falls on the just and the unjust. I have personally heard numerous people declare that they have their own relationship with God and do not need to read the Holy Bible nor gather with anyone who believes in God. Inventing god from one's own imagination is very dangerous. The Holy Bible explains God's commands and expectations for us to attain eternal life. Wandering through life without the Holy Bible is similar to driving a car on a long trip with no roadmap. Without the Holy Bible, we have no knowledge of the path to be taken, and no knowledge of the destination. By personal experience, I confess I worshipped various versions of God I invented in my mind; it did not bring peace or happiness. One cannot rely on the traditions of man, or the popular media, to teach us the truth of the gospel of Jesus Christ. Jesus is called the Word because He gave us the Word of God. We must read the living Word of God to know what God is saying.

Another false god may be one's career. Humans seek God because we want comfort and love from our creator. The Holy Spirit of God gives us strength. Christians are to build others up. Rather than getting comfort, love, strength, and a sense of belonging through God and His church, some choose their career. Companies do not actually exist physically and spiritually. Company names are copyrighted words and trademarked logos, ink on paper. The name of the company is registered with the federal government as a corporation. Companies exist to limit the liability of the owners. Companies may exist to gain investors. An owner or a board of directors control companies. Some career people may begin to place divine qualities on a company, as if it was alive and had a consciousness and a soul. Placing consciousness and a soul on a company is idolatry! Career worshippers may work long hours and neglect their family to make an offering to the company god. Career worshippers may go to work while ill, work through lunch hours, and work on their days off to gain favor from their work god. The career worshippers want to hear the company god say:

His master replied, "Well done, good and faithful servant! You have been faithful with a few things; I will put you in charge of many things. Come and share your master's happiness!" Matthew 25.23 NIV

However, the company god is a speechless idol, no different than Baal. The company god does not have an omnipotent and omnipresent consciousness that understands the sacrifices employees place at its feet.

**If we live to fulfill other people's expectations and obtain their approval, we are controlled and destined for defeat.**

Genesis 2.2 documents that God rested after creating the world. In Deuteronomy 5.14, God taught us to rest, be still, and think of Him. Humans cannot find love, joy, peace, and contentment through a career. Only God provides peace that transcends all understanding.

Some who think there is something greater than themselves may substitute education for God. Similar to pagans, some may view the earth, its creatures, or facts as a substitute for God. Thinking there is a creation, but no creator, is an attempt to acknowledge we exist, but give no glory to God and reject His sovereignty.

People have chosen to worship human beings before God.

And the LORD told him: "Listen to all that the people are saying to you; it is not you they have rejected, but they have rejected Me as their king. As they have done from the day I brought them up out of Egypt until this day, forsaking Me and serving other gods, so they are doing to you. But the people refused to listen to Samuel. "No!" they said. "We want a king over us. 1 Samuel 8.7, 8, 19 NIV

The people of Israel understood they needed protection from the invisible God, but chose a visible earthly king instead. The people of Israel rejected God as their King. Some people try to fill the void in their soul and the emptiness in their being with human idols. Recognizing and acknowledging the gifts God has bestowed on someone talented is good. However, eclipsing the worship of God by focusing on human idols is rejecting God as King. Those who worship and try to emulate human royalty, celebrities, musicians, actors, or sports figures may be rejecting God as King and making a living human idol! I am concerned for men's souls who can recite the names and statistics of professional ball players on numerous sports teams, but cannot recite a single Bible verse. I am concerned for the souls of those who idolize singers and listen to their songs, but do not be still and listen to the Word of God. Similar to Demetrius selling silver trinkets for an idol, current day merchants create idols and celebrities to sell merchandise or admission tickets. The temptation to fill the void for the invisible God in one's soul with a visible false idol has not changed in thousands of years, just the names and types of idols have changed. Yes, if we live to fulfill other people's expectations and obtain their approval, we are controlled and destined for defeat.

Seek first his kingdom and his righteousness, and all these things will be given to you as well. Matthew 6.33 NIV

Rather than worship God, false gods or idols, some people may choose to follow Satan. The children of the devil and the spiritual forces of wickedness are the enemies of the children of God. Jesus Himself told the workers at the temple that their father was the devil.

You are of your father the devil, and you want to do the desires of your father. He was a murderer from the beginning, and does not stand in the truth because there is no truth in him. Whenever he speaks a lie, he speaks from his own nature, for he is a liar and the father of lies. John 8.44 NASB

Some people are hurting so badly they do not have the desire to worship God, the devil, nor false gods. The broken and the lost may have lost faith in God when they experienced a personal tragedy in their lives. Other may have felt abandoned in life. Some try to fill their loneliness and emptiness with the excessive use of alcohol or by using recreational drugs.

When man's basic survival needs are satisfied, the risk of man placing a false god before God changes. Adam and Eve had their nutritional and environmental needs provided by God; they were well fed and naked in an evidently perfect climate. In their security, they were tempted by the devil to challenge God to become His equal. After eating of the forbidden fruit, God drove them from Eden. Humans are especially at risk to try to elevate themselves to be their own god when they feel secure, their basic survival needs are satisfied and they are not struggling. Ironically, when the needs and desires of humans are provided, some drift from the will of God and focus on their own will.

Some people on earth have acquired so many earthly treasures, they must plan where to store their treasures. Perhaps their physical strength, craftsmanship or intellect has permitted them to acquire great wealth. Those who have acquired much may reject that it was God who:

- Formed their inward parts and knit them together in their mother's womb
- Gave them the gift of craftsmanship like Bezalel the son of Uri
- Granted understanding and wisdom to their human mind like Solomon.

The self-centered worship of humans, who think they are in charge, migrates to accumulating treasures on earth. Similar to offering gifts to false gods, the self-centered offer gifts to themselves! The self-centered may accumulate earthly treasures and earthly power to lay at an alter to the god of himself.

"It is easier for a camel to go through the eye of a needle than for a rich man to enter the kingdom of God." Mark 10.25 NASB

The unseen aspects of life require belief and faith. Even pagans believe the unseen air containing oxygen is necessary for life. The continuous breathing of humans testifies for the existence of the unseen. Pagans acknowledge that unseen gravity will cause them to fall to the earth if they leap off a cliff. Belief and faith in the unseen surrounds us all daily.

**The end of the matter is clear; humans choose their god based on faith. People choose false gods or no god based on faith. Belief that the heavens and earth came into existence without a creator requires faith. Belief that the order and function of all creatures, including humans, came into existence without a creator requires faith. Belief that there is no hell to punish those who commit evil requires faith. Belief that God is the Almighty Creator is based on faith. Living and believing that Jesus died to provide eternal**

**life is based on faith. The unseen and seen power of God's majesty is understood; there is no excuse for ignoring the laws of God He placed in our hearts and He had written in our minds.**

Let us pray. God allows us to choose faith and righteousness or evil and wickedness. Let us choose faith and righteousness. Let us live and believe in Jesus such that although we die, we will live, and those that live and believe in Jesus will never die. Amen.

# CHAPTER 26

# Holy Spirit

And the earth was without form, and void; and darkness was upon the face of the deep. And the Spirit of God moved upon the face of the waters. Genesis 1.2 KJV

And the LORD went before them by day in a pillar of a cloud, to lead them the way; and by night in a pillar of fire, to give them light; to go by day and night. Exodus 13.21 KJV

The LORD spoke to Moses: See, I have called by name Bezalel son of Uri son of Hur, of the tribe of Judah: and I have filled him with divine spirit, with ability, intelligence, and knowledge in every kind of craft. Exodus 31.1-3

And in the sixth month the angel Gabriel was sent from God unto a city of Galilee, named Nazareth, To a virgin espoused to a man whose name was Joseph, of the house of David; and the virgin's name was Mary. And the angel came in unto her, and said, Hail, thou that art highly favoured, the Lord is with thee: blessed art thou among women. And when she saw him, she was troubled at his saying, and cast in her mind what manner of salutation this should be. And the angel said unto her, Fear not, Mary: for thou hast found favour with God. And, behold, thou shalt conceive in thy womb, and bring forth a son, and shalt call his name JESUS. He shall be great, and shall be called the Son of the Highest: and the Lord God shall give unto him the throne of his father David: And he shall reign over the house of Jacob for ever; and of his kingdom there shall be no end. Then said Mary unto the angel, How shall this be, seeing I know not a man? And the angel answered and said unto her, The Holy Ghost shall come upon thee, and the power of the Highest shall overshadow thee: therefore also that holy thing which shall be born of thee shall be called the Son of God. And, behold, thy cousin Elisabeth, she hath also conceived a son in her old age: and this is the sixth month with her, who was called barren. For with God nothing shall be impossible. Luke 1.26-37 KJV

As for me, I baptize you with water for repentance, but He who is coming after me is mightier than I, and I am not fit to remove His sandals; He will baptize you with the Holy Spirit and fire. Matthew 3.11 NASB

Then Jesus arrived from Galilee at the Jordan coming to John, to be baptized by him. But John tried to prevent Him, saying, "I have need to be baptized by You, and do You come to me?" But Jesus answering said to him, "Permit it at this time; for in this way it is fitting for us to fulfill all righteousness." Then he permitted Him. After being baptized, Jesus came up immediately from the water; and behold, the heavens were opened, and he saw the Spirit of God descending as a dove and lighting on Him, and behold, a voice out of the heavens said, "This is My beloved Son, in whom I am well-pleased." Matthew 3.13-17 NASB

He came to His own, and those who were his own did not receive Him. But as many as received Him, to them He gave the right to become children of God, even to those who believe in His name, who were born, not of blood, nor of the will of the flesh nor the will of man, but of God. John 1.11-13 NASB

"If you love me, you will keep my commandments. And I will ask the Father, and he will give you another Advocate, to be with you forever. This is the Spirit of truth, whom the world cannot receive, because it neither sees him nor knows him. You know him, because he abides with you, and he will be in you. "I will not leave you orphaned; I am coming to you. In a little while the world will no longer see me, but you will see me; because I live, you also will live. On that day you will know that I am in my Father, and you in me, and I in you. They who have my commandments and keep them are those who love me; and those who love me will be loved by my Father, and I will love them and reveal myself to them." John 14. 15-21

"I have said these things to you while I am still with you. But the Advocate, the Holy Spirit, whom the Father will send in my name, will teach you everything, and remind you of all that I have said to you. Peace I leave with you; my peace I give to you. I do not give to you as the world gives. Do not let your hearts be troubled, and do not let them be afraid. You heard me say to you, 'I am going away, and I am coming to you.' If you loved me, you would rejoice that I am going to the Father, because the Father is greater than I. And now I have told you this before it occurs, so that when it does occur, you may believe. I will no longer talk much with you, for the ruler of this world is coming. He has no power over me; but I do as the Father has commanded me, so that the world may know that I love the Father." John 14.25-31a

But you are not in the flesh; you are in the Spirit, since the Spirit of God dwells in you. Anyone who does not have the Spirit of Christ does not belong to him. But if Christ is in you, though the body is dead because of sin, the Spirit is life because of righteousness. Romans 8.9-10

"But you will receive power when the Holy Spirit has come upon you; and you shall be My witnesses both in Jerusalem, and in all Judea and Samaria, and even to the remotest part of the earth." Acts 1.8 NASB

And you also were included in Christ when you heard the word of truth, the gospel of your salvation. Having believed, you were marked in him with a seal, the promised Holy Spirit, who is a deposit guaranteeing our inheritance until the redemption of those who are God's possession—to the praise of his glory. Ephesians 1.13-14 NIV

In the same way the Spirit also helps our weakness; for we do not know how to pray as we should, but the Spirit Himself intercedes for us with groanings too deep for words   Romans 8.26 NASB

Or do you not know that your body is a temple of the Holy Spirit who is in you, whom you have from God, and that you are not your own?   I Corinthians 6.19 NASB

The fruit of the Spirit is love, joy, peace, patience, kindness, goodness, faithfulness, gentleness, self-control. Galatians 5.22b-23a NASB

Reiterating what Jesus mentioned in Matthew 16.6, 12 and Matthew 22.29, we are to study the word of God, the Holy Bible, and not be influenced by false teachers. This chapter includes who is the Holy Spirit, where is the Holy Spirit, and how the Holy Spirit is involved in our lives.

The Holy Bible explains the direct and personal interaction of God with mankind over many centuries. The Holy Spirit was with God the Father and

Jesus when the earth was void and dark. The Holy Spirit was with God the Father and Jesus in the beginning. The Holy Spirit of God was moving over the water when the earth was formed. The LORD spoke with Adam and Eve in the Garden of Eden. God spoke to Noah concerning the ark. God also spoke directly to Abraham and numerous prophets. God visited Moses in the form of a burning bush to announce He would free the people of Israel from captivity in Egypt. The Ark of the Covenant was designed by God and crafted by Bezalel with the help of the Holy Spirit. Divine creativity and craftsmanship come from God. The Lord guided the people of Israel during the exodus from Egypt in the form of a pillar of cloud by day and a pillar of fire by night.

In Exodus 33, Moses requested that God display his glory to him. God told Moses he must stand in a cleft in a rock to only see God's back, not his face. It appears mankind in his human sinful state is unworthy and unable to stand before God in all of God's glory without dying. God spoke directly to His people.

Leviticus 16.2 tells that God the Father appeared in a cloud above the Ark of the Covenant. The Ark of the Covenant was located behind the curtain separating the Holy of Holies. God permitted only the high priest to enter the Holy of Holies for an atoning sacrifice.

God spoke through numerous prophets to deliver His Word. The LORD told Joshua to conquer Jericho. The LORD spoke with Job regarding suffering and pain in life. Isaiah proclaimed the good news from God that a Savior would be born. God commanded ravens to feed Elijah. A widow fed Elijah and then God refilled the widow's flour and oil jars until the drought ended. God spoke though Elijah that the people are to worship God, not worship Baal. God ignited wet wood to demonstrate His power. God spoke through Elisha to provide pure drinking water. Youths jeered at Elisha and called him baldhead; God sent two bears to maul the forty-two jeering youths. The Spirit of the LORD was with Ezekiel as the valley of dry bones came together, skin covered the bones, and God gave them life. Obadiah was sent by God to declare that the country of Edom will be destroyed. God sent Jonah to preach to the people of Nineveh. Micah, Habakkuk, and others proclaimed God's message.

God sent the angel Gabriel to speak to Mary, the mother of Jesus. Gabriel told Mary that God favored her among women and wanted her to be the mother of Jesus. The Holy Spirit of God would overshadow Mary and she would give birth to Jesus, the Son of the Living God.

The parable in Matthew 21.33-45 explains the LORD and master sent numerous prophets to the wicked tenants of earth for praise, but the people on earth rejected His servants. The LORD then sent His only beloved son Jesus to earth to deliver His Word. Jesus, the Son of the Living God, became human and walked amongst us. Jesus lived as fully God and fully human, however Jesus was sinless.

The continuity between God the Father's words in the Old Testament Book of Ezekiel, chapter 36, and Jesus' words in John 3.3 and 6 is awesome. I did not comprehend that the Old and New Testaments of the Holy Bible combine in harmony to present thousands of years of God's plan.

"Then I will sprinkle clean water on you, and you will be clean; I will cleanse you from all your filthiness and from all your idols. "Moreover, I will give you a new heart and put a new spirit within you; and I will remove the heart of stone from your flesh and give you a heart of flesh. "I will put My Spirit within you and cause you to walk in My statutes, and you will be careful to observe My ordinances.  Ezekiel 36.25-27 NASB

Jesus answered and said to him, "Truly, truly, I say to you, unless one is born again he cannot see the kingdom of God." That which is born of the flesh is flesh, and that which is born of the Spirit is spirit. John 3.3, 6 NASB

God the Father told Ezekiel that He would forgive the sinful people with clean water sprinkled on them.  God the Father told Ezekiel that He would fill His people with His Holy Spirit. The symbol of baptism by water to indicate repentance and a commitment to God spans thousands of years!  Jesus Himself was baptized by John the Baptist to demonstrate His commitment to God the Father and righteousness. After Jesus was baptized, the Heavens were opened and the Holy Spirit of God descended onto Jesus.

God spoke through His beloved Son, Jesus.  Jesus devoted several years of his life preaching repentance, how to love God and love one's neighbor, and how to attain everlasting life through faith in Him.  Jesus proclaimed in Luke 13.4, 5 that we must repent to not perish, but have eternal life. A public and outward sign of repentance is expressed through baptism.  Also, Jesus explained to Nicodemus in John 3.3 and 6 that we must be born again to enter the Kingdom of God, Heaven!  John 1.11-13 explains that being born again is not of the flesh, but born by God. As an unworthy messenger of God, I humbly submit very important words of Jesus to remember: **repent** and

**be born again of the Holy Spirit**. Jesus invites us to repent and be born again of the Holy Spirit to receive Jesus' free gift of eternal life in Heaven.

Luke 23.40-43 records that while Jesus was being crucified, the thief being crucified alongside Jesus repented and indicated he deserved punishment for his sins. The thief then asked Jesus to remember him when Jesus was in His kingdom. Jesus told the thief that today, he would be with Jesus in Paradise. Although not directly recorded in scripture, it seems unlikely that the thief was a baptized Christian. The thief about to die was granted passage to paradise by his verbal repentance and faith in Jesus. However, Matthew 18 documents that Jesus commanded His disciples to be baptized in the name of the Father, and of the Son, and of the Holy Spirit. Baptism is an outward and visible sign of repentance and commitment to God.

And He said to them, "You are those who justify yourselves in the sight of men, but God knows your hearts; for that which is highly esteemed among men is detestable in the sight of God." Luke 16.15 NASB

God knows the heart of someone who may be baptized, but has a heart that is far from God. God also knows the heart of someone who may not be baptized, but is repentant and born again of the Holy Spirit of God.

Jesus taught us the Way, the Truth, and the Light. Jesus affirmed the commandments and added we are to love our neighbor. Jesus explained that we are not to worry, but keep faith in God. Jesus explained we are to be filled with peace, not as the world gives. Jesus explained that we are to be content with what we have and not gain the whole world and forfeit our soul. Jesus loved the common person and lived amongst them. The followers of Jesus were glad when Jesus walked the earth. People shouted, "Blessed be the King that cometh in the name of the Lord."

Jesus foretold in John 16.27-28 that He came into the world and would be leaving the world and returning to his Father. Jesus declared in John 14.25-31 that He would not leave us orphaned without God the Father, without the prophets of God, and without Jesus Himself! Life on earth would be very lonely without God, the prophets, or Jesus to keep life in perspective. Jesus indicated God the Father would send the Holy Spirit to not leave us orphaned.

When Jesus finished his teaching on earth, the evil forces of wickedness murdered Jesus. However, Jesus triumphed over sin and death and rose from the dead. Jesus walked the earth in his resurrected body. Fulfilling his prophecy, Jesus was taken into Heaven and sat at the right hand of

God. After Jesus returned to Heaven, God sent the Holy Spirit to teach us and remind us of all that Jesus said. God speaks now through the Holy Spirit. The Holy Spirit completes the continuity of God's presence with His people.

God spoke directly to His people. God spoke through numerous prophets to deliver His Word. God spoke through the angel Gabriel. God spoke through His beloved Son, Jesus. God now speaks through the Holy Spirit. God has not left us orphaned: Jesus is in the father, we are in Jesus, and Jesus is in us. Amen!

John 14.26 has a descriptive word for the Holy Spirit that has various meanings. The New Revised Standard Version of the Bible refers to the Holy Spirit as the Advocate. Other translations refer to the Holy Spirit as the Counselor (NIV), the Comforter (KJV), and the Helper (NASB). All these words help describe the Holy Spirit.

It would have been enough if Jesus died as a sacrifice to provide eternal life to all those who believe in Him. But in His generosity, God sent His Holy Spirit to be our Advocate, Counselor, Comforter, Helper, and Teacher during our life on earth; the Holy Spirit is God with us on earth.

John 14 records that Jesus indicated He is in the Father, we are in Jesus, and Jesus is in us. Jesus will reveal Himself to those who love Jesus and the Father. Those who love Jesus and the Father are filled with the Holy Spirit and become a temple of the Holy Spirit. Jesus proclaimed that God the Father would send the Holy Spirit to teach and remind us what Jesus said on earth.

Now that Jesus no longer walks the earth in his physical body, the Holy Spirit reminds us of Jesus' teaching. Luke 24.45-46 explains that the scriptures are not obvious and we need Jesus to open our minds to understand his Holy Word.

Without the help of the Holy Spirit of God, this book could not have been written. This book began as a collection of Bible verses I found to help me understand life. As I organized the Bible verses into chapters, I perceived the Holy Spirit of God guide me to write this book. I may only hear the Holy Spirit of God when I am still. Psalm 46.10 is precisely true; I can only perceive the awesome power of God when I am still and quiet. Ironically, at the time I began following the command of the Holy Spirit to write this book, I did not understand who the Holy Spirit was. After reading and praying about the Bible verses pertaining to the Holy Spirit, I understand the Holy Spirit dwells in humans who live and believe in Jesus and God the Father. The Holy Spirit of God began to dwell in me as my faith matured, but

I did not understand. Listening, understanding, and obeying the Holy Spirit of God involves a greater awareness of God and His Word. As a child, I had worshipped the god of the healthy, wealthy, and wise. I worshipped the false God who kept a hedge around my life that prevented all pain and misfortune. When pain or misfortune came, I rejected all gods, both the one true God and the false God of the healthy, wealthy, and wise. After I read and reread scripture with a mind opened by the Holy Spirit, I stopped complaining to God and forsaking God for any unpleasant events in my life; Jesus Himself clearly stated in John 16.33 that we will have trouble in this world. The Holy Spirit comes to those who seek the one true God.

The Holy Spirit teaches and reminds us of Jesus' teachings. The Living Word of God often can provide multiple insights in life in one scripture passage; the Holy Spirit helps us in understanding scripture. The Holy Spirit is our Advocate in the struggle with the spiritual forces of wickedness. The devil roams the earth seeking to devour us. We are to flee from temptation. We must put on the full armor of God, the helmet of salvation, and grasp the sword of the Spirit, which is the word of God, to stand firm against the schemes of the devil. The Holy Spirit comforts us in life's challenges. We will have struggles in this world, but Jesus has overcome the world. The Holy Spirit counsels us to understand the application of God's laws. Hebrews 10.16 explains that God will put the laws in our hearts and He will write the laws in our minds. The Holy Spirit dwells in us to be with us and hear our prayers.

My father-in-law, now deceased, was a kind and loving man. He was married and had a family, served in the Korean War, then came home from the war and worked for several decades until his death. My father-in-law was a generous man, to the point of sacrificing to help others. He saved a man's life by using his belt as a tourniquet to stop the bleeding when a man cut the artery in his leg in a work accident. My father-in law did not want to accept any gifts from the man whose life he saved. He saved his life as a free gift and wanted nothing in return. The rescued man instead dropped off Christmas gifts to my father-in-law's children, my future wife and her brothers. However, saving a man's life and successfully raising a family did not keep my father-in-law from feeling unworthy of God's love. My father-in-law had heard and believed the false teaching that God will give each of those who believe in Him a sign that God loves you and you are His child. My father-in-law believed this false teaching most of his life.

Jesus said to him, "Because you have seen Me, have you believed? Blessed are they who did not see, and yet believed." John 20.29 NASB

Sighing deeply in His spirit, He said, "Why does this generation seek for a sign? Truly I say to you, no sign will be given to this generation." Mark 8.12 NASB

Jesus stressed the importance of understanding the scripture for oneself. If doubting if something is in scripture or not, research it for yourself and do not believe in false teachings! The epilogue will explain how to research scripture. When my father-in-law was getting old and death seemed not far away, he became concerned he was not worthy to enter Heaven; God did not provide a personal tangible sign showing he would go to Heaven. Perhaps the root cause of my father-in-law's feeling of unworthiness came from killing the enemy in the Korean War. Jesus commanded us to "not murder."

And, behold, one came and said unto him, Good Master, what good thing shall I do, that I may have eternal life? And he said unto him, "Why callest thou me good? There is none good but one, that is, God: but if thou wilt enter into life, keep the commandments." He saith unto him, Which? Jesus said, "Thou shalt do no murder, Thou shalt not commit adultery, Thou shalt not steal, Thou shalt not bear false witness, Honour thy father and thy mother: and, Thou shalt love thy neighbour as thyself. Matthew 19.16-19 KJV

Moses took the life of an enemy in order to save one of his people from an aggressor coming to steal, kill, and destroy. The killing of the enemy to defend the weak is documented in the following scripture verses:

Now it came about in those days, when Moses had grown up, that he went out to his brethren and looked on their hard labors; and he saw an Egyptian beating a Hebrew, one of his brethren. So he looked this way and that, and when he saw there was no one around, he struck down the Egyptian and hid him in the sand. Exodus 2.11-12 NASB

My father-in-law was praying one night before his death for a sign. God did not perform a sign for him, but rather the Holy Spirit inspired him. When my father-in-law was in the Korean War, he kept a "lucky" silver dollar in a pocket of his combat trousers. While in battle, the dollar seemed to have fallen out of his pocket. He fought the remainder of the war thinking his silver dollar was gone. When he and his clothing returned from the war, he found the silver dollar had fell though a hole in his pocket, but was trapped in the lining of his trousers. His "lucky" dollar coin was with him all the time in battle, although he was unaware. The Holy Spirit explained to my father-in-law that God was with him throughout his life, like the coin was with him in his trousers; my father-in-law did not perceive God was with him. My father-in-law was comforted that God was with him and he did not need a sign to indicate he was going to Heaven. My father-in-law was heaven bound because he lived and believed in Jesus.

The fruit of the Spirit is love, joy, peace, patience, kindness, goodness, faithfulness, gentleness, self-control. Galatians 5.22b-23a NASB

Love: Love God and love our neighbor as yourself.
Joy: Happiness is fleeting and is a response to our gains and triumphs. Joy is our choice to unconditionally abide in God.
Peace: The Holy Spirit grants peace, not as the world gives, but peace in our souls.
Patience: Patience comes with the understanding that God's ways are not our ways.
Kindness: The Holy Spirit inspires to help and build up our neighbor.
Goodness: The Holy Spirit teaches to live with integrity and righteousness.
Faithfulness: Trust in the Lord and not our own understanding.
Gentleness: Endurance and love yield gentleness. A wise person gently teaches others.
Self-Control: The Holy Spirit teaches that religion without control of our tongue and our actions is worthless.

We are blessed that the Holy Spirit intercedes on our behalf to God with groans that words cannot express. God loves us so much, He sends His Holy Spirit to pray with us and for us. Our Advocate is with us always to make us strong when we are weak.

Let us pray. Thank you God for sending the Holy Spirit to dwell with us and not leave us orphaned. We need your Godly presence to remind us that you love us and we are a forgiven people. We are your sheep and need our shepherd, You God. Thank you for being our Advocate in the struggle against the spiritual forces of wickedness while we are on earth. Amen.

# CHAPTER 27

# Transform Oneself into the Likeness of Jesus

"You shall remember all the way which the LORD your God has led you in the wilderness these forty years, that He might humble you, testing you, to know what was in your heart, whether you would keep His commandments or not." Deuteronomy 8.2 NASB

Now the Lord is the Spirit, and where the Spirit of the Lord is, there is freedom. And we, who with unveiled faces all reflect the Lord's glory, are being transformed into his likeness with ever-increasing glory, which comes from the Lord, who is the Spirit. 2 Corinthians 3.17-18 NIV

Jesus answered, "Everyone who drinks this water will be thirsty again, but whoever drinks the water I give him will never thirst. Indeed, the water I give him will become in him a spring of water welling up to eternal life." John 4.13-14 NIV

Jesus declared, "Believe me, woman, a time is coming when you will worship the Father neither on this mountain nor in Jerusalem. You Samaritans worship what you do not know; we worship what we do know, for salvation is from the Jews. Yet a time is coming and has now come when the true worshipers will worship the Father in spirit and truth, for they are the kind of worshipers the Father seeks. God is spirit, and his worshipers must worship in spirit and in truth." John 4.21-24 NIV

Jesus answered him, "I have spoken openly to the world; I always taught in synagogues and in the temple, where all the Jews come together; and I spoke nothing in secret." John 18.20 NASB

And do not be conformed to this world, but be transformed by the renewing of your mind, so that you may prove what the will of God is, that which is good and acceptable and perfect. Romans 12.1-2 NASB

Do not judge by appearances, but judge with right judgment. John 7.24

Therefore, since Christ has suffered in the flesh, arm yourselves also with the same purpose, because he who has suffered in the flesh has ceased from sin, so as to live the rest of the time in the flesh no longer for the lusts of men, but for the will of God. 1 Peter 4.1-2 NASB

But he said to me, "My grace is sufficient for you, for my power is made perfect in weakness." Therefore I will boast all the more gladly about my weaknesses, so that Christ's power may rest on me. 2 Corinthians 12.9 NIV

He came to His own, and those who were his own did not receive Him. But as many as received Him, to them He gave the right to become children of God, even to those who believe in His name, who were born, not of blood, nor of the will of the flesh nor the will of man, but of God. John 1.11-13 NASB

"I am the Lord's servant," Mary answered. "May it be to me as you have said." Then the angel left her. Luke 1.38 NIV

And as he entered into a certain village, there met him ten men that were lepers, which stood afar off: And they lifted up their voices, and said, Jesus, Master, have mercy on us. And when he saw them, he said unto them, Go shew yourselves unto the priests. And it came to pass, that, as they went, they were cleansed. And one of them, when he saw that he was healed, turned back, and with a loud voice glorified God, And fell down on his face at his feet, giving him thanks: and he was a Samaritan. And Jesus answering said, Were there not ten cleansed? but where are the nine? There are not found that returned to give glory to God, save this stranger. And he said unto him, Arise, go thy way: thy faith hath made thee whole. Luke 17.12-19 KJV

And He went a little beyond them, and fell on His face and prayed, saying, "My Father, if it is possible, let this cup pass from Me; yet not as I will, but as You will." He went away again a second time and prayed, saying, "My Father, if this cannot pass away unless I drink it, Your will be done." Again He came and found them sleeping, for their eyes were heavy. And He left them again, and went away and prayed a third time, saying the same thing once more. Matthew 26.39, 42-44 NASB

Peace I leave with you; My peace I give to you; not as the world gives do I give to you. Do not let your heart be troubled, nor let it be fearful. John 14.27 NASB

Then Satan answered the LORD, "Does Job fear God for nothing? Have You not made a hedge about him and his house and all that he has, on every side? You have blessed the work of his hands, and his possessions have increased in the land. But put forth Your hand now and touch all that he has; he will surely curse You to Your face." Job 1.9-11 NASB

Though he slay me, yet will I hope in him. Job 13.15a NIV

Bear with each other and forgive whatever grievances you may have against one another. Forgive as the Lord forgave you. Colossians 3.13 NIV

"But I say to you that everyone who is angry with his brother shall be guilty before the court; and whoever says to his brother, 'You good-for-nothing,' shall be guilty before the supreme court; and whoever says, 'You fool,' shall be guilty enough to go into the fiery hell. Therefore if you are presenting your offering at the altar, and there remember that your brother has something against you, leave your offering there before the altar and go; first be reconciled to your brother, and then come and present your offering. Matthew 5.22-24 NASB

And there arose also a dispute among them as to which one of them was regarded to be the greatest. For who is greater, the one who reclines at the table or the one who serves? Is not the one who reclines at the table? But I am among you as the one who serves. Luke 22.24, 27 NASB

As a babe in Christ, I read and reread Jesus' many parables, that is, short illustrative stories. I also read the numerous books in the Bible to learn about other believers and God's teachings in their respective lives. Supernaturally, over years of study, my mind has begun to grasp the continuity of the entire

Bible itself. As I mentioned, my brain is that of an engineer and scientist. My gift from the Holy Spirit is that of technical understanding and systems. My ability to memorize sentences word for word, including Bible verses, is not good. My strength is the acquisition, retention, and retrieval of knowledge. However unworthy, I have been helped by the Holy Spirit to combine, configure, view, and decipher the Holy Bible as one entity, the sum of the parts. I feel an urgency to finish this book quickly since it has taken me over three decades to finally attain this level of understanding.

The following is a brief overview of the initial fall of man, God's punishment, and mankind's cyclic tendency to sin and perhaps repent. In the beginning, Adam and Eve ate of the tree of the knowledge of good and evil. Adam's and Eve's disobedience to God prompted toil, adversary thistles, and death to enter the world. Genesis chapter 6 indicates when mankind multiplied, every imagination of the thoughts of man was only evil. God sent a great flood to blot out all people except Noah and his family. After the great flood, mankind multiplied again. A famine occurred and the people of Israel moved to Egypt for food that Joseph had stored. Joseph's brothers had previously cast off Joseph because his father, Jacob, favored him. God changed Jacob's name to Israel. Eventually, Pharaoh imprisoned the people of Israel in Egypt. God selected Moses to lead the people out of Egypt. God sent ten plagues on Egypt because Pharaoh would not free the people of Israel. After being freed from captivity, God's people refused to enter the Promised Land. God made the people of Israel wander in the wilderness for forty years as a consequence of their lack of faith and disobedience. Deuteronomy 8.2 explains that God made His chosen people wander for forty years to humble them, to test them, to know what is in their heart, and to know if they would follow His commandments. Every year, on the Day of Atonement, the high priest presented a sin offering to God to request His forgiveness.

Isaiah 53.5 proclaims that He (Jesus) would be pierced for our transgressions and crushed for our iniquities. Jesus, the Son of the Living God, came to earth and walked amongst mankind. Jesus made the one perfect sacrifice by the shedding of his blood, the just for the unjust; all those who live and believe in Jesus will have eternal life. In John 14.6, Jesus explained He came to earth to be the way, and the truth, and the life of the world. Jesus taught us how to live in righteousness. In John 11.26 Jesus explained that those who live and believe in Him would never die, but have eternal life. Jesus explained in John 14.21-24 that a time would come when the people of God would not worship on that mountain, nor in Jerusalem; worshipers will worship in spirit and truth.

232

Although the people of God no longer wander through the wilderness as a group of nomads searching for a particular land, perhaps we each wander through the wilderness of life, where the spiritual forces of wickedness and troubles seek to devour us. We walk through the Valley of Death searching for God, God's truth, and the purpose of life. I submit that there is a consistency between the purpose of the people of God wandering for forty years after being freed from Egypt and our wandering in life today.

Life includes a sequence of experiences and choices. We have the ability to choose righteousness or wickedness. Our journey of wandering through the wilderness to be humbled, to be tested, to know what was in our hearts, and to know if we would keep His commandments may start early in our life. We move through life to gain the fruits of the Holy Spirit: love, joy, peace, patience, kindness, goodness, faithfulness, gentleness, and self-control.

Ever since I can remember as a young child, the Holy Spirit taught me to be good. God placed His laws in my heart and wrote them in my mind. As a child, I was schooled to be a productive citizen. As I mentioned previously, I stuttered after my father died in my childhood. Stuttering made me sensitive to other people's pain. I developed the fruit of kindness and gentleness. My stuttering came to an end after years of speech therapy and God's help. After high school, I attended college for five years to be trained in a variety of subjects and receive specialized training in engineering. In my mind, I prepared for twenty-two years to commence into adulthood; I enjoyed the present, but looked forward to the future.

We each are prompted by the Holy Spirit to demonstrate goodness, kindness, and gentleness. When some forsake us, we have the opportunity to become more sensitive to others.

When our adult life commences, we graduate into our careers, and people seem to continue on a training program for life initiated by God. We each start our private, but very similar wandering in the wilderness. After completing our education, and we start working in our career, money may become a primary focus for fulfillment in life. Each of us has a longing for purpose and fulfillment in life. Engineering students learn advanced mathematics, physics, chemistry, philosophy, and years of specialized training in engineering. I have witnessed the disappointment of engineering graduates when they begin working in an engineering job in industry. Engineering graduates, particularly those who have not worked during college, are especially prone to disappointment when they begin their engineering profession. The new graduates inaccurately expect to utilize all that they learned in school and find complete fulfillment in life through their job; they will not. Nearly all jobs require specific knowledge and further training. The typical engineer will not design nuclear power systems, design bridges, formulate amazing chemical compounds, design spacecrafts, design automobiles, and solve the greatest philosophical questions at any one job. Many people are shocked that all jobs eventually become familiar and routine after they develop an expertise in their industry subset. Those seeking fulfillment entirely through their job may become bored and disillusioned at work. Boredom may prompt changing jobs or returning to college for additional degrees and different lines of work.

I had worked since I was 12-years-old and knew jobs require expertise and specialization. I did not expect to utilize all my talents in one job. After working at three successive jobs after college for training, I upgraded jobs and became a senior engineer. I did not become bored in my job, but rather I focused on attaining perfection in my job and the praises of men. I worked sixty hours a week to get the job done extraordinarily well. I incorrectly projected the love and wisdom of God onto my employer; this was a gross mistake of a naive businessperson and a naive Christian. I was humbled by the rejection of man regarding my first multi-million dollar project. Being humbled early in my engineering career taught me to not conform to the world and to not receive primary satisfaction from my job. God and family are my primary priorities. After being humbled, my wife and children reached the appropriate level of importance in my life. Being rejected by man taught me to love my family more. I am content in my life balanced in God, love and work. Being rejected by man taught me to have self-control; I learned I do not have control over what others think of me. Hard work, long hours, and accomplishing the goal do not guarantee praise by one's boss. Self-control is only learned when we are tested, and losing control is normal for the natural carnal man, a creature of instinct. Self-control is demonstrated when we are treated unfairly, and we understand the carnal world is not fair. I found joy in life, rather than waiting to be honored by man. However, I still lacked peace, patience and faithfulness.

Loving others appears to come when we love people more than things that moth and rust destroy. If we love treasures more than people, we love no one. Joy is related to love. When we do not crave things of the world that prevent us from joy, we can find joy. If happiness is predicated on a marvelous mansion, perfect health and figure, a powerful career, and a fine automobile, joy will be difficult to attain. When we embrace joy unconditionally and allow God to guide us in our daily life, we can find joy.

The other fruits of the Holy Spirit, patience, peace, and faithfulness, came to me through suffering. I Peter 4 discloses that suffering leads to a reduction in sin. 2 Corinthians 12 tells that God's grace is sufficient for our weakness. My long-term challenge to keep breathing while feeling suffocated has given me supernatural patience. Understanding life is temporary and my death is simply postponed until perhaps eighty years makes life less important and gives me joy knowing I will go to heaven.

Patience seems to be developed by humans primarily by enduring suffering for a long period or by not attaining one's goal for an extended period.

Peace comes only from Jesus. Jesus gives peace, but not as the world gives. I developed peace in life after I learned love, joy, patience, goodness, kindness, and gentleness. Peace came to me when I shifted my focus to Heaven and God, rather than earthly gains and mankind.

Peace in life eludes many humans. The world teaches that happiness is attained through the acquisition of things. Those of the world may be temporarily happy when they have many things and are sad when they lose things. Carnal instincts are never satisfied. Once a treasure is attained, the carnal instinct of humans prompts us to want more. Joy remains in life when we celebrate being in God's presence. Peace in our soul comes when we embrace the Holy Spirit of God.

Faithfulness came last to me. Job 1.9-11 describes true faithfulness. Satan told God that Job would curse God if bad things happened to Job. God allowed Satan to test Job and demonstrate Job will love God although He slays him. When I had a great boss at work and I was healthy, I loved God and felt like a winner. When I was demoted at work, I would ask God why He has forsaken me. When I had colon surgery and fully recovered, I felt tested and rewarded. During my six years of enduring Sarcoidosis, I was totally humbled and my faithfulness grew to maturity.

Matthew 26. 39-42 records that Jesus asked his father three times to permit him to avoid being crucified on the cross. Since Jesus was fully human and fully God, Jesus knew He was going to experience excruciating pain. Following the path of life is not always pleasant. I am comforted in knowing Jesus asked God three times to have the cup of suffering pass from him, if it is God's will. Humans have a natural dislike of pain. Being transformed into the likeness of Jesus involves the ability to experience pain, yet still believe in God and have faith in God. Life allows us to be transformed into the likeness of Jesus Christ. However, experiencing suffering causes many to become bitter and hateful in life. We each choose to have faith in God or reject God. Matthew 7.13 explains the path that leads to destruction is wide and many take it; the road to eternal life is narrow and few find it.

My wife was tested many years ago when she was running for city council in our little town. My wife was studying Occupational Therapy at a community college. I was the only wage earner while my wife attended college full time and our expenses were extremely close to what I earned. We had a modest home in the country, one old car, and a very dilapidated old car I purchased for $400. My wife had an inspired thought and suggested she work as a city council person for our small community. As a councilperson, my wife could work as a civil servant at the town hall a few weeknights and help out citizens with their problems. My wife could earn a few thousand dollars a year as a councilperson. My wife registered to run for council at large and won the primary election. My wife survived the primary and was on the ballet! One night she received a mysterious telephone call. The caller said he would donate much money to her campaign and use his influence to bring in the votes, provided she would agree to vote the way he dictated on planned future issues. My wife indicated she would vote what is best for the city and what is ethical. The mysterious caller told my wife he would back someone else with his money and influence, causing her to lose the election. My wife cordially said goodbye. My wife prayed to God to win, so she could do good for the city and earn some money for our family. My wife felt confident that God would help her win the election because she stood for good.

On election night in November, my wife lost the election and we were disappointed. My wife said out loud to God, in my presence, "God, I do not understand why I lost the election." I began working a second job to meet our expenses. My wife worked at a retail store during the Christmas season, so we could afford to buy our two children Christmas gifts. We managed to gather money through odd jobs and pay for my wife's college tuition.

In my wife's last year in college, we were having difficulty in paying her tuition. I wrote the college President and explained we had little money, two children, and asked for help with the tuition. The college President wrote back with the most excellent news of scholarship money! We thanked the President for his much needed help. Through the years of struggles, my wife successfully graduated with her first degree. My wife and I were home one night after her graduation celebration and reminiscing about our struggles and perseverance. Later in the evening, God whispered to my wife "You did not lose. If you had taken the money in exchange for evil you would have lost your soul. Through your choice, you have won." When my wife told me what God had directly communicated to her, we were shocked. God answered my wife's question she asked years ago as if no time had passed;

my wife knew exactly what question God was answering. Her eyes filled with tears as she understood that God is with us. My wife could have joined the side of darkness and literally sold her soul to the devil. My wife did not conform to the world's corruption involving bribery and favors. We have frequent tests to choose God and eternal life or choose Satan and hell.

Mary, the mother of Jesus, was transformed into the likeness of Jesus. When the angel asked Mary if she would be the mother of Jesus, she humbly indicated she is the LORD'S servant.

A primary and critical change in the transformation to being like Jesus is the control of our instinct to sin. All humans have sinned and typically have the instinct to be selfish. However, humans have the God-given gift to choose to do good and not choose evil. Every human has the choice to set his or her mind on the Spirit and live according to the Spirit or set his or her mind on the flesh and live according to the flesh.

Being like Jesus gives us supernatural peace, not as the world gives. Peace in Christ teaches us to be thankful for all the good in the world. Jesus healed ten leapers, but only the foreigner thanked Him. A faithful person is thankful like Jesus is thankful.

In becoming like Jesus, we develop supernatural faith and we drink the water of everlasting life and present an outward sign that we are children of God.

John 18 records that Jesus indicated He spoke openly to the world and spoke nothing in secret. These concise words of Jesus make it very clear there is nothing secret in the Holy Bible.

Transforming into the likeness of Jesus involves serving others, detailed in Luke 22.27. The spiritual forces of wickedness seek to control others. Those filled with the Holy Spirit of God serve others. The power of darkness seeks to use power to dominate and control others. Much pain in life is caused by someone trying to dominate another. Jesus is the greatest, yet He served others. As a follower of Jesus, we are to be kind and serve others.

Jesus said in Matthew 5.23-24 that if our brother has something against us, we our to reconcile. A member of my family did have something against me for many years. When I read that Jesus wants us to reconcile with a brother, I was convicted. Following Jesus is difficult, not easy. I called the family member that disliked me and we had lunch. I felt a relief that I extended kindness. Loving those who do not love you is a command from Jesus that takes courage.

The journey to become like Jesus will not protect us from bad events. Jesus clearly stated there is trouble in the world. Transforming into the likeness of Jesus gives us peace and understanding that is not of this world.

Let us pray. Heavenly Father, thank you for calling us to be your sons and daughters. Let us be thankful for all the good you have created. There will be troubles in this world and men will hate us. However, let our light shine before others, so that they may give glory to God in Heaven.

# CHAPTER 28

# God and His Church

The LORD said to Aaron, "You, your sons and your father's family are to bear the responsibility for offenses against the sanctuary, and you and your sons alone are to bear the responsibility for offenses against the priesthood. "You are to be responsible for the care of the sanctuary and the altar, so that wrath will not fall on the Israelites again." Numbers 18.1, 5 NIV

And every priest stands day after day at his service, offering again and again the same sacrifices that can never take away sins. But when Christ had offered for all time a single sacrifice for sins, "he sat down at the right hand of God," and since then has been waiting "until his enemies would be made a footstool for his feet." For by a single offering he has perfected for all time those who are sanctified. Hebrews 10.11-14

After three days they found him in the temple courts, sitting among the teachers, listening to them and asking them questions. Everyone who heard him was amazed at his understanding and his answers. When his parents saw him, they were astonished. His mother said to him, "Son, why have you treated us like this? Your father and I have been anxiously searching for you." "Why were you searching for me?" he asked. "Didn't you know I had to be in my Father's house?" But they did not understand what he was saying to them. Luke 2.46-50 NIV

"Who do you say I am?" Simon Peter answered, "You are the Christ, the Son of the living God." Jesus replied, "Blessed are you, Simon son of Jonah, for this was not revealed to you by man, but by my Father in heaven. And I tell you that you are Peter, and on this rock I will build my church, and the gates of Hades will not overcome it. Matthew 16.15b-18 NIV

The kingdom of heaven may be compared to a king who gave a wedding feast for his son. "And he sent out his slaves to call those who had been invited to the wedding feast, and they were unwilling to come. "Again he sent out other slaves saying, 'Tell those who have been invited, "Behold, I have prepared my dinner; my oxen and my fattened livestock are all butchered and everything is ready; come to the wedding feast."' "But they paid no attention and went their way, one to his own farm, another to his business, and the rest seized his slaves and mistreated them and killed them. "But the king was enraged, and he sent his armies and destroyed those murderers and set their city on fire. "Then he said to his slaves, 'The wedding is ready, but those who were invited were not worthy. 'Go therefore to the main highways, and as many as you find there, invite to the wedding feast.' "Those slaves went out into the streets and gathered together all they found, both evil and good; and the wedding hall was filled with dinner guests. "But when the king came in to look over the dinner guests, he saw a man there who was not dressed in wedding clothes, and he said to him, 'Friend, how did you come in here without wedding clothes?' And the man was speechless. "Then the king said to the servants, 'Bind him hand and foot, and throw him into the outer darkness; in that place there will be weeping and gnashing of teeth.' "For many are called, but few are chosen." Matthew 22.2-14 NASB

And coming to Him as to a living stone which has been rejected by men, but is choice and precious in the sight of God, you also, as living stones, are being built up as a spiritual house for a holy priesthood, to offer up spiritual sacrifices acceptable to God through Jesus Christ. For this is contained in Scripture: "BEHOLD, I LAY IN ZION A CHOICE STONE, A PRECIOUS CORNER stone, AND HE WHO BELIEVES IN HIM WILL NOT BE DISAPPOINTED." This precious value, then, is for you who believe; but for those who disbelieve, "THE STONE WHICH THE BUILDERS REJECTED, THIS BECAME THE VERY CORNER stone," and, "A STONE OF STUMBLING AND A ROCK OF OFFENSE"; for they stumble because they are disobedient to the word, and to this doom they were also appointed. But you are A CHOSEN RACE, A royal PRIESTHOOD, A HOLY NATION, A PEOPLE FOR God's OWN POSSESSION, so that you may proclaim the excellencies of Him who has called you out of darkness into His marvelous light; for you once were NOT A PEOPLE, but now you are THE PEOPLE OF GOD; you had NOT RECEIVED MERCY, but now you have RECEIVED MERCY. I Peter 2.4-10 NASB

Each day Jesus was teaching at the temple, and each evening he went out to spend the night on the hill called Mount of Olives, and all the people came early in the morning to hear him at the temple. Luke 21.37-38 NIV

Then the chief priests and the Pharisees called a meeting of the Sanhedrin. "What are we accomplishing?" they asked. "Here is this man performing many miraculous signs. If we let him go on like this, everyone will believe in him, and then the Romans will come and take away both our place and our nation." Then one of them, named Caiaphas, who was high priest that year, spoke up, "You know nothing at all! You do not realize that it is better for you that one man die for the people than that the whole nation perish." John 11. 47-50 NIV

When Jesus saw the crowds, He went up on the mountain; and after He sat down, His disciples came to Him. He opened His mouth and began to teach them saying, Matthew 5.1-2 NASB

For I tell you that unless your righteousness surpasses that of the Pharisees and the teachers of the law, you will certainly not enter the kingdom of heaven. Matthew 5.20 NIV

"And when you pray, do not be like the hypocrites, for they love to pray standing in the synagogues and on the street corners to be seen by men. I tell you the truth, they have received their reward in full." Matthew 6.5 NIV

He replied, "Isaiah was right when he prophesied about you hypocrites; as it is written: 'These people honor me with their lips, but their hearts are far from me. They worship me in vain; their teachings are but rules taught by men.' You have let go of the commands of God and are holding on to the traditions of men." Mark 7.6-8 NIV

And he is the head of the body, the church; he is the beginning and the firstborn from among the dead, so that in everything he might have the supremacy. Colossians 1.18 NIV

"Whoever believes in the Son has eternal life, but whoever rejects the Son will not see life, for God's wrath remains on him." John 3.36 NIV

John said to him, "Teacher, we saw someone casting out demons in your name, and we tried to stop him, because he was not following us." But Jesus said, "Do not stop him; for no one who does a deed of power in my name will be able soon afterward to speak evil of me. Whoever is not against us is for us." Mark 9.38-40

The churches of Asia greet you Aquila and Prisca greet you heartily in the Lord, with the church that is in their house. I Corinthians 16.19 NASB"

Be on guard for yourselves and for all the flock, among which the Holy Spirit has made you overseers, to shepherd the church of God which He purchased with His own blood. "I know that after my departure savage wolves will come in among you, not sparing the flock; and from among your own selves men will arise, speaking perverse things, to draw away the disciples after them. "Therefore be on the alert, remembering that night and day for a period of three years I did not cease to admonish each one with tears." Acts 20.28-31 NASB

Beware of false prophets, which come to you in sheep's clothing, but inwardly they are ravening wolves. Matthew 7.15 KJV

My brethren, do not hold your faith in our glorious Lord Jesus Christ with an attitude of personal favoritism. For if a man comes into your assembly with a gold ring and dressed in fine clothes, and there also comes in a poor man in dirty clothes, and you pay special attention to the one who is wearing the fine clothes, and say, "You sit here in a good place," and you say to the poor man, "You stand over there, or sit down by my footstool," have you not made distinctions among yourselves, and become judges with evil motives? James 2.1-4 NASB

James and John, the two sons of Zebedee, came up to Jesus, saying, "Teacher, we want You to do for us whatever we ask of You." And He said to them, "What do you want Me to do for you?" They said to Him, "Grant that we may sit, one on Your right and one on Your left, in Your glory." Mark 10.35-37

Calling them to Himself, Jesus said to them, "You know that those who are recognized as rulers of the Gentiles lord it over them; and their great men exercise authority over them. "But it is not this way among you, but whoever wishes to become great among you shall be your servant; and whoever wishes to be first among you shall be slave of all. "For even the Son of Man did not come to be served, but to serve, and to give His life a ransom for many." Mark 10.42-45 NASB

How blessed is the man who does not walk in the counsel of the wicked, Nor stand in the path of sinners, Nor sit in the seat of scoffers! Psalm 1.1 NASB

If anyone considers himself religious and yet does not keep a tight rein on his tongue, he deceives himself and his religion is worthless. James 1.26 NIV

"It is written," he said to them, "'My house will be called a house of prayer,' but you are making it a 'den of robbers.'" Matthew 21.13 NIV

Pure and undefiled religion in the sight of our God and Father is this: to visit orphans and widows in their distress, and to keep oneself unstained by the world. James 1.27 NASB

The interaction between God and humans began with Adam and Eve. God loved people and cared for them. God sent His wrath on the wicked. God directly interacted with Adam, Eve, Cain, and Abel. God ejected Adam and Eve from the Garden of Eden for their disobedience resulting from their desire for control and power. God directly interacted with many other people. In Genesis 4.12, when Cain murdered Abel, God punished Cain. Over time mankind grew greatly wicked and he used his imagination primarily for evil. God determined mankind was sufficiently corrupt to drown all humans excluding Noah's family. God told Noah to build the ark and God sent a great flood to drown the creatures of the earth. After the flood, people multiplied again and became centered on themselves, not God. Genesis 11 records that the people of Babel wanted to build a tower to the heavens. God created numerous languages to humble and impede the arrogant people.

Genesis 11 explains that God sent angels to Lot concerning the destruction of Sodom and Gomorrah. God sent angels to tell Lot He will destroy Sodom and Gomorrah because the people were wicked. The angels told Lot and his family to leave and not look back. Lot's wife disobeyed God and looked back at the destruction. God punished Lot's wife by turning her into a pillar of salt.

The People of Israel moved to Egypt during a famine and were eventually held in captivity. God instructed Moses to lead His chosen people out of captivity in Egypt. It appears the concept of a congregation of followers of God began on the exodus from Egypt. In Exodus 12.3, the LORD referred to His people as a congregation. The sons and daughters of Israel began grumbling very early in their exodus. The congregation grumbled against God and Moses immediately after exiting Egypt and approaching the Red

Sea. The congregation did not trust God to deliver them from Pharaoh's army. God, through Moses, parted the Red Sea and allowed the people of Israel to cross the Red Sea, then restored the sea to drown Pharaoh's army. The people of Israel did not have a lasting faith even after witnessing the parting of the Red Sea and drowning of Pharaoh's army.

While God was giving Moses the Ten Commandments, the people of Israel made a golden calf and worshiped it. Exodus 32.35 records that God smote those who worshiped the golden calf.

Along the journey from Egypt, the congregation of the sons of Israel continued to grumble and decided to stone Moses and Aaron to death. If the congregation was successful in murdering Moses and Aaron, they planned to choose a leader to return them to captivity in Egypt. Numbers 14 records that God wanted to smote the chosen people for their sinfulness. Moses pleaded with God not to destroy the congregation. God made the people wander in the desert for forty years to humble them. The epoch from Genesis through Numbers 18 can be called the Initial Wrath of God Era. During this era, God responded to the sin on mankind with His wrath.

Numbers 18.1, 2, 5, and 7 explain that God then instituted a sin offering to be made by Priests from the tribe of Levi to avoid God's wrath. Leviticus 16.6-15 explains the actual offering by the priest. It is very important here to pause and note at this juncture that God instituted the sin offering to end His wrath. Until the sin offering was created by God to allow the people to be forgiven of their sins by the priest, sin was followed by God's wrath. God ejected Adam and Eve from the Garden of Eden for their disobedience. However, Cain did not learn from his parents' mistake and subsequent punishment; Cain murdered his brother Abel. Drowning the sinful people on the earth did not eliminate sin. When humans repopulated the earth, the people arrogantly wanted to enter heaven by building a tower. God's wrath involved creating multiple languages. Destroying Sodom and Gomorrah and its citizens did not instill the wisdom for all to fear God. God sending the plagues on Egypt, parting the Red Sea, and striking those who worshipped the golden calf with a plague did not instill the people of Israel with an understanding of God's power. When the people of Israel planned to murder Moses and Aaron, God was prepared to send a plague and destroy the people of Israel. Numbers 14.12 records that God wanted to build a new chosen people from the lineage of Moses; similar to regenerating the chosen people from the lineage of Noah through the great flood. Numbers 14.19 documents that Moses requested that God forgive the sins of the people of Israel and not destroy them. Numbers 18.5 explains that God instituted a sin offering to be made by the priests from the tribe of Levi, rather than respond to the sin of the people with His wrath. The sin offering was presented for many centuries. Jesus, the Son of the Living God, came to fulfill the law. Jesus then became flesh and walked amongst us.

Jesus replaced the sacrificial system of repentance. Jesus declared in Matthew 12.7 that He desires mercy, not sacrifice. As documented in Mark 15.38-39, when Jesus died as the perfect sacrifice, the curtain to the Holy of Holies was torn in two from top to bottom; this allowed humans direct access to God. The sacrificial blood offering was done again and again by priests, but Jesus' sacrificial death was the perfect sacrifice for all time. Salvation changed when Jesus came to earth. In 1 Peter 2.4-10, the apostle Peter explains that believers in Jesus are a royal priesthood, a Holy Nation, and a chosen people. By living and believing in Jesus, we receive God's mercy to become His chosen people and we receive God's mercy to be granted eternal life. Living and believing in Jesus makes us children of God and we receive the inheritance of eternal life in Paradise. Being a child of God fills us with the light of truth and we are filled with the Holy Spirit.

The Wrath of the Lamb, from the book of Revelation, is a powerful metaphor for the judgment of humans by Jesus Christ. Upon death, the children of the devil will incur the wrath of the lamb. John 3.36 records that Jesus indicated those who believe in the Son of God will have eternal life, but those who reject the Son will encounter God's wrath. We will each sit before the judgment seat of Christ and be recompensed for our deeds in life, according to what we each have done, whether good or bad.

The historical sequence of God's interaction with man can be summarized as follows:

- Initial Wrath of God Era
- Sacrificial Offering Era
- New Covenant Era
- Wrath of the Lamb.

Mankind's instinct to sin has not changed throughout the history of man.

Jesus' teaching of salvation through faith and mercy in the New Covenant was dramatically different than the traditions of society at the time of Jesus. Jesus warned the leaders of the religious community not to be hypocrites by externally demonstrating observation of the law, but rejecting God in their hearts:

- Praying at length to be seen by men. Their reward will be only from men, not God.
- Tithing, but neglecting justice, mercy and faithfulness.
- Being beautiful on the outside, but unclean on the inside.

The religious authorities, including Caiaphas, the high priest, arranged the execution of Jesus. John 11. 47-50 explains the Pharisees and teachers of the law wanted Jesus killed and silenced to maintain the control and power over those who attended the temple. The initial sin of Adam and Eve in disobeying God and eating of the tree of the knowledge of good and evil was rooted in the desire for control and power. Thousands of years later, chief priests and the Pharisees wanted to murder the Son of God to have control and power. The Pharisees became so corrupt at the time of Jesus that he declared that unless righteousness of the common person was greater than that of the Pharisees and the teachers of the law, they would not enter the kingdom of heaven. Jesus called some of the teachers of the law hypocrites and blind guides. When Jesus overturned the tables of the moneychangers, He indicated the Pharisees had turned the temple from a house of prayer into a marketplace. It is very revealing that Jesus identified that the Pharisees and teachers of the law were corrupted by the love of money, and the power of darkness.

The historical sequence involving the wrath of God, the sacrificial offering, the new covenant, and the final wrath of God is very informative. Mankind's instinct to sin has not changed throughout time.

The church unites chosen people into a holy nation, a people belonging to God, who God called out of the darkness and into His light of truth. Jesus established an assembly of believers through the new covenant by dying on the cross and tearing the curtain of the temple in two from top to bottom. Jesus built the church on the rock that He is the Son of the Living God. The curtain being torn in two from top to bottom permitted common humans direct access to God. Matthew 22 contains a parable from Jesus describing the invitation of the common person to God's feast for His son. Many of the chosen guests, the people of Israel, refused the invitation to rejoice at the coming of Jesus. God then invited the common people to His feast. All are invited to become children of God. However, those commoners who reject Jesus will be cast out from the feast. Only those who live and believe in God are chosen to attend the eternal feast with God the Father, the Son, and the Holy Spirit in Heaven.

Those who live and believe in Jesus comprise the chosen people, a royal priesthood, and a holy nation. Jesus, the Son of the Living God, is the head of the body of believers, His church. We become children of God when we hear and believe the gospel of Jesus Christ; we are marked with the Holy Spirit of God and He dwells in us.

Jesus established His church on the rock foundation that He is the Son of the Living God. Jesus stated that Hades would not overpower His church. God's plan for His people was unveiled through Jesus Christ. The Son of the living God became flesh and lived amongst us. When Jesus was twelve years old, He went to the temple to listen to the teachers. When Joseph and Mary asked Jesus why He stayed behind in the temple, Jesus indicated He was in His Father's house. When Jesus grew into a man, He began His teaching ministry. Jesus taught in the temple and many people came to hear His teaching. Jesus did not confine His teaching to the temple, Jesus also taught in people's homes, in fields, and on mountains.

Per Mark 9.38, the twelve apostles noticed someone not in their group was ministering in Jesus' name. The apostles tried to stop the unaffiliated follower of Jesus. Jesus told His apostles not to stop him; he who performs a deed in His name is for them, not against them. Jesus established in Mark 9.38 that no one group or person has exclusive rights to Jesus and His church. Jesus hereby authorized anyone knowledgeable to preach the true Gospel in the name of Jesus to do so.

I feel better now. I felt uncomfortable that me, an unknown common man, has spent years writing a book on Jesus and His Gospel of salvation. Jesus Himself told His apostles to let an unnamed person preach in His name. I humbly now preach the Gospel of Jesus with boldness as a nameless common man with no official manmade credentials. I wrote this book because God told me to write this book and I obey Him.

After Jesus was crucified, died, and rose from the dead, He returned to sit at the right hand of God Father in Heaven. Note here with clear awareness that the church on earth, the holy nation, is populated by imperfect human beings.

For all have sinned, and fall short of the glory of God; Being justified freely by his grace through the redemption that is in Christ Jesus. Romans 3.23-24 KJV

Jesus indeed told us the church on earth, populated by human beings, will not be overthrown by the spiritual forces of wickedness. However,

247

Matthew 4.1-10 records that the devil wants all, including Jesus, to worship him, the devil. Luke 4.13 records that the devil will tempt us, then return to tempt again at a more opportune time. The devil is the adversary of Christ's church and he is relentless in his attempt to steal, kill, and destroy.

Let us pause for a moment here and establish accurate definitions of words. In my engineering profession, words that describe processes, materials, and parts must be carefully deciphered to communicate what one wants. The same abbreviation may have multiple meanings. Likewise, the words in the Holy Bible are very important. The word "church" used by Jesus in Matthew 16.18 is translated from the Greek word meaning "assembly."[18] Jesus would build an assembly of believers. The apostle Paul indicated that Jesus is the head of the "assembly" in Colossians 1.18.[18] Paul referred to the "assemblies" of those who believe in Jesus in 1 Corinthians 16.19.[18]

After Jesus ascended into Heaven, Jesus' followers assembled into people's homes, such as the home of Aquila and Prisca, to pray to God and to teach and learn the scriptures. Since followers of Jesus were at risk to be imprisoned, assemblies of Christians were held in homes. The church Jesus spoke about is comprised of humans who live and believe in Him. The church was not a building of brick and mortar, stone, or wood. The church is the soul and bodies of believers.

The church on earth is founded on the fact that Jesus is the Son of the Living God. ALL WHO LIVE AND BELIEVE IN JESUS FOR SALVATION ARE THE CHURCH! The congregation of believers is the church. However, the meaning of the word church mutated after Jesus died and rose from the dead and ascended into Heaven.

God directly led the people of Israel in the ancient times, but 1 Samuel 8.22 records that the People of Israel wanted to be ruled by an earthly king; the people of Israel were not content with God being their King. Mirroring the actions of the people of Israel, churches on earth may be ruled by man. Centuries after Christ's death and resurrection, aristocrats, politicians and governments became earthly rulers of buildings, institutions, and hierarchies and called them their "church."

The Holy Church, comprised of the chosen people, the royal priesthood, the Holy Nation, the people of God, is the church founded by Jesus. Jesus' Church can not be overcome by the devil. Amen and praise God! The true Church is the body of believers with Christ as the head!

It is no longer I who live, but Christ lives in me; and the life which I now live in the flesh I live by faith in the Son of God, who loved me and gave Himself up for me.  Galatians 2.20b

The Church with Jesus as the head of the body is the true Church; those in the Church no longer live for themselves, but Jesus lives in them.  The church ruled by man does not have Jesus as the head of the church.

"Churches" ruled by men may contain children of God who are members of the church founded by Jesus.  However, Jesus provided numerous warnings regarding false churches, corrupt leadership, and congregations of hypocrites:

"Churches" ruled by man may be lead by a false prophet.

"Churches" ruled by man may honor God with their lips, but have hearts that are far from Jesus.

"Churches" ruled by man may be beautiful and white on the outside but on the inside be full of dead men's bones and everything unclean.  On the inside they are full of hypocrisy and wickedness.

"Churches" ruled by man may break the commandments of God and teach rules and traditions created by man.

"Churches" ruled by man may not be a house of prayer, but rather a den of thieves.

"Churches" ruled by man may contain hypocrites.

"Churches" ruled  by man may not treat others as Jesus commanded: feed the hungry, give a drink to the thirsty, welcome strangers, clothe the naked, and visit the sick.

"Churches" ruled by man may appear to contain righteous people on the outside but on the inside are full of greed, and self-indulgence.

"Churches" ruled by man may be lukewarm, and neither hot nor cold, that God would spit them out of His mouth.

The above are paraphrases of scripture from: Matthew 24.24 KJV, Mark 7.6 KJV, Matthew 23.27 KJV, Matthew 15.3 KJV, Matthew 23.14 KJV, Matthew 21.13 KJV, Matthew 23.23 KJV & Matthew 25.36 KJV, Matthew 23.25 NIV, and Revelations 3.16 KJV.

A noteworthy false prophet in a church ruled by man was Caiaphas, a high priest.  Caiaphas was a high priest of the people of Israel, the chosen people of God. Caiaphas arranged the murder of Jesus Christ, the Son of the Living God, to maintain his control and power as a church leader.  It is critical we read and understand the Holy Bible to know the truth of God, not the traditions of churches ruled by man.

I have been very disappointed and disillusioned by churches ruled by man numerous times in my life. Although I have acknowledged the sovereignty of God all my life, I had questioned if I needed to attend a church founded by man. I questioned if I could continue my relationship with God, without a physical church.

My first disappointment with a church founded by man was related to my father's death. Although my family was part of the church congregation, no clergy comforted my mother or I when my father died. As an eleven-year-old, I could not articulate my expectations, but I felt the church did not comfort a fatherless boy. Jesus spoke of this type of clergy in Matthew 23.23. They give a tenth of their income, but neglect the more important matters of the law, such as justice, mercy and faithfulness. I began to question if the church was negligent by not providing comfort in my time of sorrow. However, I still attended church on Sundays.

The next year, my brother and I went to the local church our family attended. We met with a clergy person to obtain copies of documents. Rather than ask how my brother and I were coping with the loss of our father, the clergy person asked my brother and I perverted questions pertaining to sexual gratification. My brother and I felt very uncomfortable. My brother and I were somewhat street smart and intuitively knew we were in danger. Our God-given instinct to flee from danger prevented us from becoming another statistic of children molested by clergy. We took the papers we needed and quickly escaped. Jesus warned of evil clergy in Matthew 23.27-34. The churches and men may be beautiful and white on the outside but on the inside be full of dead men's bones and everything unclean. On the inside they are full of hypocrisy and wickedness. They are like snakes, a brood of vipers. After that incident, I stopped attending church for ten years and never returned to that church.

The first church my wife and I joined was in the city, where my wife and I grew up. However many of the church members and their adult children lived in the suburbs, but attended this inner city church where the parents grew up. Members of the church with older children accepted my wife and I. Most of the people were very kind and loving. However, a couple of young suburban members seemed to view my wife and I unfavorably. Perhaps the suburban adult offspring viewed my wife and I as poor city people. The clique of young suburbanites attending the inner city church did not tell us to sit at their feet, but I perceived a distinction in the manner we were treated by some. James, the half brother of Jesus, specifically indicated we are not to differentiate fellow believers, assembled to worship God, based on perceived income.

Jesus warned in Matthew 7.15 to be aware of false prophets. At that juncture of my life, my wife and I were struggling to bank for a home and move to the suburbs. To my embarrassment, I became overwhelmed with stress and experienced symptoms of clinical depression. My wife met with our minister to share our pain and explain the situation. The minister indicated he was busy and told my wife to divorce me and move on with her life. Thankfully, my wife had no intentions of divorcing me. My wife wanted comfort from the church, but was rejected and counseled to break a marriage blessed by God. My wife and I are happily married thirty-two years later. Churches ruled by men can do more damage to the cause of Christ than the devil. When the devil attacks us, we understand he is our adversary; when a church forsakes us and tempts us to sin, we feel attacked by evil and betrayed.

My wife and I moved to a rural area and attended a local church. The second church my wife and I joined seemed normal for several years. The sermons were not always Bible based, but often self-improvement lessons. Similar to the people who fashioned the golden calf and indulged in depravity (Exodus 32), numerous people in the church began to commit adultery with one another. The minister avoided ever presenting a sermon on avoiding adultery; perhaps he did not want to offend anyone. We moved from the area and left that church.

The third church my wife and I attended for seventeen years. The church was good for a long time. Then, like Adam and Eve, the temptation for control and power began to grow. My wife and I disagreed with some managerial decisions and looked for a church that was more Bible based. We wished the church the best. My wife and I searched for a different church.

My wife and I found a church that was very much based on the Bible. The sermons were based on numerous Bible scriptures. From the first day we attended, we were warmly greeted. I was amazed by the amount of God-given musical talent in such a small church. The love and warmth shared with each other made me feel at home. In this church my knowledge of scripture grew considerably, the men's weekly Bible study with the pastor was wonderful, and my wife became more interested in studying scripture in greater detail. However, beneath the pleasant friendliness, there was a dispute regarding who had the greatest power in the church. The desire for power and control amongst the followers of Jesus is documented in Mark 10. James and John, the sons of Zebedee wanted to be powerful in Jesus' church. James and John wanted the power, but most likely had no idea that Jesus would become the greatest by becoming the servant of all by being crucified as the atoning sacrifice for mankind. The desire for control and power has accompanied humans throughout history. The desire for power and control can permeate the church. Similar to the people of Israel wanting to murder and overthrow Moses and Aaron, some members of the congregation grumbled and wanted to overthrow the pastor. My wife and I were saddened that we found a church of kind people and a teacher who preaches the Gospel, but there was a dispute over control and power. Jesus is the head of the body of believers, the church. Paul's letters to the various churches are very enlightening. Paul explained in the book of Acts that outside forces and members of the congregation will attempt to destroy the church. We, like Paul, are to admonish those causing division and ensure Christ's message is preached in the church. I felt God's presence in the church, and therefore felt called to deliver the Gospel. I rebuked the grumblers in the church. We voted and the grumblers seeking to control the church did not have a majority vote. The church is focused on teaching the Gospel. I have found an assembly of believers of Jesus where the true Gospel of Jesus is preached. Like Paul, I will admonish, or gently redirect, those who attempt to divert the focus of the church away from God.

With changes in leadership and changes in church membership, churches will change. No assembly of believers is perfect because people are not perfect. If the church drifts from its focus on Jesus, believers may need to find another church that nurtures us with the gospel. We are commanded to attend a church that is committed to Jesus.

As the deer pants for streams of water, so my soul pants for you, O God. Psalm 42.1 NIV

God designed us with a soul that longs for Him. No matter how much money or earthly treasures I have gained, my soul longs for God. Jesus established his church on earth through an assembly of those who believe in Him. I know undoubtedly that I am drawn to be with others who believe in Jesus.

As iron sharpens iron, so one man sharpens another. Proverbs 27.17 NIV

I meet with other believers to strengthen them with the love I pour out to them from Jesus. I also meet with other believers to be strengthened by seeing the love of God in them. My daughter suggested that we gather with other believers in Jesus to practice our faith. We may learn scripture from other believers. My love goes out to you as I write these words and as you read these words. As you read these words know that God loves you and I love you.

We, Jesus, you, and all those who believe in Jesus are the Church! The Church is the living body of those who believe in Jesus. Hurricanes, armies, and fires could destroy every "church" building on planet earth, but the Church of Jesus will still exist in those who believe in Him. Amen! It is critical we align ourselves with fellow believers to confirm we are the Church.

He who is not with me is against me, and he who does not gather with me scatters." Luke 11.23 NIV

Jesus indicated if we are not with Him, we are against Him; that is a very frightening statement to me. How do we demonstrate we are "with" Jesus? Although I did not read and record Luke 11.23 until the past year, I understood for many decades that God wanted me to assemble with other believers. Gathering with other believers to worship God and pray to God publicly demonstrates we are "with" God. Jesus commands that we "gather" with Jesus and other believers. Jesus is to be the head of our Church on earth.

"For where two or three have gathered together in My name, I am there in their midst." Matthew 18.20 NASB

When two or three have gathered in His name, He is there! God designed us to seek Him and gather with other believers. I gather with one or two men weekly to read and discuss the Holy Bible. My wife and I worship with other believers in Jesus weekly.

Jesus calls us to assemble with other believers and learn His ways through scripture. It is prudent to read the Bible ourselves to know the truth from the Lord. Beware of false prophets and learn the laws of God, not the rules of men. We are to gather with believers and continue on our journeys to be transformed into the likeness of Jesus.

Jesus is the Way, the Truth, and the Life. Our choice for church is quite clear. We may follow the laws of God and be a child of God, or follow the traditions of man. The church founded by Jesus, the Son of the Living God, is based on the word of God, the Holy Bible. Churches not based on the Holy Bible are based on the traditions of man. We can worship the LORD your God, who brought His people out of Egypt, or we can worship false gods. We can pray to God, serve as His ambassadors, and do His will, or we can serve our own selfish desires. We can obey the laws created by God that are documented in the Holy Bible or follow traditions created by man. God allows us to choose who we serve.

Let us pray. Dear Jesus, You are the head of Your church because You are the Son of the Living God. If we do not worship You and call You the blessed King, the stones will cry out and praise You. Let us sing praises to You, God. You, God, do not need us, but You love us as a free gift. We, however, need You, God. You made us in Your image and we are humbled You love us. We are honored to praise You in the gathering of believers you call your Church. Let us make it clear we are with You. You, God, are the light in the darkness. Let us gather together with believers, to avoid the risk of being scattered and divided in this world of darkness. Please gather the people belonging to You, God, so that as iron sharpens iron, let believers praise God. Please guide us to learn the Gospel of good news, and please grant us strength. Amen!

# CHAPTER 29

# We are to be Ambassadors of God

So we are ambassadors for Christ, since God is making his appeal through us; we entreat you on behalf of Christ, be reconciled to God. 2 Corinthians 5.20

Preach the word; be ready in season and out of season; reprove, rebuke, exhort, with great patience and instruction. 2 Timothy 4.2 NASB

"You are the light of the world. A city built on a hill cannot be hid. No one after lighting a lamp puts it under the bushel basket, but on the lampstand, and it gives light to all in the house. In the same way, let your light shine before others, so that they may see your good works and give glory to your Father in heaven." Matthew 5.14-16

Hear then the parable of the sower. "When anyone hears the word of the kingdom and does not understand it, the evil one comes and snatches away what has been sown in his heart. This is the one on whom seed was sown beside the road. "The one on whom seed was sown on the rocky places, this is the man who hears the word and immediately receives it with joy; yet he has no firm root in himself, but is only temporary, and when affliction or persecution arises because of the word, immediately he falls away. "And the one on whom seed was sown among the thorns, this is the man who hears the word, and the worry of the world and the deceitfulness of wealth choke the word, and it becomes unfruitful. "And the one on whom seed was sown on the good soil, this is the man who hears the word and understands it; who indeed bears fruit and brings forth, some a hundredfold, some sixty, and some thirty." Matthew 13.18-23 NASB

And Jesus came and said to them, "All authority in heaven and on earth has been given to me. Go therefore and make disciples of all nations, baptizing them in the name of the Father and of the Son and of the Holy Spirit, and teaching them to obey everything that I have commanded you. And remember, I am with you always, to the end of the age." Matthew 28.18-20

Just as each of us has one body with many members, and these members do not all have the same function, so in Christ we who are many form one body, and each member belongs to all the others. Romans 12.4-5 NIV

"This is my commandment, that you love one another as I have loved you. No one has greater love than this, to lay down one's life for one's friends. You are my friends if you do what I command you. I do not call you servants any longer, because the servant does not know what the master is doing; but I have called you friends, because I have made known to you everything that I have heard from my Father. You did not choose me but I chose you. And I appointed you to go and bear fruit, fruit that will last, so that the Father will give you whatever you ask him in my name. I am giving you these commands so that you may love one another." John 15. 12-17

We journey through life in our wilderness.  During our journey in the wilderness, we are humbled, we are tested to know what is in our heart, and we are presented with situations to obey the commandments of God or disobey the laws of God. The way is wide and broad that leads to destruction and many follow that path. The way that leads to eternal life is narrow and few follow that path.

Matthew 13.1-23 records the parable of a person sowing seeds. Some seeds that fell beside the road were eaten by birds. This is similar to those that hear the gospel of Jesus Christ, but do not understand it. Those that do not understand the gospel may not ponder the words of life and the evil one snatches away the gift. We are frequently bombarded with advertisements and news of the world to entice us to spend our money and to be conformed to the world. Unless we consciously focus our minds on Jesus, interests of the world may rule our hearts and minds.

Some seed fell in rocky places that had shallow soil. The seeds grew quickly, but faded quickly. These seeds are similar to people who hear the gospel and believe, but quickly lose faith when challenged or confronted by the world.

Other seeds fell among thorns and were choked out after they grew. These seeds are a metaphor for those who hear the gospel and believe, but worldly treasures or worries overtake the importance of following God. The faith of these believers did not mature.

Seeds that fall on good soil take root, grow, multiply, and bear fruit. The seeds in good soil represent those who hear the gospel and understand the word. When a person hears the gospel, believes in Jesus Christ, and repents, they are born again as a child of God and born in the Holy Spirit. When we are reborn in the spirit, we are infants in Christ; we attempt to die to the flesh and live in the spirit. As infants in Christ, we are not necessarily filled with the fruit of the Holy Spirit: love, joy, peace, patience, kindness, goodness, faithfulness, gentleness, and self-control. Luke 24.45 and John 14.26 teach that the Holy Spirit opens our minds to understand scripture and teach us God's ways.

Being born again in the Holy Spirit is the beginning of our spiritual journey and our spiritual growth. As a fatherless boy in the inner city, I was a broken follower of Jesus. I was similar to the seeds that fell among thorns and my faith was choked out and did not mature. The root cause of my loss of faith was my father's death in concert with my ignorance of the Holy Bible. I knew little of the Bible, other than historical narratives, such as Adam and Eve, Noah and the ark and Moses' parting of the Red Sea. As an innocent eleven-year-old boy, I was emotionally too young to have a mature understanding of the Holy Bible. As a naive young boy, I thought followers of Jesus would live a life free of tragedy. No one explained the Gospel of truth to me. The church where I attended as a child seemed to be filled with people who were well dressed and projected a pretense of having the perfect life. If followers of Jesus do not share their struggles and victories with one another, it is difficult for the young to learn how to walk in righteousness when struggles in life occur. My false concept of following Jesus generated a false conclusion. As a logical youngster, my false premise was that believing in God protects us from tragedy. Tragedy entered into my life prior to my understanding of the Holy Bible. I lost trust in God because I did not know what the Holy Bible actually stated.

I confess my heart was hardened as an eleven-year-old boy and I did not become receptive to God for many years. As a child, I had a heavy burden on my heart and I felt unprotected in the universe. Although I resumed attending church when my wife and I married, I thought God was not all-powerful and God was not involved in my daily life.

God did not come in person to teach me that He cares about me; He sent His ambassadors. Two of the ambassadors of God I encountered were my physician and my physician's pastor, who ministered to me. Over thirty years ago, at a time when my mind and soul ached from anxiety and panic attacks, I felt like a lost sheep in the darkness. I could no longer hear the whisper of God or feel God's reassuring presence. I was too weak to wander in life's wilderness alone. The stress of my father's suicide and my feeling of abandonment from my childhood seemed to resurface. I had no idea why, but my panic attacks mutated into an all-encompassing sense of anxiety. I felt my mind and heart racing when nothing was wrong. My anxiety worsened and I could not fall asleep. As a healthy young man in his early twenties, I did not understand why I could not fall asleep. At one point, I had two consecutive sleepless nights. After fifty-seven hours without sleep, I told my wife I was not sleeping and something was very wrong; I felt like I was encompassed by a dark confusion. My wife took me to a physician. The physician diagnosed my condition as clinical depression. The physician prescribed antidepressant medication and medication to help me sleep. I felt embarrassed and ashamed that my brain was sick. I would rather have had a heart attack and died or had terminal cancer, rather than have my brain chemistry malfunction and live. Clinical depression caused me to think slower and experience varying levels of confusion. My body had suddenly betrayed me by not properly regulating my brain chemistry. As my depression worsened, my intelligence, emotions and creativity were overshadowed by confusion, sadness and helplessness. I felt totally abandoned by God. The God I worshipped, the God of the healthy, wealthy, and wise, allowed numerous illnesses, but brain malfunctions seemed far more terrible and embarrassing.

My wife met with our minister for comfort and shared that I had anxiety that escalated into clinical depression. The minister gave my wife no comfort, but rather recommended that my wife divorce me. My wife asked the minister, "Isn't marriage for better or for worse?" The minister replied, "No. In marriage, you do not have to endure the worst." My wife had no intentions of divorcing me. She wanted understanding, but received none from the church. My wife loved me for better or for worse, in sickness and in health. My wife understood unconditional love for her weak and sick husband at his worse time.

My extraordinarily angelic wife, more precious than rubies, helped make me become strong when I was weak. God created physicians to act on His behalf; the healing of physicians comes from God. The physician's medication did not improve my mental confusion immediately, but it did permit me to sleep at night. Ironically, the physician told me I needed more faith in God and recommended I meet with his pastor who believes in unconditional love. One church founded by man abandoned me, but a pastor from a Church led by Jesus, the Son of the Living God, loved me as God loves us: unconditionally. My wife experienced a huge growth in her transformation toward a greater likeness of Jesus. My wife learned that loving someone who is weak and sick is a demonstration of the unconditional love of Jesus, not a sign of weakness. I grew in my walk with Jesus also. I learned I am too weak to walk through life without the love of God and His ambassadors! I learned my wife has the faith and righteousness of an angel. I met weekly with my physician's pastor and grew in faith by his ministry. Thank you Pastor Black for teaching me God loves me unconditionally and when I am weak, I can be strong in God.

My recovery from clinical depression was much slower than I ever imagined. I was able to get out of bed after two weeks. I went to work daily and utilized all of my ability to concentrate to function as an engineer. For the first few months, I was so exhausted after each day of work, I ate dinner and went to sleep. I smiled once after six months of treatment. My joy of life, love of people, intelligence, and creativity gradually returned over the course of a full year. Clinical depression is an emotionally painful disease. Those inflicted with clinical depression experience somewhat of an out-of-body experience. The spiritual part of me, my soul, knew I was intelligent enough to graduate from a challenging engineering program, but my physical brain and my biochemical mind found it very difficult to decide what brand of cola to purchase. For the first time, I comprehended that the soul, the brain, and the mind are three entities that co-exist in the human body while we are alive. When the physical brain chemistry malfunctions, the mind experiences confusion, but the everlasting soul is present in the body and understands the brain and mind are broken. Perhaps sadness occurs because the everlasting soul wants to praise God, experience joy, and love others, but the physical brain and the biochemical mind keep the soul silenced and imprisoned. Although my episode of clinical depression occurred over thirty years ago, recalling and documenting the illness brings tears to my eyes for everyone who has experienced or who is currently experiencing depression. I pray that everyone affected by depression be comforted by the Holy Spirit and be healed by earthly physicians and the great physician, God.

Worse than the isolation, confusion, sadness, and exhaustion of depression, I personally felt abandoned by God. God did not abandon me;

He was with me through the illness. However, I was not able to sufficiently calm my brain to be still and know He is God. When I finally recovered, my joy reappeared because I felt God's presence once again. I prayed to God and forgave my father for abandoning me; harboring anger toward my father for robbing me of a normal childhood did no good. Clinical depression can be so isolating, and horrifying by the self-awareness of the illness, death may appear to be a suitable surrender to the pain. When in a clinical depression, it is critical that those involved remember that this is a struggle that will pass. God blessed me with my own personal ambassador, my wife. Finishing the race of life, while in a clinical depression, takes more strength than surrendering and admitting defeat. My ambassador wife gave me unconditional love and the strength to trust in the LORD with all my heart and not rely on my own understanding. The journey in the wilderness of life may include the valley of darkness. I walked through the valley of darkness with the help of my wife, physician and my pastor. Walking through the valley of darkness humbled me. For the first time in my life, I needed others to help me emerge on the other side of the valley. These three ambassadors of God guided my path. Perseverance in life does not imply we succeed alone; perseverance and spiritual maturity may be only possible with the assistance of ambassadors of God to help us in our journey through the wilderness. I learned to persevere in times of trouble with the teaching by God's ambassadors.

Clinical depression is indeed a brain biochemical malfunction. I personally have managed to reduce my risk of enduring another clinical depression for over thirty years. Out of love for you, my reader, I share a common man's method of minimizing my risk for clinical depression; perhaps the information may be beneficial to you. My action plan to reduce my risk of clinical depression includes:

- Remembering to read the Holy Bible and build my house on the rock of God's Word
- Like Bartimaeus in Mark 10.51, I pray to God for His help in my daily activities
- Living as a temple of the Holy Spirit and serving as God's ambassador
- Knowing God hears our prayers and loves us
- Humbly acknowledging that I am not perfect; perfection is reserved for God
- Understanding that what is seen is temporary and what is unseen is eternal

- Balancing worship, family time, sleep and work
- Doing my best, then being content with God's gifts
- Storing up treasures in Heaven, not treasures that moth and rust destroy
- Remembering that the worst outcome for any situation we can imagine seldom occurs
- Visiting my physician immediately if I have clouded thoughts or am not sleeping (this happened when my mother and my brother-in-law died in the same week).

With love, I suggest my readers seek treatment from a physician immediately if one cannot sleep, feels overwhelmingly sad and isolated, or it is difficult to concentrate. Be especially aware if clinical depression has affected members of your family. I disclose I am not a physician; I am a survivor of clinical depression.

My spiritual understanding continued to grow when I attended a Christian men's weekend retreat. We met in groups to discuss applying the Bible to our daily lives. My group's topic was "Does God have sovereign control of all?" The leader of our group shared that his daughter died of a disease at eleven years old. The speaker indicated the duration of his daughter's illness and eventual death exceeded a year. During the time of his daughter's illness, he continually prayed to God to heal his daughter. To the speaker's immense disappointment and grief, his daughter died. He shared that he felt abandoned by God and angry with God after his daughter died. Eventually he came back to God. After much prayer and reading the Bible, the leader acknowledged that God controls all.

He stated we either believe Genesis 17.1, where God declares He is almighty, John 1.3, clarifying that all things came into being through Jesus and without Jesus not one thing came into being, or we believe the Holy Bible is false. The leader declared that he concluded that God is in charge.

The speaker in the men's group sited Job 2 as an example that God controls all. Satan did not have the power to cause harm to Job. The leader read aloud Job 2.5, explaining that God alone is all-powerful. The common man teacher explained Matthew 10.29: even the death of sparrows occurs by the will of God. The leader shared one more scripture verse:

Trust in the LORD with all your heart, and do not rely on your own insight. Proverbs 3.5

The sharing of the death of his daughter and his ultimate surrender to God inspired me to bow humbly before God, the King of the universe. I acknowledged that clinical depression is a struggle in life that occurs with God's knowledge. As a created being, I understood for the first time that anger at God is futile; God is all-powerful and only by His will does a sparrow die!

I logically agreed with the speaker that someone is ultimately in charge of the universe and His name is God.

"For my thoughts are not your thoughts, neither are your ways my ways," declares the LORD. "As the heavens are higher than the earth, so are my ways higher than your ways and my thoughts than your thoughts." Isaiah 55.8, 9 NIV

In his hand is the life of every living thing and the breath of every human being. Job 12.10

Every breath we take is a gift from God. God has the authority to stop our breath in His timing. A common man taught me that God is all-powerful, but I did not yet understand God's love. My friend and neighbor Dave S. and I were talking one day and I mentioned that I thought God did not care about my daily life. I thought perhaps we meander through life on our own and then die. After we die, then God acknowledges the existence of our soul and sends us to heaven or hell. Dave quoted Luke 12.7, indicating that God knows the numbers of hairs on our head and we each are valuable to God. Dave's brief and powerful scripture quote changed my view toward God and my outlook on life.

When I returned home from talking with Dave, I read Luke 12. This Godly man taught me the missing knowledge of God my soul thirsted for.

For many years, I read the Bible as a history book. My Godly friends inspired me to read the Bible; I started reading the Bible, not as a meaningless dead history book, but as the Living Word of God.

I was shocked that Jesus loves me and knows me. The Bible states God knew me before I was formed in my mother's womb. I was like a lost sheep. Luke 15 records that Jesus is like a shepherd that will leave his flock and hunt for a lost sheep. When the shepherd finds the lost sheep, he puts the lost sheep on his shoulders and carries it home with joy. Likewise, Jesus loves His lost sheep and wants them safe.

My wife, my physician, my pastor, the leader of the men's group and Dave S. served as God's ambassadors to me. Without these five ambassadors from God listening to me and redirecting my path, my faith would have remained choked by the thorns of my struggle and false religion in my childhood. Once I was freed from the thorns of my false religion, my faith began to grow and mature. Yes, God sends the rain on the righteous and unrighteous; God's ways are not our ways and are beyond our understanding.

God sent these five ambassadors into my life to do His work of healing and teaching. Jesus came to earth and provided His message of salvation, died to grant us eternal life, and ascended into Heaven. Jesus chose to no longer physically walk the earth and preach His message.

Jesus tells us to go and teach what He taught. The five ambassadors of God taught me the true gospel of the personal friendship and love of Jesus. The root seeds of my transformation into the likeness of Jesus were the personal disclosure by God's five ambassadors. We, as common people, have the God-given power and responsibility to teach the gospel. As believers saved me, we too may save the wanderers, the broken and the lost.

Let us pray. Heavenly Father, thank you for sending five ambassadors to tell me You, God, are alone Almighty and You, God, care about us. I am humbled You came to earth and walked amongst humans to teach Your gospel of love and salvation. Please give the readers of this book and me the power and courage to be Your ambassador. Let the quality of our efforts as ambassadors be pleasing to You Lord. Send us out to preach Your Holy Word. Send us out to proclaim that God knows the numbers of hairs on our heads and loves us. Send us out to feed the hungry, clothe the poor, and minister to the lonely, those who mourn, the sick, and the broken. Whatever we do to the least of these, we do unto you Lord. Encourage us to use all of our talents as Your ambassadors, such that when we are in Your presence in Heaven You say to each of us "Well done my good and faithful servant." Amen.

# CHAPTER 30

# Death

For everything there is a season, and a time for every matter under heaven:
a time to be born, and a time to die;
a time to plant, and a time to pluck up what is planted;
a time to kill, and a time to heal;
a time to break down, and a time to build up;
a time to weep, and a time to laugh;
a time to mourn, and a time to dance;
a time to throw away stones, and a time to gather stones together;
a time to embrace, and a time to refrain from embracing;
a time to seek, and a time to lose;
a time to keep, and a time to throw away;
a time to tear, and a time to sew;
time to keep silence, and a time to speak;
a time to love, and a time to hate;
a time for war, and a time for peace. Ecclesiastes 3.1-8

"No one knows about that day or hour, not even the angels in heaven, nor the Son, but only the Father. Be on guard! Be alert! You do not know when that time will come. It's like a man going away: He leaves his house and puts his servants in charge, each with his assigned task, and tells the one at the door to keep watch. "Therefore keep watch because you do not know when the owner of the house will come back—whether in the evening, or at midnight, or when the rooster crows, or at dawn. If he comes suddenly, do not let him find you sleeping." Mark 13.32-36 NIV

"All men are like grass, and all their glory is like the flowers of the field. The grass withers and the flowers fall. Isaiah 40.6b-7a NIV

The length of our days is seventy years -- or eighty, if we have the strength; yet their span is but trouble and sorrow, for they quickly pass, and we fly away. Psalm 90.10 NIV

They will say, "Where is this 'coming' he promised? Ever since our fathers died, everything goes on as it has since the beginning of creation." The Lord is not slow in keeping his promise, as some understand slowness. He is patient with you, not wanting anyone to perish, but everyone to come to repentance. 2 Peter 3.4, 9 NIV

Brothers, we do not want you to be ignorant about those who fall asleep, or to grieve like the rest of men, who have no hope. We believe that Jesus died and rose again and so we believe that God will bring with Jesus those who have fallen asleep in him. According to the Lord's own word, we tell you that we who are still alive, who are left till the coming of the Lord, will certainly not precede those who have fallen asleep. For the Lord himself will come down from heaven, with a loud command, with the voice of the archangel and with the trumpet call of God, and the dead in Christ will rise first. After that, we who are still alive and are left will be caught up together with them in the clouds to meet the Lord in the air. And so we will be with the Lord forever. I Thessalonians 4.13-17 NIV

The poem recorded in Ecclesiastes 3.1-8 is an amazing collection of opposing events that occur in our journey through the wilderness of life. There is indeed a time for every matter under heaven. Most of us can relate to the events mentioned in Ecclesiastes 3.1-8. I remember planting raspberry bushes, then plucking them out many years later. My wife and I danced on our wedding day over thirty years ago. I remember wailing at my aged mother's funeral service. My wife and I mounted our name on the mailbox of our first home. I remember removing our name plate from the mailbox when we relocated for a better job. I remember boldly speaking the truth of righteousness. I am quiet when I listen to the voice of God. I have lived through several periods of war and short durations of peace. Birth and death are engrained in the cycle of life. Humans have the intelligence to observe crops grow in the spring and be harvested in the autumn. All of nature proclaims a progression from start to finish, birth to death.

My wife and I are blessed with two grown children. I never conceived that the human mind is designed by God to acquire, retain, and retrieve detailed information for one's entire life. I remember when my wife gave birth to our two children. Our children are now adults. However, images of my son as a two-year-old are still clear in my mind. Images of my daughter at seven-years-old playing in the backyard of our country home are also clear in my mind. The memories stored in my mind are a gift from God. A fellow at work asked for some tutoring on mathematics involving statistics. Although I had not used the formulas from my college days thirty-five years ago, I successfully helped him with his homework. Suddenly, I fully recognized I am getting chronologically old. Both of my children are now older than my age at the time when they were born.

Although we humans possess the knowledge that we will each die one day, we tend to live each day and not dwell on death. Psalm 118.24 declares that the Lord made each day and we are to rejoice and be glad. Ironically, the way one views death greatly affects how one lives on earth. Observing how a person lives may indicate that person's view of death! The word death is more complex than the ending of physical life. The Bible distinguishes the death of the body and the death of the soul:

- A time to be born, and a time to die. Ecclesiastes 3.2 KJV
- For thou hast delivered my soul from death. Psalm 116.8a KJV

The way one views the existence of the soul directly impacts how one views the death of the body:

- If one disregards the existence of the soul, then the death of the body is viewed as the end of life.
- If one acknowledges the existence of one's soul, then the death of the body can be viewed as a transition from carnal life to eternal life.

Then he told them a parable: "The land of a rich man produced abundantly. And he thought to himself, 'What should I do, for I have no place to store my crops?' Then he said, 'I will do this: I will pull down my barns and build larger ones, and there I will store all my grain and my goods. And I will say to my soul, Soul, you have ample goods laid up for many years; relax, eat, drink, be merry.' But God said to him, 'You fool! This very night your life is being demanded of you. And the things you have prepared, whose will they be?' So it is with those who store up treasures for themselves but are not rich toward God." Luke 12.16-21

The above parable by Jesus in Luke 12 explains the story of a landowner with an unusually plentiful harvest. The landowner was in the agriculture business and was very wealthy. Agriculture is a very detailed business that requires supplemental workers, good planning, sourcing good seeds, precise planting, weeding, strenuous harvesting, transporting the crops to market, and sales. To achieve wealth in agriculture, the rich man likely worked long and difficult hours. It appears the rich man was focused on his work, his achievements, his wealth, and his things. Luke 12.19 suggests the rich man accumulated many earthly treasures, enough to last for years. Despite his immense wealth, the rich man evidently had no intention of sharing his plentiful harvest with his neighbors or the poor. Instead, the agricultural tycoon considered the bumper crop to be a challenge; the rich man decided to build bigger barns to store his grain and his ever-increasing collection of treasures.

God abruptly interrupted the rich man's plans to build more barns to contain his amassed wealth. God called the rich man a fool and indicated his life on earth was being taken that night. The word fool is a supernatural choice. A fool can be described as a person smitten for a particular earthly possession or someone lacking in understanding. This rich man was a fool in two applications of the word. The rich man was a fool for devoting his earthly life to the accumulation of wealth and treasures. The man accumulated so much grain and treasures, he needed to build more barns to store his possessions. The rich man was also a fool for storing up things for his selfish desires on earth and not storing up treasures toward God in heaven. The rich man was not concerned with the judgment of his soul. Perhaps the rich man rejected or ignored that he had a soul, but focused on only the visible things of this world. The rich man apparently did nothing to feed the poor or clothe the naked. Jesus taught in Matthew 25.35 that we are to share our food. God tells the selfish rich man that he will get what he prepared for himself. The rich man stored his entire treasure on earth and stored nothing for heaven. The rich man apparently had no concern for the death of his soul. The rich man's treasure will remain on earth and the rich man will not receive treasure in heaven. God further indicates anyone who stores up things for himself, but nothing for God, will receive nothing for heaven.

This parable of the self-centered rich man, fully focused on life in the flesh, can describe the prevalent philosophy in modern society. Marketing experts and society in general promote focusing on oneself, similar to the rich man in Luke 12.16-21. The carnal world attempts to entice us to focus on ourselves. Previously, man was tempted to buy bigger mansions, bigger barns, bigger wardrobes, and bigger treasures. In modern society, nothing much has changed; we are prompted to buy bigger mansions, bigger garages, bigger wardrobes, bigger vehicles, bigger entertainment centers, and the latest technological advancements. Our lives in civilized societies may be quite similar to the rich man in Luke 12. Being wealthy is a gift from God, but from whom much is given, much is expected. God ended the man's life before he could build bigger barns to hold his bigger grain harvest and treasures. He stored things up for himself, but was not rich toward God. Those who deny or disregard the existence of the soul view death as the end of their carnal life of food, drink, and earthly treasures. Like the beautiful flowers of the field in all their glory, flowers and men will die and wither. The rich man stored nothing for God. God warns that this is how it will be for anyone who stores up things only on earth; there will be no riches for God. The parable indicates the man focused on hording his grain and treasures. Perhaps the rich man did not sin by commission. There was no mention that the rich man committed murder, committed adultery, or committed robberies. Perhaps the rich man sinned by omission. There was no mention of the rich man providing food for the hungry, providing clothing for the naked, or visiting the sick. The parable stated the rich man was not rich toward God, perhaps indicating he omitted worshipping God. The rich man lived a carnal selfish life. The rich man may have never considered the spiritual aspects of life and love. However, Jesus warns:

"He who is not with Me is against Me; and he who does not gather with Me scatters." Matthew 12.30 NASB

Eternal life is a gift from Jesus to those who live and believe in Him. The rich man evidently chose to reject Jesus and his command to love one another. Death for the rich man is most likely a frightening concept. Death for the rich man is something to be avoided.

Where the rich man sinned by omission, others sin by commission. Children of the devil acknowledge there is a spiritual aspect of existence; they endorse the spiritual forces of wickedness. The children of the devil may want to be like and be with their father, the devil. I personally love God and prefer a cooler climate; I have no desire to spend eternity in the lake of fire with the devil. However, images of the devil are commonplace. I never conceived of the concept of choosing evil on earth and embracing hell after death until I am typing these words. Some children of the devil indeed acknowledge a spiritual aspect of life, but live in defiance of God's laws, and actively seek to steal, kill, and destroy.

By this the children of God and the children of the devil are obvious: anyone who does not practice righteousness is not of God, nor the one who does not love his brother. I John 3.10 NASB

The children of the devil may fill their days by hating and hurting others, lying, hiding in the darkness, and stealing that which is not theirs. The devil and his children seek to tempt and devour the children of God. The devil and his children are enemies of God and enemies of God's children. The children of the devil will commit their acts of theft, murder, and destruction until they die.

The broken and the lost may not know how to live and may not understand the consequences of death. The Son of Man will come when we do not expect Him. The lost and the broken may think there is time in the future to repent and find faith. The lost and the broken may think their life will end at old age. There is no guarantee that anyone will reach seventy to eighty years old. Cemeteries have graves of people who died of illnesses or accidents at an early age. The lost and the broken may be kind to one another. The lost and the broken may share their food and love their neighbor. However, we are justified by faith in Jesus. The parable of the laborers in the vineyard in Matthew 20 indicates laborers who started at various times received the same pay (a metaphor for Heaven). If the lost or the broken commit to faith in Jesus at a later time in life, they are still saved. However, the lost or broken are at risk to die before they repent and find Jesus.

Those that live and believe in Jesus Christ are to live each day to the fullest. Although the children of the light comprehend that death is inevitable, followers of Jesus are to rejoice and be glad in the day that the Lord has made. Jesus' parable of the talents in Matthew 25.14-28 teaches that we are to fully utilize our God-given talents. The followers of Jesus are to be a shining beacon of light to others, so that others may see their good works and give glory to God. Those who understand we each have an eternal soul are to serve as God's ambassadors. Followers of Jesus of Nazareth are not to sleep their life away and stare into the sky waiting for Christ's return; Jesus commands us in Mark 13 to successfully perform our assigned tasks in life. God gave me the talents in engineering, logical thinking, and communication, then biblical research and understanding. My assigned task is to work as an engineer and also learn and teach the gospel. Writing this book is my task assigned by God. Jesus teaches we are not to be preoccupied with death, but rather occupied with doing our assigned task. We each are called to love God and love our neighbor as our self. We are to serve in the church of Jesus with other followers. If we follow Jesus' command to visit the sick, feed the hungry, and welcome strangers, and serve as His ambassador, we can be active for many years. We are to minister to the lost and the broken.

Those who live and believe in Jesus, even though they die, will live. Those who live and believe in Jesus are justified by faith; we are imperfect forgiven sinners. The righteous may live up to seventy or eighty years old and die individually. The righteous may be called to heaven and gather with Jesus when He comes again. Regardless, those who believe must do their assigned task until our life on earth ends.

The children of the light acknowledge Jesus may return at any moment and His angels will gather together people belonging to God in the sky. The children of the light also acknowledge they may be called home individually by God prior to Jesus' return. Jesus specifically said in Mark 23.32 that the angels, nor Jesus Himself, know when Jesus will return. Regardless if we die individually or if we are collectively called to heaven, the destination is identical. Let me repeat, if we die individually or if we are collectively called to heaven, the destination is identical. Some people seem fixated on Jesus' return to gather the elect. Whether I die of old age or I am called into the sky to meet Jesus, it is fine with me.

Ironically, some people professing to be Christians claim to know when Jesus is returning to call the righteous and send wrath to the wicked. My deceased grandfather falsely proclaimed he and others knew when Christ was returning. Their false date of Christ's return in the 1950's came and passed uneventfully. Anyone who claims to know when Jesus will return is a false teacher. Do not follow false teachers; discern people of the truth and people of the lie.

2 Peter 3.4, 9 records that after Jesus rose from the dead and subsequently ascended into Heaven; some thought He would return quickly. Peter rebuked these people who pompously thought God was slow in initiating Jesus' second coming. Peter indicated that life is proceeding as it has since creation. Peter profoundly stated that God is patient in His return. I have heard born again believers share that they think that the current era is so wicked, Jesus must be coming soon. God's ways are not our ways. In 2 Peter 3.9, Peter indicated Jesus may allow ample time for people to repent and be saved! In a divine mystery, perhaps the children of the light are called to preach the Word of God in good times and in the wicked times to rebuke and instruct the wicked, the broken, and the lost! In the Initial Wrath of God Era, prior to the time of Numbers 18, God did pour out his wrath when humans sinned. The destruction of Sodom and Gomorrah are fine examples

of God's wrath. However, God instituted the sacrificial era and then the new covenant. We are living in the new covenant era. Jesus is allowing time for His ambassadors to make disciples. Followers of Jesus of Nazareth are to preach the word with great patience and instruction.

Let us pray. Heavenly Father, please give us the deductive logic skills to understand death is not the end of us. Our existence on earth includes a mind and a soul. Our mind and soul work in concert to encompass our yearning for God, awareness of existence, personality, behavior, conscience, intelligence, ethics, creativity, and memories. The mind and soul function within our human brain and body. Upon death, the human physical brain dies and withers; the functioning of the mind, manifested within the electrochemical and biological structure of the brain, will end. However, our consciousness and soul are eternal. Death is not the end of our existence; death is simply the transition from the temporary life in the flesh to eternal life in the spirit. Jesus, please remind us daily of your wise council from Matthew 6, that we are not to store up our treasures on earth, where moth and rust destroy or where thieves break in and steal. We are to store up for ourselves treasures in heaven, for where our treasures are, there our hearts will be also. Death of the body is not a possibility; death of the body is an inevitability. Let us live and believe in Jesus to prepare treasures for heaven during our lifetime on earth and avoid the sting of death. Amen.

# CHAPTER 31

# Judgment of One's Soul

Now there is in store for me the crown of righteousness, which the Lord, the righteous Judge, will award to me on that day—and not only to me, but also to all who have longed for his appearing. 2 Timothy 4.8 NIV

"I tell you, my friends, do not be afraid of those who kill the body and after that can do no more. But I will show you whom you should fear: Fear him who, after the killing of the body, has power to throw you into hell. Yes, I tell you, fear him." Luke 12.4-5 NIV

Do not be deceived; God is not mocked, for you reap whatever you sow. If you sow to your own flesh, you will reap corruption from the flesh; but if you sow to the Spirit, you will reap eternal life from the Spirit. Galatians 6.7-8

And you were dead in your trespasses and sins, in which you formerly walked according to the course of this world, according to the prince of the power of the air, of the spirit that is now working in the sons of disobedience. Among them we too all formerly lived in the lusts of our flesh, indulging the desires of the flesh and of the mind, and were by nature children of wrath, even as the rest. But God, being rich in mercy, because of His great love with which He loved us, even when we were dead in our transgressions, made us alive together with Christ (by grace you have been saved). Ephesians 2.1-5 NASB

Then the kings of the earth and the great men and the commanders and the rich and the strong and every slave and free man hid themselves in the caves and among the rocks of the mountains; and they said to the mountains and to the rocks, "Fall on us and hide us from the presence of Him who sits on the throne, and from the wrath of the Lamb; for the great day of their wrath has come, and who is able to stand?" Revelations 6.15-17 NASB

273

His winnowing fork is in his hand, to clear his threshing floor and to gather the wheat into his granary; but the chaff he will burn with unquenchable fire." Luke 3.17

I have fought the good fight, I have finished the course, I have kept the faith; in the future there is laid up for me the crown of righteousness, which the Lord, the righteous Judge, will award to me on that day; and not only to me, but also to all who have loved His appearing. 2 Timothy 4.7-8 NASB

All who sin apart from the law will also perish apart from the law, and all who sin under the law will be judged by the law. For it is not those who hear the law who are righteous in God's sight, but it is those who obey the law who will be declared righteous. (Indeed, when Gentiles, who do not have the law, do by nature things required by the law, they are a law for themselves, even though they do not have the law, since they show that the requirements of the law are written on their hearts, their consciences also bearing witness, and their thoughts now accusing, now even defending them.) This will take place on the day when God will judge men's secrets through Jesus Christ, as my gospel declares. Romans 2.12-16 NIV

If your hand or your foot causes you to sin, cut it off and throw it away. It is better for you to enter life maimed or crippled than to have two hands or two feet and be thrown into eternal fire. Matthew 18.8 NIV

For we must all appear before the judgment seat of Christ, so that each one may be recompensed for his deeds in the body, according to what he has done, whether good or bad. 2 Corinthians 5.10 NASB

Jesus' statement in Matthew 10.28 regarding only fearing God is profound in multiple ways. Jesus indicated we are not to fear anyone who can only kill our body, but unable to kill our soul. We are to rather fear Him who is able to destroy both soul and body in hell. I embrace this statement in my daily life. I will not allow myself to be bullied into committing sin on the threat of being fired from a job or killed. This scripture should prompt all humans to understand that life is temporary and God has the power to send our souls to hell for eternity.

God made the stars. God formed our inward parts while we were in our mothers' wombs. God knew us before we were born. God designed the hawk to soar and to fly south. Not even a sparrow will die and fall to the ground without God's will. God clearly differentiates obedience from disobedience and righteousness from evil throughout His Holy Word, the Bible. All of God's creation teaches consequences. If we plant tomato seeds in good soil, the harvest will be tomatoes. If we plant corn, corn will grow. If we do not tend our land, thistles will grow.

Sir Isaac Newton's third law of motion is: "For every action there is an equal and opposite reaction."[19] As every work reflects the designer, nature and God reveal that every action has an opposite reaction. Luke 12 records that God has the power to send unrepentant wicked souls to hell. However, Jesus died in our place such that those who live and believe in Jesus will be saved by His grace. God is a righteous judge.

What we sow while we are alive in the flesh determines the judgment we will receive. Rereading the aforementioned scriptures brings me to my knees with the awesome power of God; God's ways are not our ways. We each choose to live and believe in God or reject God. God gave Adam and Eve, Cain and Abel, and each of us the ability to follow God's command to love God and love our neighbor or reject it. Adam and Eve wanted to obtain the knowledge of good and evil and disobeyed God to get it. Cain killed his brother Abel because God favored Abel's heartfelt offering. Numerous people who believe in God reject God's laws. Satan believes in God and opposes God. It appears that humans who know God, and choose to live wickedly, intentionally forfeit Heaven to gain the treasures or pleasures of the flesh. Broken or lost people, who do not have faith, risk not being invited to Heaven.

Jesus saith unto him, Thomas, because thou hast seen me, thou hast believed: blessed are they that have not seen, and yet have believed. John 20.29 KJV

I knew a little girl who died and met Jesus. The body of the little girl experienced a trauma and she stopping breathing. Her mother ran to her daughter's body sprawled on the ground. The mother lifted her daughter up and cradled her limp body in her arms and carried her into the house. The little girl was unresponsive and had stopped breathing. Her mother started wailing because her daughter's body was lifeless. The little child was soon in the presence of Jesus, the Son of the Living God. Jesus said to the little girl, "You may come with me to Heaven." The little girl then perceived the spiritual forces of wickedness lurking nearby. She was not afraid; she felt happy and safe with Jesus. The little girl did not see a bodily image of Satan; he hates the Light and lives in darkness. The little girl started to follow Jesus into the light. She knew if she went with Jesus there would be no returning to her life on earth. Satan then said, "She belongs to me."

Jesus replied, "You know all children belong to me!" The little girl looked back and saw her mother crying and praying to Jesus to not take her little girl. The little girl turned to Jesus and said, "My mother needs me." Jesus replied, "If you come with me today, you belong to me. If you choose to stay, the next time you see me, you will have made your choice where to spend eternity." The little girl was suddenly looking up at her mother's tear-filled face. Her mother saw the life return to her daughter's face and rejoiced.

While being held in her mother's arms, the little girl's first words were, "I talked with Jesus." The mother, terrified and in denial of the incident, replied, "No, you just had a dream. You are safe now." The little girl replied to her mother, "It was not a dream. I talked with Jesus and saw you holding me and crying. I asked Jesus if I could come back." For years thereafter, whenever the girl mentioned she saw Jesus on the day she was injured, the mother told her that her interaction with Jesus was a dream.

Many years later, when the little girl matured into a teenager, she told her mother, "I still remember with perfect clarity the time I talked with Jesus as a child. Jesus invited me to go to heaven with Him because I was a child. However, if I came back to be with you, mom, I would decide for myself to choose Heaven or Hell. That incident was not a dream; seeing Jesus was a spiritual experience that I will never forget." The mother paused and replied, "I thought you were dead in my arms and when you suddenly spoke, I did not want to frighten you." The daughter replied, "I was never frightened because Jesus loves me and is always with me. I choose to live as a child of God. I was frustrated all these years that you said my spiritual experience was a dream. I have no fear of death because I have seen and believe." That little girl and teenager grew into a woman who became my wife.

My wife had the opportunity to personally see Jesus and believe. Romans 1.20 teaches that creation itself and God's eternal invisible power is sufficient for understanding; no one has an excuse to deny God's existence. Anyone who denies the existence of God and denies the laws of God has no excuse; all will be judged according to their deeds.

2 Timothy 4.8 clarifies that Jesus is a righteous judge. Jesus indicated in John 14.6 that no one comes to the Father, but through Him. Jesus, the Son

of the Living God, lived as a human being and died for our sins; Jesus died once for all, the just for the unjust. The following four scripture selections clarify grace and eternal life are gifts from Jesus:

Those who believe in him are not condemned; but those who do not believe are condemned already, because they have not believed in the name of the only Son of God. John 3.18

Jesus said to her, "I am the resurrection and the life; he who believes in Me will live even if he dies, and everyone who lives and believes in Me will never die. John 11.25-26a NASB

For by grace you have been saved through faith; and that not of yourselves, it is the gift of God; not as a result of works, so that no one may boast. Ephesians 2.8, 9 NASB

Since all have sinned and fall short of the glory of God; they are now justified by his grace as a gift, through the redemption that is in Christ Jesus, whom God put forward as a sacrifice of atonement by his blood, effective through faith. He did this to show his righteousness, because in his divine forbearance he had passed over the sins previously committed; it was to prove at the present time that he himself is righteous and that he justifies the one who has faith in Jesus. Romans 3.23-26

Scripture clearly teaches that we are saved by the redeeming grace from Jesus. Jesus taught that all who live and believe in him will have eternal life. I approach the throne of God with confidence because I know I am a forgiven sinner by the grace of God. God tells us not to judge others; God said He will be gracious to whom He will be gracious and He will show mercy on whom He will show mercy. God exclusively has the right to invite people to heaven at His discretion.

As for me and my house, we will serve the LORD. Joshua 24.15 KJV

Some humans believe that there will be no judgment of their soul; they believe when they die, there will be no recompense for their sins. Some believe when they die, there is no conscious existence of the soul, just peaceful non-existence in death. Regardless if people try to deny the recompense for their sin after death, they will sit before the judgment seat of Christ. Scripture declares that some people will try to avoid judgment by hiding themselves in the caves and among the rocks of the mountains. Some will be terrified of He who sits on the throne, and from the wrath of the Lamb. Revelations 6 has a very interesting phrase: the wrath of the lamb. Jesus and His angels will clear his threshing floor and gather the wheat into his granary; but the chaff he will burn with unquenchable fire." The wrath of the Lamb is not a possibility; the wrath of the Lamb is prophesied in the Holy Bible!

Perhaps the prophecy regarding the wrath of the Lamb is the final warning to not sin and be thrown into the eternal fire of hell! The *wrath of the Lamb* has a clear relevant teaching for me. I know the commandments of God very well. I have tried to retain as much of the teaching of the Holy Bible as I could. However, when the spiritual forces of wickedness and the children of the devil come to steal my dignity, kill my self-esteem, and destroy my life, the desire for revenge fills my heart and mind. I confess I am a warrior at heart and am a trained martial artist. Without God, the Holy Bible, my wife, and my pastor to guide me, I could be very tempted to take revenge against my adversaries. When we humans are attacked, our natural response, and the instinct of our carnal nature, is to defeat those who attack us! Years ago, a large attack dog charged to devour me. I fought the dog off with my martial arts skills. The beast and I both parted alive and unharmed. However the fight filled my body and mind with endorphins and adrenaline that provided a physical and mental peace that was amazing. I confess I am a barbaric cave man at heart with a fight or flight instinct. My carnal instincts for fairness and righteousness make me a better cave man, warrior, hunter-gatherer, than an engineer and a child of God. Our dual nature of a carnal creature of instinct and a follower of Jesus diametrically oppose one another.

Now that you, the reader, and I live in a society where the spiritual forces of wickedness may seek to steal, kill, and destroy in covert ways, we must adjust our defense against evil. The children of darkness may not seek to slay us with swords, but destroy us with insults and persecution. God tells us vengeance is His, He will repay. If the children of darkness insult you, persecute you and falsely say all kinds of evil (Matthew 5) know your reward in heaven will be great; the evil ones persecuted the prophets who came before you.

Do not repay evil with evil or insult with insult, but with blessing, because to this you were called so that you may inherit a blessing. 1 Peter 3.9 NIV

Jesus indicated in Matthew 18.8 that we are to cut off anything that causes us to sin in order to enter eternal life and avoid being thrown into the eternal fire of hell! I was humbled and enlightened when I acknowledged that anything that causes me to sin might cause me to be thrown into eternal fire in hell! We may be tempted to seek revenge. We are not to repay evil for evil, nor insult with insult. If evil is done to us, cut off the relationship. If we are insulted, cut it off. Evil and insults will tempt us to seek revenge. Bless those who hate us and cut them off. It is better to cut off abuse that tempts us to sin, than spend eternity in hell! Vengeance is the LORD's.

We are to cut off the temptation for fleshly lusts. Joseph, son of Jacob, ran away from Potiphar's wife when she wanted him to commit adultery. Like Joseph, we are to cut off any temptation of fleshly lusts that cause us to sin.

Whether we acknowledge there is a war between good and evil, Jesus will one day judge us; we will be recompensed for our deeds. God gave us each the freedom to choose where we will spend eternity. God has the power to send our souls to the location our deeds have chosen.

Let us pray. An unrighteous master may punish his servants for unspoken expectations or conflicting goals. Thank you Jesus for teaching us in advance the criteria for our judgment when we die. A righteous master tells His people how they will be judged. You, Jesus taught us those who live and believe in You would have eternal life. Your command for judgment is clear: love God and love your neighbor as yourself. Amen.

# CHAPTER 32

# Hell

"Now there was a rich man, and he habitually dressed in purple and fine linen, joyously living in splendor every day. "And a poor man named Lazarus was laid at his gate, covered with sores, and longing to be fed with the crumbs which were falling from the rich man's table; besides, even the dogs were coming and licking his sores. "Now the poor man died and was carried away by the angels to Abraham's bosom; and the rich man also died and was buried. "In Hades he lifted up his eyes, being in torment, and saw Abraham far away and Lazarus in his bosom. "And he cried out and said, 'Father Abraham, have mercy on me, and send Lazarus so that he may dip the tip of his finger in water and cool off my tongue, for I am in agony in this flame.' "But Abraham said, 'Child, remember that during your life you received your good things, and likewise Lazarus bad things; but now he is being comforted here, and you are in agony. 'And besides all this, between us and you there is a great chasm fixed, so that those who wish to come over from here to you will not be able, and that none may cross over from there to us.' "And he said, 'Then I beg you, father, that you send him to my father's house-- for I have five brothers--in order that he may warn them, so that they will not also come to this place of torment.' "But Abraham said, 'They have Moses and the Prophets; let them hear them.' "But he said, 'No, father Abraham, but if someone goes to them from the dead, they will repent!' "But he said to him, 'If they do not listen to Moses and the Prophets, they will not be persuaded even if someone rises from the dead.'" Luke 16.19-31 NASB

If anyone does not abide in Me, he is thrown away as a branch and dries up; and they gather them, and cast them into the fire and they are burned. John 15.6 NASB

And there was war in heaven, Michael and his angels waging war with the dragon. The dragon and his angels waged war, and they were not strong enough, and there was no longer a place found for them in heaven. And the great dragon was thrown down, the serpent of old who is called the devil and Satan, who deceives the whole world; he was thrown down to the earth, and his angels were thrown down with him. Revelations 12.7-9 NASB

But for the cowardly and unbelieving and abominable and murderers and immoral persons and sorcerers and idolaters and all liars, their part will be in the lake that burns with fire and brimstone, which is the second death." Revelation 21.8 NASB

"Who then is the faithful and sensible slave whom his master put in charge of his household to give them their food at the proper time? "Blessed is that slave whom his master finds so doing when he comes. "Truly I say to you that he will put him in charge of all his possessions. "But if that evil slave says in his heart, 'My master is not coming for a long time,' and begins to beat his fellow slaves and eat and drink with drunkards; the master of that slave will come on a day when he does not expect him and at an hour which he does not know, and will cut him in pieces and assign him a place with the hypocrites; in that place there will be weeping and gnashing of teeth. Matthew 24.45-51 NASB

And the devil who deceived them was thrown into the lake of fire and brimstone, where the beast and the false prophet are also; and they will be tormented day and night forever and ever. And if anyone's name was not found written in the book of life, he was thrown into the lake of fire. Revelations 20.10, 15 NASB

Jesus' parable regarding the rich man and Lazarus was relevant years ago and is relevant today. The rich man in Jesus' parable did not believe hell existed. The rich man was focused on himself and gave none of his riches to help others. The rich man was so exceedingly selfish, he would not give Lazarus his discarded food. Lazarus was poor, sick, and hungry. Both the rich man and Lazarus died. The rich man was sent to hell and angels carried Lazarus to heaven. Scripture indicates that hell is a place of torment. It is frightening that those in hell, although they are in the spiritual realm, experience the discomfort of thirst and the agony of burning flesh in a fire.

The arrogant rich man mistakenly thought his earthly status and power to dominate others on earth transferred beyond the grave and into hell.

The rich man had the audacity to ask Abraham to send Lazarus to fetch him water. Abraham told the rich man Lazarus would not provide him water; Lazarus was now comforted. This portion of the parable illustrates the hypocrisy of those who live in luxury and demand to be treated well, yet have no concern for others. The rich man enjoyed living in luxury, but would not give Lazarus the crumbs that fell from his table. However when the rich man wanted water, he wanted Lazarus to provide him water. Jesus commands us to:

"Treat others the same way you want them to treat you." Luke 6.31 NASB

Jesus came to serve, not to be served. Jesus explained in Matthew 25 that we are to give a drink to the thirsty, visit the sick and feed the hungry. The rich man did not help Lazarus. The rich man was a hypocrite regarding reciprocity and fairness. After his death, the rich man wanted pity from Abraham, but during his life he gave no pity to Lazarus. Abraham indicated to the rich man that now Lazarus would be comforted and he would be in agony. Being hard hearted and still arrogant, the rich man asked that Lazarus be sent as a messenger to his brothers to warn them hell exists. This insightful parable of the rich man and Lazarus illustrates that the first shall be last and the last shall be first. The rich man had the misconception that his earthly wealth and status would extend beyond death. It is critical that we understand what is seen is temporary and what is unseen is eternal. God's ways are not our ways. We come from dust and return to dust; we take no earthly treasure or earthly power with us in life after death.

Once again, Abraham denied the rich man's request to use Lazarus as a servant. Abraham told the rich man that if his five brothers did not listen to Moses and the prophets, they would not believe in heaven or hell if someone rose from the dead. Ironically, Jesus raised a widow's son from the dead (Luke 7.12-17), Jesus raised a little girl from the dead (Luke 8.54-56), Jesus' raised his friend Lazarus from the dead (John 11.42-44), and Jesus Himself rose from the dead (Matthew 28.5-10). Although people were indeed raised from the dead, many still do not believe in God and the gospel. Jesus indicated in His parable found in Luke 16 that we are to listen to Moses and the Prophets by reading the Holy Bible. The Holy Bible teaches the Truth. The parable of the rich man and Lazarus brings me peace. Jesus blessed us with His Holy Word. Jesus' death and resurrection was a gift that provides the forgiveness of sin and salvation for those who live and believe in Jesus Christ.

Like the rich man and his five brothers, God gives us the choice to love God and love their neighbor or forsake God and disregard those in need. Those who repent of their sins, love God, and love their neighbor shall be carried to heaven as Lazarus was carried to heaven. Those who live as the rich man, forsaking God and disregarding the needs of their neighbor, will be condemned to eternity in hell. Jesus declared that He spoke openly and told nothing in secret. Jesus openly taught that hell awaits all who disregard the law and the prophets.

Those who believe in Jesus are to gather together with other believers and to build one another up. After learning of the good news of Jesus, believers are to go forth into the world, share the good news of Jesus, save sinners, and make disciples. Those who do not abide in Jesus will scatter.

The devil is not currently in hell; as in the time of Job, the devil roams the earth seeking to steal, kill, and destroy. As with Adam and Eve, the devil seeks to destroy peoples' faith, prompt them to sin, and have their souls sent to hell. The wages of sin is death, that is, eternal punishment in hell.

Please understand there is no reward for the devil and the children of the devil in destroying the righteous; Jesus already won the war over evil. The destination for the devil and his followers is hell. Satan and his followers were thrown out of heaven for their evil ways. Satan is sentenced to hell and wants to destroy the lives of as many as he is able. The devil and his children torment others to make them weary and tempt them to sin. The wicked motivation of the devil is precisely what Jesus said: to steal, kill, and destroy. Like a jealous vandal who destroys another's treasure because he cannot have it, the devil and his followers seek to prevent us from going to heaven because he and his followers will not go to heaven.

Jesus' parable in Matthew 24 is instructive and conveys the awesome power of God to judge our deeds and consequently our souls. The master in the parable gives each servant activities to perform and leaves. When the master returns, the master is to find the servants performing their assigned jobs. The master in the parable is Jesus Christ and we are the servants. Jesus wants us to perform our Godly duties until He returns and we meet Him. Jesus wants each of us to use our God-given talents to do good work.

Let your light so shine before men, that they may see your good works, and glorify your Father which is in heaven. Matthew 5.16 KJV

In doing good works, our neighbors see the light of Christ in us. Our kindness before people demonstrates we are children of God; this gives glory to God who art in heaven. While we are alive on earth, we are to continue to be the salt and the light of Jesus in a fallen world. We are to love God and treat others the same way we want them to treat us.

God is not the author of confusion. I Corinthians 14.33a KJV

God does NOT cause confusion. Jesus has spoken the truth openly; Jesus has not spoken in secret to the rich nor the powerful on earth. Through the living Word of God, Jesus continues to talk to the common man and woman.

The servant in the parable in Matthew 24 behaves in a wicked manner by beating his fellow servants. The wicked servant chose to act as a child of the devil and beat his fellow servants, thinking the master will not return soon. The parable explains the master will return when he is not expected. The master will have the wicked servant cut to pieces and assign him a place where there will be weeping and gnashing of teeth.

Jesus openly and clearly taught that unrepentant wicked people would be sent to hell. The wicked servant chose to abuse his fellow servants. All of us have sinned and fall short of the glory of God. Jesus told us numerous times in the gospels to repent. Jesus gives each of us the opportunity to repent. After we repent of our sins, Jesus can forgive us through our faith. We have salvation only because we are justified by his grace as a gift; we are redeemed because Jesus died as a sacrifice of atonement, the just for the unjust.

We each have the ability to reject the gift of eternal life in heaven offered by Jesus. We each have the choice to be evil or righteous. Our choice has severe consequences. Those that reject Jesus' gift of life and choose evil over righteousness will be sent to hell.

Jesus' describes hell as a lake of fire where there is unrelenting and eternal torment, agony, thirst, weeping, and gnashing of teeth. I wept at my mother's funeral service; weeping is caused by extreme sorrow. I have gnashed my teeth when I experienced extreme pain.

Jesus is being kind by providing a written warning of danger. Electrical appliances have a danger message of electric shock. I mounted several danger signs on my powerful lawn mower that indicates a cutting danger; I wanted to remind myself not to place my feet or fingers near the powerful spinning sharp blades. The radiator caps on our cars and trucks state "Danger, do not open when hot, burn hazard." If we open the radiator cap when the vehicle is hot, pressurized scalding hot radiator fluid may burn us. The windshield washer fluid for our cars and trucks is marked "Danger, Poison, Do Not swallow."

I have not electrocuted myself, cut off my fingers on my lawn mower, opened a radiator cap on a hot engine, or drank windshield washer fluid. I comprehend that the dangers are real and understand the warnings are truly intended to keep us safe from harm.

Jesus warned us of the dangers of hell: excessive heat, torment, agony, thirst, weeping, and gnashing of teeth! Let us comprehend the dangers of hell are real and understand the warnings by Jesus are truly intended to keep us safe from harm.

Let us pray. Dear Jesus, thank you for informing us of the dangers of hell. Like a good friend, you love us enough to direct us to the path of eternal life and warn us to avoid hell. You are a very loving and open God without secrets. I believe hell is a real and a terrible place of torment and isolation from Your presence oh, God. My body has been filled with Your Holy Spirit during my time on earth; I do not want to lose Your presence for eternity. I pray all who are reading **Jesus is Our Friend** understand that hell is real and we will each be recompensed for our deeds in the body. Eternal life in heaven is a gift from You, oh God, paid for by Your death on the cross for us sinners. Hell is the eternal punishment for the children of the devil. Let us each choose to be children of God and inherit the kingdom as sons and daughters of God. Eternity in hell being isolated from God's love is the worst form of torment. Amen.

# CHAPTER 33

# Heaven

"Do not store up for yourselves treasures on earth, where moth and rust destroy, and where thieves break in and steal. But store up for yourselves treasures in Heaven, where neither moth nor rust destroys, and where thieves do not break in or steal; for where your treasure is, there your heart will be also." Matthew 6.19-21 NASB

Jesus said to her, "I am the resurrection and the life; he who believes in Me will live even if he dies, and everyone who lives and believes in Me will never die. John 11.25-26a NASB

"Blessed are those who have been persecuted for the sake of righteousness, for theirs is the kingdom of heaven. Blessed are you when people insult you and persecute you, and falsely say all kinds of evil against you because of Me. Rejoice and be glad, for your reward in heaven is great; for in the same way they persecuted the prophets who were before you." Matthew 5.11-12 NASB

"You will be hated by all because of My name, but it is the one who has endured to the end who will be saved. Matthew 10.22 NASB

"The kingdom of heaven is like a merchant seeking fine pearls, and upon finding one pearl of great value, he went and sold all that he had and bought it." Matthew 13.45b, 46 NASB

"Our Father who is in heaven, Hallowed be Your name." Matthew 6.9 NASB

When the angels had gone away from them into heaven, the shepherds began saying to one another, "Let us go straight to Bethlehem then, and see this thing that has happened which the Lord has made known to us." Luke 2.15 NASB

And he was saying, "Jesus, remember me when You come in Your kingdom!" And He said to him, "Truly I say to you, today you shall be with Me in Paradise." Luke 23.42-43 NASB

Let not your heart be troubled: ye believe in God, believe also in me. In my Father's house are many mansions: if it were not so, I would have told you. I go to prepare a place for you. And if I go and prepare a place for you, I will come again, and receive you unto myself; that where I am, there ye may be also. John 14.1-3 KJV

Surely goodness and mercy shall follow me all the days of my life: and I will dwell in the house of the LORD for ever. Psalm 23.6 KJV

And I heard a loud voice from the throne, saying, "Behold, the tabernacle of God is among men, and He will dwell among them, and they shall be His people, and God Himself will be among them, and He will wipe away every tear from their eyes; and there will no longer be any death; there will no longer be any mourning, or crying, or pain; the first things have passed away." And He who sits on the throne said, "Behold, I am making all things new." And He said, "Write, for these words are faithful and true." Then He said to me, "It is done. I am the Alpha and the Omega, the beginning and the end. I will give to the one who thirsts from the spring of the water of life without cost. He who overcomes will inherit these things, and I will be his God and he will be My son." Revelations 21.3-7 NASB

Jesus clearly tells us in Matthew 6.19-21 that we are not to store up our treasure on earth, where treasure can be destroyed by moth and rust or be stolen. Jesus tells us to store up our treasure in Heaven. Treasure stored for Heaven is eternal. Where people accumulate their treasure indicates what is most important in their heart. We actually choose where our soul will spend eternity during our life in the flesh. Loving God with all our heart, soul, and mind will prompt us to store up our treasure in Heaven. People have the ability to store up their treasures on earth and not be concerned with their soul. However, all earthly treasure that people accumulate will remain on earth when they die.

I want to make an aside here. Per Psalm 118.24, the LORD gives each day to us as a gift and we are to rejoice and be glad. We store up our treasures in Heaven by being God's ambassadors on earth. Heaven is indeed our destination, but we are to love God and love our neighbor while we are alive in the flesh. We wander in the desert of life to conquer our carnal instinct and be transformed into the likeness of Jesus. Life teaches us that when we are weak, Christ's power rests on us.

Jesus indicated He is the resurrection and the life. If we live and believe in Jesus, we will have eternal life in Heaven. Jesus' profound declaration in Matthew 5.11-12 that we will be persecuted for believing in Jesus, establishes the seriousness of the struggle between good and evil. As my commitment to follow Jesus became more focused and serious, the spiritual forces of wickedness seemed to focus their efforts to disrupt me from sharing the good news of Jesus. As I get older, I fully understand the gravity of the war between good and evil around us. My goal of being invited to Heaven by Jesus is very real to me. I am committed to being an ambassador of Jesus Christ and sharing the good news of salvation by loving God and loving my neighbor as myself. The children of the devil seem to perceive when a follower of Jesus is committed to the kingdom of God. Jesus said he blesses us when we are insulted and persecuted because we are committed to living and believing in God. Children of the devil, some masquerading as Christians, have persecuted me and tried to disrupt my path to finishing this book, *Jesus is Our Friend*. Remember that Jesus gave His stern rebuking to hypocrites involved with the church. Remember that there are wolves attending churches that seek to draw believers away from God and cause confusion among believers. I will not be surprised if cold and timid souls insult me for writing this book to spread the gospel of Jesus Christ.

In Matthew 10.22, Jesus tells us plainly that believers will be hated by the world. Yes, I expect to be hated by some for writing this encouraging and truthful book about Jesus. The children of the devil have hated the children of God since the beginning. Acts 7.57-58 describes that Stephen was stoned to death for his faith in Jesus. However, Jesus' words in Matthew 10.22 explain that those who endure being insulted and hated, because they love Jesus, will be saved. THE GOAL FOR EACH OF US IS ETERNAL SALVATION IN HEAVEN! Sometimes life is very pleasant and sometimes life has struggles. Regardless of how we are being treated, we must endure to the end. Proverbs 3.5 tells us we are to trust in the LORD with all our heart and not rely on our own insight. We will be insulted and hated by the children of darkness, but our Savior already won the war; Jesus is victorious over death and evil; we shall fear no evil! The Holy Spirit intercedes for us to

God and dwells in us; the Holy Spirit gives us joy and peace that transcends all understanding.

Jesus' perfect blood sacrifice was a free gift for all mankind for the forgiveness of sin; those who live and believe in Jesus have eternal life. The path to righteous and eternal life is difficult, but worth more than anything we could ever pay. Jesus paid our admission to Heaven by His perfect love for us; He laid down His life for His friends!

Heaven is unlike any place on earth. Jesus told us in His prayer that God the Father is in Heaven. The angels, who informed the shepherds in the field near Bethlehem of Jesus' birth, returned to Heaven after they shared the good news. The gospel indicates angels live with God in Heaven. Luke 15.10 indicates the angels in Heaven rejoice when humans repent and love Jesus.

In Luke 3.22, the Holy Spirit descended to Jesus, when He was being baptized. The Holy Spirit is both in us and intercedes with God in Heaven.

When Jesus was being crucified on the cross, there were two other men being crucified. One of the men being crucified along side Jesus repented of his sins and asked Jesus to remember him. Jesus told the repentant believer, who was about to die, that he would be with Jesus in paradise later that day! Both Jesus and the forgiven sinner are in Heaven.

Jesus said there are many mansions in Heaven. Jesus prepares a place for us in Heaven. Jesus will come again to take us to be with Him in Heaven. Amen and praise the LORD!

It would have been enough if Jesus died to provide forgiveness for our sins, but He granted us eternal life. It would have been enough if Jesus granted us eternal life, but He prepared a mansion for us. It would have been enough if Jesus prepared a mansion for us, but He prepared a mansion for us in paradise.

Heaven is the reward and destination for those who walk through the narrow gate. Heaven is the reward for those who live and believe in Jesus.

In our years on earth, we wander through the desert of life. We experience joy and endure suffering. Our suffering may include mourning over the death of loved ones, crying over unkind treatment by others, and physical pain of the body. Heaven is very different than life in the flesh. Those who live and believe in Jesus, although they die, will have everlasting life in Heaven. When Jesus comes again, He will take believers to Heaven. In Heaven, we will be in the presence of God the Father, Jesus, the Holy Spirit, the Angels, and the souls of the faithful departed. We will live in the light of truth and love. Holiness and goodness will fill Heaven. Being in the presence of God in Heaven will bring peace to our souls because our void in our soul will be filled!

Revelations 21 explains that in Heaven God will wipe away any tears from our eyes. Jesus is triumphant over death and there is no death in Heaven. In Heaven, there will be no mourning, crying, or any more pain. Everlasting life in Paradise with God and His followers is a gift from the Almighty without cost.

"His master replied, 'Well done, good and faithful servant! You have been faithful with a few things; I will put you in charge of many things. Come and share your master's happiness!'" Matthew 25.21 NASB

The above words from Jesus in Matthew 25.21 are very interesting to me. Jesus stated in Matthew 25.21 that we are to utilize our talents on earth. Perhaps Jesus is also indicating that we will utilize our talents in Heaven. Perhaps "Well done my good and faithful servant" may also refer to Jesus' words to the faithful departed. Those who faithfully utilize God's gifts to benefit the kingdom of God may be given additional responsibilities in Heaven. We humans are created in God's image. God was in the beginning and did not need to create the universe. God worked and used His talent to create the universe and living creatures, including humans. Adam and Eve cultivated the Garden of Eden prior to their sin. God Himself invented work and He worked to create all. Jesus, being God and the Son of God, chose to work as a carpenter while He lived as a human on earth. If God worked to create the world and Adam and Eve worked in the Garden of Eden, perhaps we will somehow work in Heaven. Jesus indicated that those who were faithful with the talents God gave them would be put in charge of many things. Scripture seems to indicate that work in Heaven will utilize our creativity.

May God bless you for seeking to know more about the Father, Son, and Holy Spirit. May the Holy Spirit remind you of the scriptures. Remember, Jesus is with you always, to the end of the age. I pray that this book was beneficial to you in sharing God's good news. We occasionally encounter struggles during our journey in the desert of life, but Jesus conquered death and sin. Know also that I love you and pray for you.

If you, the reader, have not committed your life to Jesus, know that Jesus welcomes you and loves you. Scripture tells us to repent of our sins and live and believe in Jesus to be saved; as a child of God, you will start your journey toward spiritual maturity.

If you call out for insight and cry aloud for understanding, and if you look for it as for silver and search for it as for hidden treasure, then you will understand the fear of the LORD and find the knowledge of God. Proverbs 2.3b-5 NIV

I want to thank God for immersing me in His Holy Word and in His Holy Spirit to write this book, *Jesus is Our Friend*. Although writing this book was a tremendous effort that exceeded my intelligence and knowledge of the Bible, God filled me with His light of truth and love and gave me undeserved spiritual gifts. This book truly records the spiritual journey of a common man to find Jesus Christ.

Let us pray. Heavenly Father, thank you for your perfect sacrifice that tore the curtain of the temple in two, from top to bottom. By your death on the cross, you allow common men and women to approach the throne of God and ask for grace and mercy. God, you give eternal life to all who live and believe in Jesus as a gift of love. While we were sinners, you laid down your life for us and called us your friend. We do not deserve your friendship; your cleansing blood justifies us. Thank you Jesus for choosing us to be your people.

# Epilogue

The Holy Bible is the living Word of God. For many, the Holy Bible may be difficult to read from the beginning to the end. I would recommend the purchase of a study Bible for those interested in reading the Bible for the first time. Study Bibles have comments and cross-references pertaining to the scripture listed. I personally own multiple translations of the Holy Bible, many in a study Bible format. *Jesus is Our Friend* lists actual Bible verses from four different translations. Numerous scholars translated ancient texts into the New Revised Standard Version, New American Standard Bible, New International Version, and the King James Version of the Holy Bible. These translations, and others, are committed to accurately translating the ancient texts into English and many other languages with the literary quality preserved.

Some other versions of the Bible may paraphrase the words of the Holy Bible and change the actual sentence structure. Be cognizant if the Bible one reads is a translation of the actual ancient texts or a paraphrased version.

The four gospel books, Matthew, Mark, Luke, and John, are four separate accounts of the life of Jesus Christ. The book of John is good to read first with respect to the events in Jesus' life. The book of John does not appear to record Jesus' parables. Matthew, Mark, and Luke record the parables of Jesus.

The apostle Peter wrote the books of 1 Peter and 2 Peter; these concise books are very powerful and share experiences and beliefs of a Christian at the time of Christ.

The book of James is brief and I very much enjoy the book. James was an earthly half brother of Jesus. James teaches practical ways to be like Jesus in an easy-to-understand writing style. When reading the book of James, it gives me the impression the author spent much time listening to Jesus and understood His message.

After reading the four gospels, both of Peter's letters, and James's book, I recommend viewing the word-for-word Gospel of John by Visual Bible International (2003). We are blessed to live in an era of motion pictures. I did not fully comprehend that Jesus mentioned a man was not born blind as a punishment for sin until I viewed the scene of John 9.3 in the film. Viewing the motion picture is a good supplement to reading the book of John.

The book of Acts documents the events immediately after Jesus' resurrection. Acts chapter 9 reveals that a Jewish man named Saul was imprisoning Christians. After Jesus rose from the dead and ascended into Heaven, Jesus returned to visit Saul on the road to Damascus. Jesus blinded Saul for three days. Saul then believed in Jesus and was referred to as Paul. Much of the remainder of the New Testament contains letters from the apostle Paul.

A dedicated reader may read the Old Testament in approximately nine months. The Old Testament and New Testament form one integrated and harmonious book. I found it easier to read the New Testament first, then read the entire Holy Bible from cover to cover.

Listening to an audio version of the Holy Bible while commuting is an excellent and efficient use of one's time. I continue to listen to a recorded Holy Bible frequently while commuting to and from work.

The Holy Bible is the Living Word of God. In a true miracle, reading the same portion of scripture at different times often provides a different message from God. When several people gather and read the same Bible passage, God may give a unique message to each reader. When reading the entire Holy Bible for the first time, it may be easier if one joins a study group.

It was during my many times of reading and re-reading the Holy Bible that I began to acquire, retain, and retrieve the scripture verses for **Jesus is Our Friend**. When we understand the joy and peace that comes from God, we are called to be God's ambassadors. Let us share the good news of God's love to all people. Amen.

# Work Cited*

1.  Moynahan, Brian. <u>God's Bestseller: William Tyndale, Thomas More, and the Writing of the English Bible---A Story of Martyrdom and Betrayal.</u> New York, New York: St. Martin's Press, 2002. 56-57, 378.

2.  Smithsonian Education IdeaLab. "Calvin Coolidge Thirtieth President, 1923–1929." Mr. President, Profiles of our Nation's Leaders. http://smithsonianeducation.org/president/detail.aspx?id=29. Accessed on 1/6/2011

3.  Roosevelt, Theodore. Excerpt from "Citizenship in a Republic Address at the Sorbonne, Paris, April 23, 1910." <u>Letters and Speeches by Theodore Roosevelt.</u> New York, New York: The Library of America, 2004. 781-782.

4.  National Aeronautics and Space Administration (NASA). "Newton's Laws of Motion." Glen Research Center. http://www.grc.nasa.gov/WWW/K-12/airplane/newton.html. Accessed on 1/6/2011.

5.  Tiner, J.H. <u>Isaac Newton: Inventor, Scientist and Teacher.</u> Fenton, Michigan: Mott Media, 1975. 107.

6.  Copi, Irving M. <u>Introduction to Logic</u>, Fourth Edition. New York, New York: The Macmillan Company, 1972. 85.

7.  Berry, George Ricker. <u>Interlinear Greek-English New Testament</u>, Twenty-eighth printing 2008. Grand Rapids, Michigan: Baker Academic, 1897. 2, Lexicon 108.

8.  *The Gospel of John.* Produced by Chris Chrisafis, Garth H. Drabinsky, Martin Katz, Joel B. Michaels, and Clyde Wagner. Directed by Philip Saville. 180 minutes. Visual Bible International; 2003. Videocassette.

9.  Centers for Disease Control and Prevention (CDC). "Homicides and Suicides --- National Violent Death Reporting System, United States, 2003--2004". Morbidity and Mortality Weekly Report (MMWR). http://www.cdc.gov/mmwr/preview/mmwrhtml/mm5526a1.htm. Accessed on 1/6/2011.

10. United States Nuclear Regulatory Commission. "Backgrounder on the Three Mile Island Accident." http://www.nrc.gov/reading-rm/doc-collections/fact-sheets/3mile-isle.html. Accessed 1/6/2011.

11. United States Holocaust Memorial Museum. "Anti-Jewish Legislation In Prewar Germany." Holocaust Encyclopedia. http://www.ushmm.org/wlc/en/article.php?ModuleId=10005681. Accessed 1/6/2011.
United States Holocaust Memorial Museum. "The Final Solution." Holocaust Encyclopedia.
http://www.ushmm.org/outreach/en/article.php?ModuleId=10007704. Accessed 1/6/2011.

12. Milgram, Stanley. Obedience to Authority. New York, New York: First Perennial Classics, an Imprint of Harper Collins Publishers, 2004. 32-122

13. United States Code of Federal Regulations. TITLE 42 - The Public Health and Welfare, Chapter 21B - Religious Freedom Restoration. 42C21B. http://uscode.house.gov/download/pls/42C21B.txt. Accessed 1/6/2011.

14. Roosevelt, Theodore. Framed quotation. Centerville, Virginia: The Artist's Proof Vintage Photography & Memorabilia, 1995.

15. Lewin, Leonard C. Report from Iron Mountain on the Possibility and Desirability of Peace. Dial Press, 1967

16. The White House. "40. Ronald Reagan 1981-1989." Our Presidents. http://www.whitehouse.gov/about/presidents/ronaldreagan/. Accessed on 1/6/2011.

17. DeMello, Anthony. Awareness: The Perils and Opportunities of Reality. New York, New York: Image Book published by Doubleday, 1990. 76, 80.

18. Berry, George Ricker. Interlinear Greek-English New Testament, Twenty-eighth printing 2008. Grand Rapids, Michigan: Baker Academic, 1897. 45, 468, 521.

19. Tiner, J.H. Isaac Newton: Inventor, Scientist and Teacher. Fenton, Michigan: Mott Media, 1975. 108.

Society. Use of either trademark requires the permission of International Bible Society.

Where scripture is noted NASB: the Scripture taken from the NEW AMERICAN STANDARD BIBLE®, Copyright © 1960, 1962, 1963, 1968, 1971, 1972, 1973, 1975, 1977, 1995 by The Lockman Foundation. Used by permission.

Scripture noted as KJV is from the King James Version set forth in 1611 and is in public domain.

# About the Author

When Carl Butcher was eleven years old, his father committed suicide. Carl wandered in the wilderness of life through his teenage years, then earned a Bachelor's degree of Industrial Engineering, and began to climb out of spiritual and financial poverty. The author began his research of the Holy Bible to understand suffering in life and fill the void in his soul. The author has worked in manufacturing engineering management for over thirty years, and has written numerous technical guides and manuals regarding product design and manufacturing. The writer is gifted in researching and deciphering vast amounts of complex data and organizing the information for efficient acquisition, retention, and retrieval. The author has taught Bible application classes for grade school children, high school students, and adults. What began as Carl's personal longing to research, analyze, and understand God's Word, became a thirty year endeavor that resulted in the writing of *Jesus is Our Friend*.

Made in the USA
Charleston, SC
08 May 2012